Military to Federal Career Guide

Ten steps to transforming your military experience into a competitive Federal resume

Kathryn Kraemer Troutman

Published by The Resume Place, Inc.,
Baltimore, MD
Phone: 888-480-8265
Email: resume@resume-place.com

Published by The Resume Place, Inc.,
Baltimore, MD
Phone: 888-480-8265
Email: resume@resume-place.com
Website: www.resume-place.com

Printed in the United States of America
Library of Congress Control Number: 2005930671

ISBN 13: 978-0-9647025-7-6
ISBN 10: 0-9647025-7-6

We have been careful to provide accurate information in this book, though it is possible that errors and omissions may have been introduced.

AUTHOR'S NOTE: Sample resumes are real but fictionalized. All Federal applicants have provided permission for their resumes to be used as samples for this publication. Privacy policy is strictly enforced.

PUBLICATION TEAM:
Interior Design and Covers: Brian Moore, MJR Media
CD-ROM Designer: Brian Moore, MJR Media
Development Editor: Emily K. Troutman
Technical Federal HRM Editor: Harry C. Redd, III
Military Federal Resume Sample Development Editor: Patricia Alvarez and Sarah Blazucki
CD-ROM Editors: Mark Hoyer, Patricia Alvarez, Kelly Roscoe
Associate Editor: Sarah Blazucki and Bonny Day
Indexer: L. Pilar Wyman

Contributing Authors and Researchers:
Step 8, KSA Writing, Rita Chambers
Step 4, Find Your Federal Job Chart: Harry C. Redd, III, Mark Hoyer, Kelly Roscoe

Other Books by Kathryn Kraemer Troutman

The Student's Federal Career Guide & CD-ROM; Co-authored with Emily K. Troutman

Ten Steps to a Federal Job & CD-ROM

Ten Steps to a Federal Job – Jobseeker's Guide

Ten Steps to a Federal Job – Trainer's Guide

Federal Resume Guidebook & CD-ROM, 1st, 2nd, and 3rd Editions
(Published by Jist, Inc., Indianapolis, IN)

Electronic Federal Resume Guidebook & CD-ROM

Reinvention Federal Resumes

Creating Your High School Resume, 1st and 2nd Editions
(Published by Jist, Inc., Indianapolis, IN)

DEDICATION

For all the men and women of the U.S. Army, Navy, Air Force, Marine Corps, and Coast Guard who dedicate their lives to our Nation's defense.

ACKNOWLEDGEMENTS

I'd like to thank all of the Military Career Transition Counselors, Spouse Employment Assistant Program Managers, Family Support Center Counselors, Army Transition Assistance Program Managers, Army Community Support Center Counselors for their insight, stories and experiences. Their daily counseling, teaching and Federal job support services inspired me to write this book. And in particular Ed Roscoe, Commander, Navy Installations, Family Readiness Programs, for recognizing the importance of Federal Job Search Training for U.S. Navy Fleet & Family Support Center Spouse Employment & Assistance Program Managers.

Special thanks to Cathy Knight, Master Certified Federal Job Search Trainer, who had the vision to implement and lead the *Ten Step* training program to Air Force MAJCOM Europe and trained 15 career counselors in Europe. And to Fred Mitchell from USMC, Camp Pendleton, CA, who showed me their current resumes and inspired me further to create a new Military Federal Resume – that was MORE military!

I sincerely thank Ligaya Fernandez, Sr. Human Resources Policy Analyst for the Merit Systems Protection Board, who developed the popular Federal Hiring System program presented at the Certification Training Programs since 2002. Ligaya has been instrumental in keeping us up-to-date with Federal Hiring Processes, Hiring Authorities, and the Civil Service Merit System. Ligaya's friendly training style and informative PowerPoint presentations have contributed to our understanding of the complex journey of the Federal employment process.

Thanks also to Harry C. Redd III, retired Sr. Human Resources Policy Analyst for Merit Systems Protection Board, for excellent research and writing for this publication. He researched the human resources information, military conversion charts, and vacancy announcement summaries, focusing on material relevant to military enlisted personnel and officers.

A special thank you to Patricia Alvarez who helped me create the final versions of the Military Federal Resume. And to Sarah Blazucki for editing, finalizing and creating the final Word files and templates that will be used by many resume writers.

Sample resumes contributed to the book were graciously offered by Tracey Bell, Benjamin Fairbanks, Richard Flory, Margaret Gersh, Thad Larson, Vaughn Lately, Jose Lopez, Geraldo Martinez, Steve Odom, Timothy Rittman, Morgan Smith, Shirley Caban and Fred Mitchell. We thank you for your contribution; your job search stories and information will help thousands of others write outstanding resumes for federal jobs.

And finally, to every military jobseeker that I meet and to whom I write. I was inspired to write this book for you. To help you draft a better first resume that will get better and faster results with resume builders, on-line applications and Human Resources!

TABLE OF CONTENTS

TABLE OF CONTENTS

TABLE OF CONTENTS

TABLE OF CONTENTS

CD-ROM CONTENT
- Glossary of Federal Employment Terms
- List of Federal Agency Names
- List of Federal Occupational Series and Job Titles
- Core Competencies for Marine Corps, Defense Logistics Agency, Veteran's Administration, Senior Executive Service
- 26 Military Federal Resume Samples and Templates, including Electronic Resume samples for Resumix, CHART, STAIRS, QuickHire, AvueCentral, USAJOBS.
- Other resume formats include: paper resume formats, corporate resumes and job fair resume samples. Read the full list of samples on the next page.

TABLE OF CONTENTS – ON THE CD-ROM

Name	Service	Rank	Grade	Target Occupational Series and Title	Resume Format
Billings	USCG	E-5	GS-05/06/07	1802 - Registration Technician (OA) 1811 - Criminal Investigator (Special Agent) 1896 - Border Patrol Agent	Electronic Federal
Rodriguez	USMC	E-6	GS-07/09	301 - Administration, Program Management 343 - Management Analyst 501 - Fina ncial Administration 512 - Internal Revenue Agent 560, 561 - Budget Analyst / Technician 2200 - Administrative work in Information Technology	Electronic Federal
Tarka	USN	E-6	GS-09/11	343 - Management Analyst, Resource Management 346 - Logistics Management 2001 - General Supply Specialist 2003, 2005 - Supply Management Analyst / Specialist 2010 - Inventory Management Specialist	Electronic Federal Air Force Builder Paper Federal Corporate
Snyder	USN	E-7	GS-07/09	201, 203 - Humarn Resources Specialist (Military) 343 - Program or Management Analyst	Electronic Federal
Grayson	USA / USAR	E-7	GS-11/12/13	201 - Human Resources Specialist 1810 - Criminal Investigator	Paper Federal AVUE Resume KSAs
Herboso	USA	E-8	GS-09/11	201 - Human Resources Specialist (Military) 1750 - Training Instructor	Electronic Federal
Simmons	USA	E-8	GS-11/12	201 - Human Resources Specialist 301, 341 - Administration, Program Management 343 - Management Analyst, Resource Management	Electronic Federal
La Rue	USMC	E-9	GS-09/11/12	101 - Work Life Specialist, Family Advocacy Specialist 303 - Career Transition Counselor 1701, 1702 - Education and Training Specialist 17 12 - Training Instructor 1720, 1740 - Education Program / Services Specialist	Electronic Federal
Benedetto	USA	CW-2	GS-09/11/12	2152 - Air Traffic Contoller 2181 - Airline Pilot / Helicopter Flight Instructor 2183 - Aircraft Electronic Warfare Specialist, Officer	Electronic Federal USAjobs Resume
Perkins	USA	CW-4	GS-11/12/13	346 - Logistics Management Specialist 2181 - Airline Pilot / Helicopter Flight Instructor 2183 - Aircraft Electronic Warfare Specialist, Officer	Electronic Federal Navy Resume
MacArthur	USAR	CW-4	GS-11/12	201 - Human Resources Specialist (Military)	Before Resume Electronic Federal Job Fair, 1 pg KSA
Roberts	USA	O-4	GS-13/14	301, 341 - Administration, Program Mgt. Spec. 343 - Management Analyst, Resource Management 346 - Logistics Management 1102 - Contracting, Procurement Specialist	Electronic Federal Corporate, 1 pg Job Fair, 1 pg
Lester	USANG	O-5	GS-13/14	301, 341 - Administration, Program Management 343 - Management Analyst, Resource Management 346 - Logistics Management 1101 - Business, Industry Specialist	Electronic Federal CPOL Resume

Military to Federal Career Guide

Ten steps to transforming your military experience into a
competitive Federal resume

PREFACE

Having completed a highly successful twenty-six year Navy career I thought it was time to move on and try my hand in the civilian world while I was still at an acceptable age to contribute to a company deserving of my talents and skills. The challenges that I faced were many, and the expectation of grass on the other side of the fence being greener, or at least what I thought would be greener did not turn out that way at all. It was more like a light brown. This was contrary to what I was expecting since I had attended the Navy's Transition Assistance Program (TAP) workshop approximately 9 months before retirement. I guess all the preparation in the world cannot guarantee you will land the perfect job, however, that doesn't mean that you shouldn't continue to look. I always had a hard time accepting rejection.

The first thing that I was instructed to accomplish during the TAP workshop was to write a resume, and oh by the way, you were told to demilitarize the wording. Not sure what that meant, I asked the question, and the answer was simple. Translate your military skills and all acronyms to civilianese. I didn't think that was going to be hard so I sat down and started what I thought would be a simple task. Two reams of paper and three weeks later I thought that I had a winner and set out to find the perfect job to start my second career.

After beating my head against the wall for nearly seven months, and numerous interviews which basically said that you have a lot of experience, knowledge, skills and abilities, but we can't afford you. I was even thinking of offering to forego the benefits; you know the medical, dental, 401K etc. since I had my military benefits. This was really selling oneself short, they knew it, and so did I.

I had never given very much thought in working for the Federal Government until one of my shipmates called and we were discussing retirement and finding employment. He said, "Have you tried the federal government?" "Your learning curve would be much shorter and you are already familiar with policies, chain of command, and terminology, not to mention your experience and background."

Now if you think writing a federal resume 7 years ago was easy, I have two words for you, "Think Again!" Navigating the Federal Government/Human Resource system was worse than trying to navigate a mine field using a rowboat, a compass, and you are the only crewmember onboard. Once you submitted your application it seem to take forever to get classified, meaning they assigned you an occupational series based on your background and experience. No one ever told me about key words they use to pull your application for job vacancies, but luckily I was finally called for an interview and was accepted for the position. I thought to myself, if an individual is familiar with the federal government and has now acquired an idea of how the system works, what about the average civilian who knows nothing about the federal government, terminology or the process at all ever get a job working for the federal government?

Three years later I had the opportunity to meet Kathryn Troutman during a conference in Nashville. Kathryn Troutman had almost 30 years experience in assisting people with securing federal jobs and was considered the "Guru" among government officials. Kathryn Troutman's presentation introduced her new book and certification training program, called "Ten Steps to a Federal Job."

Needless to say, I purchased the book and CD. I was now employed as the Program Manager for the Navy's Spouse Employment Assistance Program. I was looking for ways to help spouses find federal employment and other partnerships with corporations giving spouses every opportunity to seek employment that would add portability to their mobile military lifestyles. Moving around every two to three years did not afford spouses the opportunity to amass retirement benefits, such as 401Ks, sick and vacation time, or retain their seniority. Starting over after every move was their norm. Employment with the federal government would afford them that opportunity, especially since it offered spouse hiring preference.

The "Ten Steps to a Federal Job" became so popular that soon the program was available to all military spouses and written into the training curriculum for the Spouse Employment Assistance Program. This program has now expanded to the transitioning military service member.

Now is a perfect opportunity for retiring military members, military spouses, and transitioning military to find employment within the federal government. You have served your country with honor, dedication and commitment. With your experience you bring a wealth of knowledge that the federal government values and needs to ensure we maintain a strong government. The greatest feeling to me is that I am now in a position to give something back to those that support and defended our great nation.

This book will make your search for a federal job a much smoother process and will open a door that will lead to a rewarding career. The process is becoming easier and you no longer have to demilitarize your resume, the government and government agencies understand the language. Go Federal, it will be the best move you ever made.

Ed L. Roscoe, Bio YNCM(SW), U.S. Navy (Retired)
Mr. Ed L. Roscoe completed a highly successful twenty-six year military career before joining the civilian workforce. Mr. Roscoe joined Commander Navy Installations in October 2004 where he uses his knowledge of the needs of military personnel and family members to improve Family Readiness Programs and training curriculum for family members, including: Family Employment Readiness, Volunteer, Deployment Readiness, Ombudsman, Sponsorship, and Information and Referral Programs. As the Project Director, Ed revised the DoD Standardized Volunteer Desk Guide for DoD Family Employment Readiness Programs throughout DoD. In order to meet the changing needs of military family members, Ed lead an Interaction Process Team to develop a strategic plan for better utilization of human capital throughout the regions that will bring standardization of training and delivery of all programs throughout CNI and all 16 regions. Mr. Roscoe and his wife Karen are from Concord, North Carolina. They have five children, three of whom are currently serving their country in the Navy or the Army.

Making the Decision to Serve

As a former or current member of the U.S. armed forces, you have already demonstrated personal dedication, perseverance and a strong commitment to service. Unfortunately, in previous decades, there were few career choices for you after separating from your job. Today the U.S. Government is better prepared than ever to offer you new, economically competitive employment opportunities that may help you find fulfilling life work. The events of September 11, 2001 changed many of the missions of U.S. government agencies. Your skills are now in very high demand and can help the nation respond to complex new global security threats.

Your military service can also help you start a new and totally different career. Whether you were an officer, a bookkeeper, an air traffic controller, a sailor, a soldier or a marine—this book is for you. Employment in the Federal government is unbelievably diverse.

You also have an inherent advantage: the government has numerous preference programs for both veterans and families of veterans.

In an easy-to-follow, step-by-step process, this book will teach you:

Where you can work—	Names of agencies Job titles which match every experience level Contracting vs. Federal jobs
How to find jobs—	Crucial web addresses Job databases Networking tips Advice for job search novices Managing your career transition from abroad
How much you can earn—	What it takes to move up in government How your military service can help your salary
How to apply—	Help for people who have *never* written a resume Tips to translate complex military jargon Expert advice for online application processes
How to interview—	Restating military experience for civilians Basics for beginners
Extensive samples—	CD-ROM includes ready-to-use templates

Military to Federal is different from other resume books because it presents a new, cutting-edge format for resume writing. You will learn how to write your "Military Federal Resume." **The Military Federal Resume is a Federal resume that includes some of your precise military experience and jargon.** In the past, career counselors may have told you to remove all military lingo from your resume. Not anymore! Since the missions of U.S. government agencies are increasingly focused on National Security, your military service gives you just the competitive edge you need! *Military to Federal* helps you navigate that fine line between too much technical information and not enough.

Why Federal?

If you're reading this book, you are probably aware that the private industry job market is a jungle. This is even true for recent college graduates—today, college graduates are more likely than high school dropouts to be unemployed. Having a college degree no longer ensures that a person will have the job of his or her dreams after graduation. In fact, in today's competitive job market many college grads find themselves in competition with those who have 5 to 10 years of job experience!

The U.S. Federal government employs 2.6 million people in jobs that range from biology to art restoration to law enforcement. In addition, the average Federal employee is over 46 years of age, and two of every five are eligible now to retire. Agencies are scrambling to find new, highly-qualified employees… YOU! Your previous job experience will slow the pace of brain-drain in government and help agencies lower their training costs. In other words: congratulations. You are way ahead of the curve.

Work in the Federal government is often more financially rewarding than work in private industry. The average *entry* level starting salary in government is $26,000 to $37,000 per year. With your military experience, you are probably qualified for mid-level positions. The government may also offer full benefits: including comprehensive health insurance, 401K with matching funds, 10 paid holidays annually, plus 13 days paid vacation to start. This is far beyond the average in private industry. Working for the Federal government often offers more workplace flexibility than corporate America. If you have a family, then you already know how important flexibility is.

Why Military to Federal?

Military to Federal is just the latest in a series of *10 Step* books. The *10 Step* formula is now widely adopted in military and government agencies around the world. The content for this book was culled from 30 years of experience helping people advance in the Federal government. Kathryn K. Troutman is the leading expert in Federal employment. The content of the book represents the accumulated knowledge of hundreds of applicants, career counselors and human resource experts. You can be certain that the information you find here is both cutting-edge and tried-and-true.

Kathryn Troutman understands the unique challenges you face and trains people *just like you* at numerous Federal government agencies and bases around the world:

Defense agencies:
Pentagon
Defense Logistics Agency
Defense Finance and Accounting Service (20 military bases and sites)
Defense Reduction & Threat Agency
Defense Contract Management Agency
Defense Intelligence & Supply Service

More than 50 Federal agencies, including:
Federal Bureau of Investigation
U.S. Marshall's Service
National Science Foundation
National Institutes of Health
Bureau of Land Management
Environmental Protection Agency
Department of Interior
Federal Highway Administration
Center for Medicare & Medicaid Services
Pension Benefit Guarantee Corporation
U.S. Department of Agriculture
Department of Energy
Environmental Protection Agency

More than 40 military bases, including:
U.S. Marine Corps Bases: Albany, GA; Kanaohe, HI; Parris Island, SC
U.S. Navy Bases: Norfolk, VA; San Diego, CA; Pearl Harbor, HI
U.S. Army Bases: Heidelberg, Wurzburg, Weisbaden, Mannheim, Germany; Ft. Meade, MD
U.S. Air Force: Aviano, Vicenza, Italy; Kaiserslautern, Germany; Bolling, Washington, DC; Offutt, Omaha, NE; Wright-Patterson; OH

Make your move

Daunting as it may seem, you are ready to move on-and you will. *Military to Federal* is a perfect starting place and will see you through to your goal. In addition to the information here and on the CD-ROM, you will find important references to answer any unanswered questions you may have. You can learn who to contact for help writing resumes, finding jobs, applying to jobs and moving up the salary ladder. Your future Federal career is just around the corner. Best wishes!

—*The Editors*

Step 1　Networking – Who do you Know?
How can a network of contacts help you find and land a Federal job?

Step 1: Networking – Who do you Know?
How can a network of contacts help you find and land a Federal job?

In addition to www.usajobs.gov, agency and contractor websites for job listings, sometimes "who you know" does make a difference, even for Federal or government contractor jobs.

A supervisor is THE best network contact you can have!

A supervisor in an agency of your field of interest may be your #1 contact in your network for pursuing a Federal job vacancy announcement or government contracting. Here's why:

If you know a supervisor:
⊙ He/she can tell you when they are hiring – THAT IS A GIFT!
⊙ He/she can hire you directly, if they have the authority to do that.
⊙ He/she can hire you non-competitively if they are using the Veterans' Hiring Programs (more on this in Step 2).

If you know someone who has contact with a supervisor, this person may be able to tell you:
⊙ When a supervisor is going to be hiring.
⊙ When the supervisor receives the List of Eligible resumes from the human resources office.
⊙ If your name is on the List of Eligible resumes.
⊙ The supervisor's name and email, so that you may personally make contact.
⊙ If the resume is forwarded to the supervisor, and if you are being considered.
⊙ Who they hire, or may hire, and perhaps even why.

A Federal employee is a great ally!
An employee of a Federal agency or government contracting firm can relate relevant information that you will NOT read in the paper or online. These are hot tips that you can learn from. For example:

⊙ If the agency is in a growth posture, i.e., increasing budget, additional jobs—this is good for you!
⊙ If many people are retiring, again more jobs.
⊙ If the agency is moving part of the operations – if so, where are they going?
⊙ If it's reducing in workforce – if so, how many, and who?
⊙ If it's going to be on the Base Realignment and Closure (BRAC) list. BRAC closings take 2-5 years and may not happen at all. This is interesting and just good to be aware of.
⊙ If the agency is part of a future commercial activity study – also good to know. The agency could win the competition and jobs will remain. The agency could lose the competition and contractors will take the jobs. You could work for the contractor in that case.

A Federal human resources, a civilian human resource (HR) specialist, or a special emphasis program (SEP) manager is a real find!

Even if you don't know someone in these supportive positions well, you can write or call and ask a question. An HR specialist or SEP manager can be a great help with understanding the application system, conveying insight into your resume, and sharing information regarding upcoming announcements, job fairs, and more.

Recognize your 2nd, 3rd, 4th and 5th circle of friends and other contacts expands your opportunities for employment.

A person in your network might know someone else who knows about a job or opportunity coming up. Dick Bolles, author of *What Color is your Parachute*, talks about the importance of 2nd, 3rd,4th and 5th circle of friends and contacts. I saw him speak at a career conference in Sacramento, California. He drew a picture of a pond and a rock being thrown into the middle of the pond. The first circle around the rock represents your immediately family. The 2nd circle is your best friends. The 3rd circle is your friends' friends. The 4th circle is friends of friends. The 5th circle is your friends' network. The 3rd, 4th and 5th circle can be your best network because they are not THAT CLOSE to you, and that circle is much larger than circle 1 and 2.

Make a point to communicate with more than just your close friends and family. Envision Dick Bolles' rock falling into water when you are thinking, "I don't know anyone who works for the government." You probably do know someone, but that person could be in your 4th or 5th circle around the rock (which is you).

How to approach your 3rd through 5th circle of friends/contacts

Ask your close friends and family who they know in the Federal government and, if possible, for their contact information. Write an email to each of them introducing yourself and telling them about your Federal job objectives and your interests. Establish a writing friendship by asking about their job and agency. Ask about the growth of their agency, jobs that could be opening up and ideas they might have for positions and opportunities. Ask them if they know anyone who works in your favorite agency. You never can tell who they might know and may refer you to. This distance writing could result in networks and contacts for your future.

How to get hired through your network, without competing with other applicants

The Federal government has special hiring programs for veterans that supervisors may use to hire qualified candidates WITHOUT going through the competitive process. Complete details are listed in Step 2, Federal Hiring Benefits for Veterans and Family Members.

What can you learn from your Circle of Friends/Contacts?

Relevant training and continuing education ideas

A person in your network could recommend training or assignments that would be good for your career that you may not have considered. The Federal government is looking for specialized knowledge employees. Whatever your field of interest, it is extremely important to continue specialized education, meet and learn from industry experts, and read current information. This is critical to your ongoing career and for promotions!

Insider resume writing and agency culture tips

Network contacts within an organization can tell you important information to help you decide if this is the ideal agency for you. They can tell you:

- How to write a competitive, insightful resume for the position and the agency.
- About the agency's mission, work culture, objectives, challenges and upcoming changes.
- About the workforce – is the work light, heavy, effective? Is there overtime? Are the employees friendly or distant? Is the office team-based? Not all agencies are equally well-managed or staffed. It's good to know before applying for a job.

Upcoming job fairs and national conferences

Obtain information on local job fairs and national conferences sponsored by professional organizations and minority groups. Learn about special meetings hosted by Federal agencies and departments sharing information on employment opportunities.

Job Fair "Meet and Greet" Strategies and the "Sticky" Job Fair Resume

Never miss an opportunity to go to a job fair!

The agencies that purchase exhibits, send materials and friendly recruiters are SERIOUS ABOUT MEETING AND HIRING YOU! The agency representatives at the booth may be human resources recruiters, who have the power to remember you, speak about you to someone else, refer your resume, read your resume again after they get back to the office, and actually HIRE YOU! This is a powerful opportunity for you to break into an agency.

Dress for Success

Men should dress professionally - a suit or slacks, button-down shirt and jacket. An interesting tie adds color. A small boutonniere or pin of personal distinction adds personality.

Women may wear classic black and white, with a splash of color to stand out. Either slacks or skirt work, as long as they are professional and attractive. Wear healthy-looking make-up and conservative jewelry. Stockings and comfortable closed-toe shoes are best.

In either case, remember, self confidence is your best look!

The emotional approach to job fairs

First impressions are important. Combat operations and daily life in the military is a far cry from today's modern job market. Negativity, however justifiable, will come across to other people. It is important to be positive and hopeful that this experience WILL benefit you, and may result in meeting someone at a booth, or in a conversation that may result in a lead for a job or career!

Be aware of your mood and body language. You don't have to smile all the time, but do not frown or grimace. Look pleasant, relaxed and friendly. Walk tall and sit up straight. And be prepared to shake hands!

What to carry to the job fair

A portfolio is best with resumes on one side along with your business card if you have one. I recommend a business card for job searching. Collect brochures and business cards from exhibitors' booths that you visit and store them in the other side of your portfolio. Take note of the recruiters' name and the time you visit them, and obtain their business cards if possible. Note: never let a noisy cell phone interrupt an important conversation! Ladies, if you carry a purse, make it a small with essentials only. Keep your hands free for the portfolio, writing and hand-shaking.

Plan your itinerary before you go into the exhibit area of the job fair

Take the time to read the exhibitor list before you go into the job fair. Plan and list your target booths and number them in order of importance and interest. Look at the floor layout for the exhibit locations to save yourself time and footwork!

Informational Interviews, the Neglected Job Search Tool

1. Identify the Information You Want.
2. Make a List of People You Know.
3. Make the Appointment.
4. Plan an Agenda for the Session.
5. Conduct Yourself as a Professional.
6. Show Interest.
7. Be Prepared to Answer Questions About What You're Looking For.
8. Get Names.
9. Send Thank-You and Follow-Up Letters.
10. Take Advantage of Any Referrals You Receive.

Carol Martin, Monster.com Contributing Author
http://interview.monster.com/articles/informational/

Here is a list of organizations that attended the Corporate Gray Job Fair in Greenbelt, Maryland:
See the list of Job Fairs here: *www.corporategray.com*

7-Eleven	ManTech International
ABC Supply Company	Maryland Air National Guard
Advanced Technologies	Maryland Dept of Public Safety & Correctional Services
AFLAC	Metropolitan Police Department
American Express Financial Advisors	Military Officers Association of America
American Infrastructure	MilitaryResumes.com
Ameritas Acacia Companies	Milton Hershey School
Anteon Corporation	Minerva Engineering
ARAMARK	MPRI
AT&T Government Solutions	National Geospatial-Intelligence Agency
Beta Analytics / Analex Corporation	National Security Agency
Books Are Fun, Reader's Digest Company	NCI Information Systems
CACI	Northrop Grumman Corporation
Capstone Corporation	Office of Naval Intelligence
Career Beginnings	OMNIPLEX World Services Corporation
Centers for Medicare & Medicaid Services	Owens & Minor
Comcast Cable	Pitney Bowes Government Solutions
Computer Sciences Corporation	PricewaterhouseCoopers
Crane Pro Services	Prince George's County Public Safety
CVS Pharmacy	Pro-Telligent.com
DC Air National Guard	Raytheon
dcjobs.com	Remote Surveillance Technology Solutions
Decisive Analytics Corporation	RS Information Systems
Defense Intelligence Agency	Shapiro and Duncan
Delaware Department of Correction	Strayer University
EDO Corporation	Swales Aerospace
EG&G Technical Services, a division of URS	Target Corporation
Eiden Systems	The Resume Place
GEICO	The Wexford Group
General Dynamics Network Systems	Trawick and Associates
GMRI	Troops to Teachers
Home Depot	U.S. Army Reserve / Reserve Recruiting
Indian Health Service	U.S. Secret Service
KBR (Kellogg Brown & Root)	United States Department of State University Alliance
L-3 Communications GSI	University of Maryland Dept. of Public Safety
LB&B Associates	University of Phoenix - Maryland Campus
Lockheed Martin	Verizon Federal Network Services
Logistics Management Resources	Virginia Linen Service
McNeil Technologies	Weichert, Realtors
MAMSI -- United Healthcare	Xerox

Booth Strategies – how to be memorable with the HR recruiters

There will be two or three friendly recruiters there to meet and greet you. They are there to meet the best and brightest people to potentially hire. Think of this as a "mini" job interview. For best results, shake hands firmly, look the recruiter in the eye, smile and introduce yourself. This first impression is important!

Sample introduction:

"Hello, I'm Susan Wilson. I'm pleased to be attending this job fair (pause, smile). I will be separating from the Army in 6 months after four years of active duty in the _____. I'm interested in a Federal career in information technology. Here's a copy of my resume (pause, if they don't speak, continue with a question)."

Sample questions for agency recruiters:

This is the time to ask questions and get some excellent information. If there is a LONG line of jobseekers behind you, be prepared to ask your top 3 questions because of time-constraints. Be sure to write down their answers after you leave the booth. Remember to get the recruiter's business card so that you can contact them later with any additional questions:

- ⊙ Is your agency hiring now?
- ⊙ What jobs are coming available?
- ⊙ Are you collecting resumes for current positions, or to scan into your database for future positions?
- ⊙ What kinds of people or positions are you hiring for?
- ⊙ What are the typical salaries or grades?
- ⊙ Do you have positions with advancement potential?
- ⊙ Where are most of the jobs located?
- ⊙ How would I apply for jobs with your agency?
- ⊙ Do you have any insight to improve my resume?
- ⊙ Does your agency require KSAs in addition to a resume?
- ⊙ Is your agency offering recruitment incentives or tuition reimbursement?

Say something memorable if you get the opportunity

Make a comment showing personal interest in the job fair, the booth, the agency, your experience, or other topic that relates. Mention this item in your follow-up email. It may trigger a memory response of your face and personality.

When you get to Step 8 in this book, Knowledge, Skills & Abilities Writing, you could memorize one or two of your most memorable accomplishments in case you get the opportunity to talk about anything that stands out in your military career.

Writing a "Sticky" Job Fair Resume

"Sticky" is a term coined by Malcolm Gladwell in his book, *Tipping Point*. He says that sticky (impressive, relevant) content, sticks to the reader and results in an action or chain of events. The action you desire is to have increased interest in you after the job fair, resulting in a job offer! Examples of a Sticky Job Fair Resume are in Step 7 and on the CD-ROM. You can also learn about sticky Core Competencies in Step 7.

- Your Job Fair resume should be formatted so that it is easy to read by humans. Do not use your electronic resume format that you would submit into the Resume Builders online. The electronic resume is formatted for automated systems only.
- Print your resume on gray, tan or ivory paper so that it will stand out among hundreds of resumes. Keep the color conservative, but do NOT use white copier-type paper for a job fair!
- Use heavier weight or textured paper if possible.
- Your Job Fair resume should not be more than 2 pages.
- Type font should be 11 or 12 point for ease of readability.
- Focus your Job Fair resume toward your stickiest skills—the ones you are hoping to use in your next job. If you can give specific job titles, even better!
- Include a sticky accomplishment on the top of page two to encourage the reader to continue reading!
- Two samples of a Job Fair resume are on the CD-ROM and in Step 7. One sample focuses on skills for jobseekers who do not know their exact future job title; the other sample lists job titles for jobseekers who know their future job titles.

How to manage networking long-distance

With email and the internet, networking long distance is absolutely possible and very effective. You can make solid contacts and develop relationships with others without ever meeting them. You do have to be assertive, creative, resourceful in your research and downright clever to develop a great network via email and internet. If you like challenges and opportunity, you will be successful at this part of the job search.

Write a "cold-call" introduction to a supervisor listed on an organizational chart

Occasionally you can find an agency's organizational chart on their website. You might find the name of an agency hiring official in a certain geographic location where you are interested in living. You could write to that person directly to ask if there are hiring opportunities for a person with your experience, qualifications and interest. They will probably point you toward usajobs.gov, but they might also give you job titles or insight into the future positions at that agency. AND … this person could be a NETWORK / CONTACT for you in the future.

Follow the news and write to people who are quoted in the media

People who are quoted or have stories about their government programs or careers generally have their names, titles and agencies listed in the articles. You can receive these types of articles if you sign up for such automatic email services from www.govexec.com, Steve Barr's Federal Diary, or The Federal Times email announcements.

Write to the individual(s) about the article in which they were quoted. You may locate their email address on the agency's website. If not, you can try guessing their email address by other emails for the agency. Most agencies have a consistent format for all emails. Defense Finance & Accounting Service format is firstname.lastname@dfas.mil. The Navy format is firstname.lastname@navy.mil. If there are two people with the same name, you won't know the email address.

When you write, introduce yourself and tell them what your plans are for your future Federal career. Ask them if they have any insight, job leads or ideas for positions in their agency or office. This person could become a network or contact for future use.

You should also read www.govexec.com as regularly as you can. They send a daily email as well that can keep you on top of agencies that are hiring, human resources policies, new Department of Defense personnel rules, new or re-invigorated hiring incentives (this is very important), and which agencies are "hurting" to hire more people. This extra insight can help you in an interview and in searching for jobs with agencies that are most in need of quality new employees.

No matter where you are, you can listen to www.Federalnewsradio.com online. You can listen to the interviews online and even write questions to the interviewers when they are Live Online. Mike Causey interviews Federal managers concerning varied topics. Mike takes email questions and gives you an opportunity to introduce yourself to managers. You might learn valuable information. These interviews are archived for listening when you can manage the time.

Write to your college or high school alumni members

Find your college or high school online and see if they have an alumni association. Join it, get their membership list, read the list and see if anyone works for the government or for a contractor. Write to introduce or reacquaint yourself to them. Tell them about your plans and objectives and see if they have ideas for employment, agencies, or other insight.

Read the college or high school alumni newsletter and write to alumni

Maybe one of your alumni published an article or is listed in the "Member News" section because they landed a great new job or were promoted in a Federal agency. Write and congratulate them on their achievement. Introduce yourself and talk about your objectives.

Join a professional association and write to speakers

Even if you can't attend any meetings or conferences right now, join anyway. You will receive their newsletter which will give you information about the industry, upcoming events and people in the news. Pay attention to the people in the news in case there is someone who works in an agency that is of interest to you. Maybe they even perform a job that is similar to the one you are seeking. You could write to this person and introduce yourself. Tell them about your objectives and ask for any ideas or jobs that they may know about. This person could become a NETWORK / CONTACT for your future.

Attend a professional association conference and write to the speakers or attendees

If you can attend the conference, that's great. But if you are away and cannot attend the conference, you can read the conference speaker and break-out workshop list anyway on the association's website.

Look at the keynote speaker list, breakout workshop titles and speakers. Read the bios of the speakers and trainers. Usually you can "Google" the speakers and write to them if you think they may have information that can help you find your target position in government or government contracting.

Introduce yourself and tell them your situation. You can tell that that you really wish you could come to their presentation. Maybe they would even send you their handout – you never know. Maybe they could recommend any information about job search, skills or opportunities so that you can land on your feet when you complete your military service. This person could become a member of your NETWORK / CONTACTS for your future.

Write to people on relevant message boards

Check out the Public Service / Government Message Board, www.monster.com. Write to me, Kathryn Troutman! I'm the Federal Career Coach™ and Career Advisor for the Government/Public Service pages. You might read about someone who is in your situation. Read the advice they receive from other jobseekers and from me. You can share your experiences, questions and even contact people on this board.

Keep a mailing list

Create an Outlook or other email group folder to keep your network email contact list. Keep your contacts, job titles, and information in a file that you will not lose. Email it to a friend. Ask them if you can stay in touch with them during your transition into the private sector and if they would please contact you if they find a great article, speaker or book that you should read.

Read books on your topic and to prep for an interview

Authors of books are so impressive and inspiring. Keep reading books on leadership, teamwork, change management, personal motivation so that you can stay positive and organized in your career change. Changing your career from military to civilian is a giant change, and you will need inspiration and reinforcing knowledge. A popular interview question: What's your favorite book? What book have you read last? Who do you most admire?

NETWORK—WHO DO YOU KNOW?

1

Read a book or articles on marketing to learn more about self-marketing and networking

All of the tips and insight in this step are basic marketing concepts for a new product, service or a business. You are a product right now. You are marketing yourself to a new job. Networking, relationship development, research and contacts are all elements of marketing. Anything that you read about marketing could be applied to you and your job search objectives! Get creative and insightful with your job search!

Additional opportunities to meet people who work for the Federal government or a contractor

- ⊙ Managers and workers at non-appropriated fund organizations at your base or post, such as the commissary, post, or base exchange.
- ⊙ People in your place of worship may be able to assist (including your minister, priest, or rabbi, or other members of the staff).
- ⊙ Adults in organizations where your children are involved, such as PTAs, Boy Scouts or Girl Scouts.
- ⊙ The civilian personnel office on your base or post, if there is one, or any organization on the base or post that has a significant concentration of Federal civilian employees.
- ⊙ Job or transition support counselors on your base or post.
- ⊙ Nearby Federal civilian agencies. A simple "fishing" visit can provide valuable leads.

Summary

Networking is the human side of your job search. The people you know and like can help you with your career and job search. Networking should be on your "List of Things to Do" when you are nearing separation or retirement from the military. If possible, start the process a year or two ahead, or as soon as you finish reading this book!

Keep your list of contacts and networks. Create an email file and stay in touch with people. Successful networking can certainly help you with your first career after the military, but it will also help you with your 2nd and 3rd move. Start planning your network right now for your future career!

Keep up-to-date about Federal managers, jobs, incentive, recruitment and employment programs at these websites:

www.govexec.com   www.washingtonpost.com – Steve Barr's Federal Dairy
www.federaltimes.com   www.federalnewsradio.com – listen live on the Internet
www.federaldaily.com   www.monster.com – Government/Public Service Career Advice

Step 2　Federal Hiring Benefits for Veterans and Family Members
Advantages in applying for Federal jobs for veterans

Step 2: Federal Hiring Benefits for Veterans & Family Members
Advantages in applying for Federal jobs for veterans

Can your military service (or your family member's) give you an advantage in applying for Federal jobs?

Quick answer: Yes, your military service is definitely an advantage. You can apply for jobs that are otherwise open only to current Federal employees, and under certain conditions, get preference in hiring including extra points added to your passing score. Under certain conditions family members of veterans and of active duty personnel also receive some advantages in applying for jobs or hiring. Because of these advantages you can compete and beat first-time private sector applicants!

Hiring Preference

Veterans' Preference
5 points added to your passing score!
Many former service members are eligible for veterans' preference. These applicants are called "preference eligibles." You qualify for 5-point veterans' preference if you meet at least one of these criteria:

1. You served on active duty during a war in a campaign or expedition for which a campaign badge has been authorized.
2. You served on active duty during certain periods defined by specific dates. A list of these dates and more veterans' preference information is available on the CD-ROM.

You must have been discharged under honorable conditions. If an agency is using numerical scores when assessing applicants, these candidates have 5 points added to their passing scores, and must be offered jobs before non-veterans with equal or lesser scores.

10 points added to your application score!
Some military applicants who have been disabled during their service have 10 points added to their passing scores when agencies use numerical scores to assess applicants and must be offered a job before non-veterans with equal or lesser scores. For most jobs, disabled veterans with a compensable service-connected disability of 10 percent or more are listed ahead of all other applicants eligible to be hired. Some family members also may qualify as 10-point preference eligibles. You qualify for 10-point veterans' preference if you meet at least one of these criteria:

⊙   Service members who served on active duty, were separated under honorable conditions, and who establish the present existence of a service-connected disability, or who are receiving compensation, disability retirement benefits, or pension because of a law administered by the Department of Veterans Affairs.

⊙ Unmarried widows or widowers of veterans whose active duty service was during a war, and who served in a campaign or expedition for which a campaign badge was authorized, or during the period beginning April 28, 1952 and ending July 1, 1955.

⊙ Under certain conditions, the spouse of a service-connected disabled veteran or the mother of a service-connected permanently and totally disabled veteran.

Veterans Service Organizations, OPM, and the Department of Labor can provide additional information about these three conditions and more benefits for veterans.

http://www.va.gov/ - Veteran's Service Organizations
http://www.opm.gov/veterans/ - Office of Personnel Management
http://www.dol.gov/vets/welcome.html - Department of Labor

When agencies use "category ranking" instead of numerical scores to assess applicants, veterans are listed ahead of non-veterans in whatever category their qualifications put them, and must be offered jobs ahead of non-veterans in that category. For most jobs, qualified applicants with a 10 percent or greater service-connected disability are placed at the top of the highest category.

A special advantage granted to 10-point preference eligibles. You can still apply after an announcement has closed!

If you meet the definition of a 10-point preference eligible (see above), you have an advantage not granted to other applicants—you can submit an application for a closed announcement and the agency must accept it. If a selection has not been made when the agency receives your application, it must treat your application as timely. If a selection has been made, the agency must hold your application for consideration for any similar vacancy announced in the calendar quarter following your submission of your application. (Your authority to do this is based on law: 5 USC 3305.)

If you file under this special provision we recommend you email, fax or overnight your application according to the vacancy announcement instructions and include a cover letter stating clearly that you are a 10-point preference veteran applying for this position.

Military Spouse Preference (MSP)

Spouses of active duty members of the armed forces (including the Coast Guard) are eligible for military spouse preference within the Department of Defense when their active duty spouses receive a permanent change in station.

This preference may be used for many vacant positions in DoD, but the jobs must be in the commuting area of the permanent duty station of the sponsor. While all military services operate under the same DoD guidance, there are variations in how they operate their MSP programs. Generally, when the applicant is "Best Qualified" and eligible for MSP, the selecting official must hire the military spouse or have the installation commander approve a decision not to. *(NOTE: MSP does not supersede*

Veterans' Preference.) Always check with the local civilian personnel office in the target area to find out specific policies and application procedures.

Application Preference

Veterans' Employment Opportunity Act (VEOA)

The VEOA does not give you an advantage in actual hiring, but it allows you to apply for jobs that are otherwise open only to Federal employees! Even if your active duty military service does not qualify you as a "preference eligible," service in the armed forces can work to your advantage. The VEOA allows former service members to apply for vacancies that are open only to current Federal civilian employees and those who have "status" because they previously worked as Federal civilians. If an agency has announced a vacancy limited to applications from current Federal employees and is accepting applications from other Federal agencies, it must accept applications from VEOA applicants.

Being allowed to apply under the VEOA does not give an applicant any advantage in scoring his or her application (does not convey veterans' preference). The advantage you gain is being able to apply for jobs that are not open to the general public. Federal agencies usually have more job listings for internal candidates than for external candidates. To qualify for VEOA you must have served on active duty and have been separated under honorable conditions.

Special Hiring Programs

Veterans' Recruitment Appointment (VRA)

The VRA provides a Direct Hire opportunity. This special authority allows agencies to hire you "without competition" for white-collar positions through GS-11 and equivalent jobs under other pay systems. You have to meet basic qualifications, but do not have to be on a list of eligible candidates who are competing for the job. If you submit an application in response to a vacancy announcement you can be hired without having to compete with other applicants.

Get Hired Directly!

The VRA means that you can get hired DIRECTLY by the agency. Your application does not have to be ranked in competition with other applicants--you merely have to be basically qualified for the job. If you know a hiring supervisor, or meet one at a Job Fair, your VRA eligibility could lead to a noncompetitive appointment. Networking can be very helpful for VRA employment opportunities.

The following individuals are eligible for a VRA appointment:

- ⊙ Disabled veterans
- ⊙ Veterans who served on active duty in the Armed Forces during a war declared by Congress, in a campaign or expedition for which a campaign badge has been authorized.
- ⊙ Veterans who, while serving on active duty in the Armed Forces, participated in a military operation for which the Armed Forces Service Medal was awarded.
- ⊙ Veterans separated from active duty within the past 3 years.
- ⊙ There is no minimum service requirement, but the individual must have served on active duty, not active duty for training.

Use of this authority is at the discretion of the agency. Agencies can recruit candidates and make VRA appointments directly, which are initially for 2 years. Successful completion of the 2-year period may lead to a permanent civil service appointment. Persons selected for VRA appointments who have less than 15 years of education must agree to participate in a training or educational program. 15 years means a high school diploma plus three years beyond high school.

30% or more Disabled Veteran Program

Federal agencies have the authority, by law, to give noncompetitive appointments to any veteran who has a service-connected disability of 30 percent or more. Like the VRA, use of this authority is discretionary with the agency. The disability must be officially documented by the Department of Defense or the Department of Veterans Affairs. In addition, the job for which you are hired must be publicly posted.

> 30% or more Disabled Veterans can also be HIRED DIRECTLY. Networking may pay off here. Having this eligibility can get you the job without competition as long as you are basically qualified.

This authority covers jobs in all grade levels and occupations. You must meet all qualification requirements for any position to which you are appointed. This could include the requirement to achieve a passing score on a written test.

Certain Former Overseas Employees (Family Members)

This is often called (incorrectly) "spousal preference" and applies to spouses and unmarried children under 23. This hiring authority allows an individual to be noncompetitively appointed to a stateside position following employment overseas. To qualify, an individual must be a family member of a military sponsor who was officially assigned to an overseas area, have completed 52 weeks of creditable overseas service in an appropriated fund position (for example, not a military base recreation center or bar), have a performance rating of successful or better, and apply within 3 years of returning to the U.S.

The complete text of the authorizing regulation can be found in 5 CFR 315.608, "Noncompetitive appointment of certain former overseas employees." (www.gpoaccess.gov/ecfr)

Veterans Preference Does NOT Apply to the Following:

- ⊙ Jobs in the Senior Executive Service (SES)
- ⊙ Certain medical occupations in the Department of Veterans Affairs (VA is under a separate personnel system—Title 38)
- ⊙ Retired members of the armed forces UNLESS
    - ○ They are disabled veterans or
    - ○ They retired below the rank of major or equivalent
- ⊙ Scientific or professional jobs at or above GS-9 do not have "float to the top" provisions for disabled veterans with 10% or greater disability

Summary

The U.S. Government supports service members, veterans, and sometimes family members in three important ways:

- Preference in competitive hiring;
- The right to apply for jobs otherwise closed to the public; and
- Special hiring programs for veterans and some family members

Step 3 Write Your Basic Military Federal Resume
Getting started, find your documents and write your basic resume

Step 3: Write Your Basic Military Federal Resume
Getting started, find your documents and write your basic resume

Writing your first basic Military Federal Resume

Your Military Federal Resume is the most important career document you will write as you pursue your new Federal career after military service. According to Federal human resources specialists, the Work Experience section in your resume is THE most important section of the resume, because it describes your experiences, knowledge, skills and abilities. The Federal resume will be your job application, your "examination" for the job, and sometimes even your interview. Some supervisors do not interview applicants, they simply choose the best candidates and give a job offer. Some job offers are even made online in electronic job databases! (more on this in Step 9).

DEFINITION: Military Federal Resume – a federal-style resume for job applicants with active duty and reserves military experience who are targeting Federal agencies, missions and jobs. This resume style and content includes details of military experiences and duties, ranks, Military Operations and Campaigns, specific training and certifications, security clearance levels, awards and honors, projects and accomplishments.

The Military Federal Resume is used for applying for Defense, Intel, Homeland Security and other Federal agencies with missions supporting Defense, Homeland Security and Anti-terrorism Operations to protect America.

This book dedicates two chapters/steps to Federal resume writing: Step 3 and Step 7. Step 3 will get you started with finding your training and employment documents, and writing a basic resume based on the Office of Personnel Management's instructions in OF-510, Applying for a Federal Job.

Step 7 will give you proven, successful tips and strategies to focus your basic resume toward particular job announcements. We'll give you samples and instructions for writing accomplishments, keywords, a skills summary, nouns and headlines to help your resume STAND OUT!

Introducing a new resume format: the Military Federal Resume

Prior to September 11, 2001 most military-to-civilian resumes were generic, with few specifics about actual military experience. The resume terminology was simply translated into civilian language. You may still find career services personnel who recommend this strategy. The civilian resume is correct and preferred for private industry job searches as many corporate and small business managers do not understand military job duties, ranks, training or situations.

However, things in government today are different. The Federal government has a pressing need for civilian employees with military experience. For example, the Department of Homeland Security is now hiring thousands of border patrol employees. In such a case, your precise military history can give you a competitive edge. It is desirable to incorporate specific military details in your resume including rank, service name, base or post locations, operation names in which you served, relevant experiences with numbers and particulars, specialized training course titles, accomplishments and quotes. Military job assignments will be written with a description of the military activities, operations and duties.

Military Federal Resume vs. Civilian Resume:

Military Federal Resume	Civilian Resume
Rank	No Rank
Names of bases, posts and locations	No specifics about bases or posts, countries or locations
Specific accomplishments	Accomplishments generalized
Description of technical work	General descriptions
Some military terminology okay	Military terminology decoded
Clearance listed	Clearance listed
Training described, including location of training, hours of training, title of course, certification (if any)	Training may or may not be included, depending on relevance to your new career objective.
Average length: 3 to 4 pages	Average length: 2 pages

Military Federal Resume vs. Civilian Private Industry Resume

Take a FIRST LOOK at a Military Federal Resume. The next two resume excerpts demonstrate the language difference between the Military Federal Resume and a Civilian Resume. This applicant is applying for military personnel / human resources positions in either government or human resources (recruiting) in private sector. See the differences in the writing style. The Federal version keeps more of the military language. The Civilian version is shorter and includes less details about military and more about personnel operations.

Military Federal Resume targeting Military Personnel Positions

02/2003 to 05/2004; 44 hrs/wk, PERSONNEL MANAGER, MANAGEMENT SUPPORT BRANCH (CW4), United States Army Reserve, Headquarters, 63d Regional Readiness Command, Los Alamitos, CA 90720; Supervisor: Larry Wilson, 562-777-2234 (may contact).

MANAGED HISTORIC RECRUITMENT OF ACTIVE DUTY / HUMAN RESOURCE OPERATIONS. Managed military personnel services for Command Special Actions for one of the largest Army Reserve Commands in U.S. Planned, designed, implemented active duty recruitment notices (written and phone) requiring personnel to report to active duty within 2 weeks. More than __ Reservists were called to active duty for assignments in Iraq and Afghanistan over a period of 6 months.

WROTE NEW PERSONNEL REGULATIONS, IMPLEMENTED NEW PROCEDURES TO ACHIEVE LARGE CALL-UP DEMAND. Initiated and recommended guidance and policy to implement actions to best resolve complex and sensitive issues. Wrote instructions to announce / implement procedures on diverse military personnel management programs. Composed instructions to officer and enlisted personnel concerning promotions, education benefits, officer selection boards and career management.

RESEARCHED SENSITIVE, IMPORTANT CONGRESSIONAL / WHITE HOUSE INQUIRIES. Case Manager for inquiries from Army Office of Chief Legislative Liaison concerning Reservist actions and events involving diverse set of performance issues. Responded quickly to inquiries and sensitive correspondence. Investigated issues by conducting interviews with commanders, staff, and subject matter experts. Analyzed interview information and documentary evidence and compiled findings to develop and submit official responses to headquarters.

Civilian Resume Seeking Human Resources (Recruitment Position in Corporation)

02/2003 to 05/2004; 44 hrs/wk, PERSONNEL MANAGER, MANAGEMENT SUPPORT BRANCH, United States Army Reserve, Headquarters, Los Alamitos, CA 90720; Supervisor: Larry Wilson, 562-777-2234 (may contact).

MANAGED HISTORIC RECRUITMENT OF PERSONNEL AND MANAGED HUMAN RESOURCE OPERATIONS. Managed personnel services for one of the largest Army Reserve Commands in U.S. Planned, designed, implemented successful recruitment program. Developed methods of communication to recruit and present position duties and benefits.

WROTE NEW PERSONNEL REGULATIONS TO ACHIEVE LARGE NEW RECRUITMENT. Initiated and recommended guidance and policy to implement actions to best resolve complex and sensitive issues. Wrote instructions to announce / implement procedures on diverse military personnel management programs. Wrote instructions concerning career promotions, education benefits, officer selection boards and career management.

RESEARCHED SENSITIVE, IMPORTANT VIP AND PERSONNEL INQUIRIES. Case Manager for inquiries concerning personnel actions and events involving diverse set of performance issues. Responded quickly to inquiries and sensitive correspondence. Investigated issues by conducting interviews with managers and staff.

What do supervisors consider when making selections?

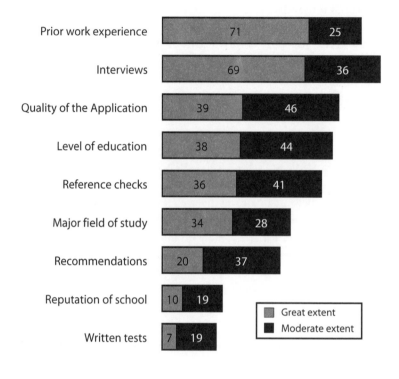

Prior work experience — Great extent: 71, Moderate extent: 25
Interviews — Great extent: 69, Moderate extent: 36
Quality of the Application — Great extent: 39, Moderate extent: 46
Level of education — Great extent: 38, Moderate extent: 44
Reference checks — Great extent: 36, Moderate extent: 41
Major field of study — Great extent: 34, Moderate extent: 28
Recommendations — Great extent: 20, Moderate extent: 37
Reputation of school — Great extent: 10, Moderate extent: 19
Written tests — Great extent: 7, Moderate extent: 19

- Great extent
- Moderate extent

Supervisors look closely at your Work Experience section of your resume to determine if you are qualified for the position.

U.S. Merit Systems Protection Board,
2000 Merit Principles Survey.

Getting Started – Find your Documents

Writing your first Federal resume means finding your career documents, evaluations, past resumes and other paperwork so that you can identify the dates of your assignments, training courses and awards. This is critical to writing your first resume or federal resume. Here's a list of documents you can compile.

Assemble your career documents and begin your basic Military Federal Resume

Separation papers

DD-214

Current LES

Performance appraisals
> Coast Guard: Performance Reviews
> Navy: Fitness Reports (Officers) or Performance Evaluations (Enlisted)
> Army: Evaluation Reports (Officer, Non-Commissioned Officer or Enlisted)
> Marine Corps: Fitness Reports (E-5 & above) or Proficiency Conduct Marks (E-4 & below)
> Air Force: Officer Performance Evaluation Report or Enlisted Performance Appraisal

DD 2586-Verification of Military Experience and Training (VMET), Military Training Record
> Coast Guard: Educational Assessment Worksheet (CGI 1560/04e) - used to evaluate USCG military experience and training.
> Navy: Electronic Training Record
> Marine Corps: Basic Training Record (BTR)
> Army: Education & Training Section of the OMPF

Training certifications and forms

Previous resumes or employment forms

Award citations

Letters of commendation and letters of appreciation

Articles or letters concerning military activities

Professional organization memberships or conference attendance materials

College transcripts

Military transcripts
> Navy & Marine Corps: Sailor & Marine Transcript (SMART)
> Army: Army/American Council on Education Registry Transcript (AARTS)
> Air Force: Community College of the Air Force Transcript

Course descriptions for courses relevant to your objective

Specialized training (include joint or other training which may not be listed elsewhere)

Military Federal Resumes require either Rank or Salary

In order to evaluate your qualifications, knowledge, skills and abilities for a target position, it helps the human resources recruiter if you include your rank.

Office of Personnel Management's Form OF-510 instructions:

You must include your grade, rank or beginning and ending salary for each position for the last 10 years.

Decision 1: **Rank** – Use your rank if it is to your career search benefit. If your current rank is equivalent to your target career objective, then the rank would help the HR specialist know that you are qualified for a certain grade.

Decision 2: **Salary** – If you don't want to use your rank because you are performing duties which are much higher level than the rank would imply, you should include your salary plus allowances. Your annual salary review will give you the salary, plus housing and allowances so that your compensation is not just what is shown on your Leave and Earnings Statement.

Decision 3: **Grade** – Include this if you are currently a permanent, temporary or term civilian employee in the government.

"With getting started writing their resume, to spark their memories and make the resume writing process easier, we ask all military personnel to come in with a copy of their DD Form 2586, the Verification of Military Experience and Training which can be downloaded at www. dmdc.osd.mil/vmet. We also ask them to bring their annual performance appraisals. In the Navy, these are called Evaluations (enlisted) or FITREPS- fitness reports (officer). From Marine Corps personnel we ask for Fitness Reports (for E-5 and above) or Proficiency and Conduct Marks (E-4 and below). Marines can also bring a printout of their Basic Training Record (BTR)- this includes a listing of local and military courses and Marine Corps Institute (distance learning) courses. These important documents should all become part of the Career Catalog".

—Enochia T. Anderson, FJST, CFRWC,
Transition Assistance Program Manager, Fleet & Family Support Center, Rota, Spain

Get more help with your Basic Resume here: www.resume-place.com/military

Sailor/Marine/American Council of Education Registry Transcript (SMART)

SMART transcripts translate military education and job experience into civilian language by listing college-equivalent credit recommendations to assist colleges and universities in credentialing Sailors' and Marines' experience and knowledge.

SMART transcripts are available to active-duty Sailors and Marines, enlisted members and officers, reserve component personnel, and separated or retired Sailors and Marines. You can find out more online at: *https://smart.cnet.navy.mil/*

To Obtain Your Verification of Military Experience and Training (VMET) Document

To get your verification document, go to the VMET web site at *http://www.dmdc.osd.mil/vmet*. All separating military personnel can electronically download and print their VMET from the VMET Web site. Follow the instructions and download your document. You can now get your verification document at any time online; however, you should retrieve it no later than 120 days prior to your separation. If you have problems getting your VMET and need assistance, check with your Transition Counselor.

Once You Receive Your Verification Document

Identify the items that relate to the type of work or education you are pursuing and include them in your resume. If there are problems with information listed on the form, follow the guidance indicated below for your respective service:

* **Army:** Review and follow the guidance provided by the Frequently Asked Questions (FAQs) listed on the VMET online website.
* **Air Force:** Follow the instructions in the verification document cover letter or contact your Transition Counselor.
* **Navy:** Contact your Command Career Counselor or your local Fleet and Family Support Center Transition Office.
* **Marine Corps:** Follow the instructions in the verification document cover letter. If you need further assistance, contact your Administrative Office.

Michael J. Spiltener, Work and Family Life Consultant, Fleet and Family Support Center, Yokosuka, Japan

What's the Difference between a Government Contractor Resume and a Military Federal Resume?

The contractors who are working side-by-side with Federal workers are performing the same Federal jobs, so your Military Federal Resume can be used for contractor applications as well!

The good news is that a government contractor resume could be basically the same resume as a Military Federal Resume, except that you TAKE OUT your Social Security number and veterans' preference information from the top of the resume. Your Federal resume might be 3-4 pages long. The contractors might prefer 2-3 pages, but they want all of the information about your experience, so length is not a consideration. Government contracting recruiters are using electronic resume submissions, so they can receive a 3-page resume in the same amount of time as a 2-page resume. Length is not the question, the descriptions of your experience and specialized skills is what's important to the contracting recruiter. Most contractor resume websites do not specify resume length; they are focusing on relevant experience.

Recruiters from major government contractors, such as Boeing, Lockheed Martin, SAIC will appreciate the details of your experiences, skills, and specifics of locations and training, so that they can decide if your skills are appropriate for certain contracts. You will usually submit the electronic resume format into their online resume application systems. Military personnel are in great demand because you have the security clearances they need for immediate contract performance.

What to include in your Federal resume, based on OF-510, Office of Personnel Management's flyer, "Applying for a Federal Job".

http://www.opm.gov/Forms/pdfimage/of0510.pdf

Job Information: Announcement number, title, and grade.

Personal Information: Full name, mailing address (with ZIP code), day and evening phone numbers (with area code), social security number, country of citizenship, veterans' preference, reinstatement eligibility, and highest Federal civilian grade held.

Education: Colleges or universities, name, city and state, majors, type and year of any degrees received (if no degree, show total credits earned and indicate whether semester or quarter hours). High school name, city, and state, date of diploma or GED (some announcements do not ask for high school).

Work Experience: Job title, duties and accomplishments, employer's name and address, supervisor's name and phone number, starting and ending dates (month and year), hours per week, salary, and indicate whether or not your current supervisor may be contacted. Prepare a separate entry for each job.

Other Qualifications: Job-related training courses (title and year), job-related skills, current job-related certificates and licenses, job-related honors, awards, and special accomplishments.

Military Resume Writing Section-by-Section, Based on the Instructions in the OF-510

PERSONAL INFORMATION:

Full name, mailing address (with ZIP code), day and evening phone numbers (with area code), social security number, country of citizenship, veterans' preference, reinstatement eligibility, and highest Federal civilian grade held.

Email: Sign up for an internet email that includes your last name if you can, so that your email can be searchable.

Address: Some Federal job announcements require that you live within a 50-mile radius of where the job is located, and others state that they will not pay for relocation. This is difficult to handle because you cannot live in multiple locations while job hunting. Read the information about the location and "who can apply" carefully. If you see a job that's in the Washington, DC area and it requires that you live within a 50-mile radius, disclose in your resume that you are willing to relocate at your own expense, or that you have a military move coming to you.

Telephone: Cell phones are great for job searches because you can set up a professional voicemail and take most of the calls yourself (instead of family or co-workers). On the other hand, job interviews are *not* great on a cell phone!

Social Security number: You must include your Social Security number (SSN) on your Federal or Military Federal Resume. The government securely manages employees and job applicants via the SSN number. If you do not include your SSN, you will not be considered for a job. It's as simple as that.

Country of citizenship: Most Federal jobs require U.S. Citizenship, but some allow non-citizens with working visas to apply for jobs. Read the vacancy announcements.

Special note on citizenship: If the applicant is a non-citizen, he/she may not be eligible for Federal jobs. Most agencies require U.S. citizenship, but some are able to hire non-citizens. Each vacancy announcement will indicate whether U.S. citizenship is required for the job. If citizenship is an issue for you or a family member, be sure to read the vacancy announcement carefully before applying. For more information go to: *www.opm.gov or www.usajobs.com*

Veterans' Preference or Veterans' Hiring Program: 5-Point Preference or 10-Point Preference, if eligible (see Step 2 for more information).

Reinstatement eligibility and highest Federal civilian grade held: If you previously worked for the U.S. government as a civilian, include your highest job title and grade, and the dates held here.

Andrew P. MacArthur

6748 Smithey Avenue
Dallas, TX 75201
Home: (555) 123-4546
Work: (555) 789-1212
Email: andrew@us.army.mil

Social Security Number: 333-33-3333
Country of Citizenship: United States of America
Veteran's Preference: 5 points

JOB INFORMATION:
Announcement number, title, and grade.

Objective: This information can be added to the top of the resume, or you may simply include the title of the position, grade and announcement number in the agency's Profile or Registration pages when you set up your resume and information into the agency's database. For example,

> *Objective: Human Resources Specialist, GS-201-11, Announcement No. 10505*

"There is a "job description" of each MOS that I have found to be very helpful in writing Federal resumes as well as developing resumes for those who are in the military and are seeking civilian employment. It is very complete and it assists me in understanding their job a little better so I can translate it into a civilian position or match it to another Federal position. Every job description/classification instruction/classification regulation is in a book that can be found in all training departments and personnel offices. The military member may contact their personnel department to receive one of these descriptions/classification instructions/classification regulations or they can click on the publications button in the website for each branch of the military."

—*Susanne Blanton, CFRW, Grand Island, NY,*
Air Force/Air National Guard Dependent

WORK EXPERIENCE CHRONOLOGY:

Job title, duties and accomplishments, employer's name and address, supervisor's name and phone number, starting and ending dates (month and year), hours per week, salary, and indicate whether or not your current supervisor may be contacted. Prepare a separate entry for each job.

Which positions will you include in your resume? Some agency resume builders give you space to include only six jobs. Some online resume sections are unlimited. An effective strategy is to aim for about six job entries because earlier experience can be summarized. Some positions which were short or repetitive can be left off.

What about gaps in dates? Federal HR specialists are looking for recent and relevant positions. If you have unrelated job or assignment entries, they may be summarized or unlisted according to the circumstances. Accounting for every day and month is not necessary. Hiring specialists are most interested in your experiences that are relevant to the job.

Sample:
02/2003 to 05/2004; 44 hrs/wk, PERSONNEL MANAGER, MANAGEMENT SUPPORT BRANCH (CW4), United States Army Reserve, Headquarters, 63d Regional Readiness Command, Los Alamitos, CA 90720; Supervisor: Larry Wilson, 562-777-2234 (may contact).

Job title: PERSONNEL MANAGER, MANAGEMENT SUPPORT BRANCH
Employer's name and address: United States Army Reserve, Headquarters, 63d Regional Readiness Command, Los Alamitos, CA 90720
Supervisor's name and phone number: CPT John Smith, 49-999-888-2222
Starting and ending dates (month and year): 02/2003 to 05/2004
Hours per week, salary or rank: 40 hours per week; CW4
Indicate whether or not your current supervisor may be contacted: (may be contacted)

Duties and accomplishments:
SENIOR MANAGEMENT ADVISOR / CONSULTANT. Analyzed, interpreted, and reported Special Actions case-oriented program information to senior managers. Problem cases often became high profile and occasionally attracted involvement from senior staff. Provided oral briefings on a case-by-case basis, addressing issues and concerns expressed by senior managers. Supervised the utilization of the Army Personnel database systems to update, maintain, and manipulate information and to ensure the most current and accurate information was available. Personnel systems consisted of 3 databases addressing Congressional inquiries, casualties, and Line of Duty (LOD) investigations.

RESEARCHED SENSITIVE CONGRESSIONAL / WHITE HOUSE INQUIRIES. Case Manager for inquiries. Expedited congressional inquiries and other sensitive correspondence.

Investigated issues by interviewing commanders, staff, and subject matter experts. Analyzed interview information, documentary evidence, and regulatory guidance. Compiled findings to develop and submit official responses to headquarters.

MANAGED LINE OF DUTY INVESTIGATIONS. Coordinated initiation, completion, and approval of formal and informal LOD investigations. Ensured accurate documentation and validation of service connected injuries, diseases, or deaths. Reviewed documentation for completeness and compliance with regulations; forwarded to senior management. Advised soldiers on regulations regarding LOD approval requirements.

COMMAND POSITION MANAGEMENT / COMMAND SELECTION BOARD SUPPORT: Managed staffing and reassignment actions for tenured senior command positions. Wrote, distributed vacancy announcements and application instructions. Received, reviewed applications for completeness. Referred applications to board of senior commanders for review and selection. Provided results to the Board President for review. Composed official memo for Commanding General's signature approving results. Made public distribution of official results.

TEAM LEADER / TRAINER: Trained employees in benefits administration. Coached employees in bereavement counseling. Promoted cooperative working relationships and fostered cohesive team work. Recommended performance recognition or corrective action, when necessary. Recognized outstanding performance of staff in areas of multi-tasking, deadline management, problem-solving, and teamwork.

SPECIAL ASSIGNMENTS: Managed Casualty Mission during dramatic increase due to deaths related to Operations Enduring Freedom and Iraqi Freedom.

Prepared and presented an oral presentation at the annual G-1 Personnel Conference.

ACCOMPLISHMENTS:

IMPROVED LINE OF DUTY CASE MANAGEMENT SYSTEM. Assessed need, used problem-solving skills to revise and improve case tracking systems and communications with supporting agencies. Liaison with Military Medical Support Office, Command Health Services Coordinator, Military Treatment Facilities, LOD senior managers to ensure claims were processed and soldiers received medical treatment and compensation.

RECOGNITION: "CW4 McArthur epitomizes a senior warrant officer with technical expertise, experience, and professionalism. His performance materially improved the operation of the Management Support Branch during a very arduous period of increased LODs, Congressional Inquiries and casualties caused by the high level of mobilizations and deployments. His calm, professional attitude set the example for his branch." *Performance Evaluation, January 2004*

EDUCATION:

Colleges or universities, name, city and state, majors, type and year of any degrees received (if no degree, show total credits earned and indicate whether semester or quarter hours). High school, name, city, and state, date of diploma or GED.

Sample 1

Ohio State University, Columbus, OH, Bachelor of Arts, History, 1980
Troy High School, Troy, OH, Diploma, 1975

Sample 2

MPA: Major, Public Management, Leadership; In-Progress; Completed 25 credit hours
Troy State University, Fort Belvoir, VA.
MS in Administration with Honors; Major, Organizational Behavior, 2004. GPA, 3.64, Central Michigan University, Mt. Pleasant, MI.
BA with Honors: Major, Human Resource Management, 2003. GPA, 3.89, Strayer University, Woodbridge, VA. OUTSTANDING SCHOLAR
Anderson High School, Anderson, IN; Graduated 1975

If you graduated recently, a list and/or description of your research papers or team projects may be included in your resume.

Are you a college grad?

If you are a recent graduate, or if your education is critical to your target job objective, you could consider more information and recent grad samples from the award-winning book and CD with samples, *The Student's Federal Career Guide,* by Kathryn and Emily Troutman, pub. 2004, The Resume Place.

If your GPA is 3.45 or higher for your undergraduate degree, you are an OUTSTANDING SCHOLAR

If you are applying for entry-level GS-5 or -7 positions, the Outstanding Scholar Program could help you stand out. The Outstanding Scholar Program is a special, court-approved hiring method that agencies may use to fill entry-level (GS-5 and -7) jobs in over 100 professional and administrative occupations. This special hiring method allows agencies to hire individuals who meet the definition of Outstanding Scholar without competition.

This program is widely used by some agencies and not used at all by others. Although the Outstanding Scholar Program allows agencies to hire individuals without competition, some agencies have established Outstanding Scholar hiring programs that include competition. These agencies accept applications from college graduates who meet the Outstanding Scholar definition and then make their selections based on how well the qualifications of the people in this restricted applicant pool meet their job needs.

An Outstanding Scholar is defined as someone who earned a bachelors degree from an accredited school and who meets either of the following criteria:
1. Earned a 3.5 Grade Point Average or higher during their undergraduate education (3.45 also qualifies because it rounds up to 3.5, **or**
2. Graduated in the upper ten percent of their undergraduate class or major university subdivision, such as the College of Arts and Sciences.

The Outstanding Scholar Program does not require that the degree be recently earned, which may help explain why OPM data show that the average age of all outstanding scholars hired in fiscal year 2000 was nearly 30 years. Neither does the Program require a specific relationship between the degree earned and the job being filled.

Most agencies clearly identify on the vacancy announcements their Outstanding Scholar job openings. If you meet the qualifications, this is a hiring possibility you should consider. Most hiring should be at GS-7 because Outstanding Scholars meet Superior Academic Achievement criteria, but the agency can choose to offer only GS-5. This is an agency decision, just as accepting or rejecting the terms of a job offer is yours. Agencies may accept your application before you are a graduate, but they will require verification of your eligibility before actually hiring you. You will be required to prove you meet one of the eligibility criteria through a transcript (GPA) or certification by the appropriate school or academic department (top 10% requirement).

OTHER QUALIFICATIONS:
Job-related training courses (title and year). Add classroom hours if more than 8 hours.

It is your choice how far back you go with the dates and course titles. If the courses are job-related, you can include all courses that support your objective. This Federal jobseeker included aviation training throughout his career because of his interest in working with FAA in the aviation industry. Other resume writers will not include courses beyond 10 years because of the relevancy of technology and training.

Sample:
U.S. Army Training Modules completed:
Command and General Staff College, 1998; Supply Management Officer, 24 hrs., 1996; Battle Focused Instructor Training, 16 hrs. 1995; Aviation Commanders Safety Course, 40 hrs., 1991; Aviation Accident Prevention Course; Dynamics of Employee Behavior, 1986; Combined Arms Staff

School, 1986; Instructor Training Course, 1985; Aviation Officer Advanced Course; 101st Aviation Maintenance Officer Course, 1983; 101st Aviation Maintenance Officer, 1983; Rotary Wing Flight School, 1981; Air Assault School, 1980; Armor Officer Basic Course, 1980; Airborne School, 1978.

Job-related skills

This is an important section to add important keywords, skills, specialized qualifications, knowledge of systems and programs and other information that could help you to stand out when the supervisor reviews resumes.

Sample:
Proficient in contract negotiations. Successfully practiced in purchasing and manufacturing supervision in support of cellular manufacturing. Experienced with Total Quality Management to incorporate quality during manufacturing. Talented at source development, including locating new parts, technology, lower cost items for purchase, and product development worldwide. Successful supervisor, managing, monitoring, coordinating work, and mentoring up to 53 employees.

Technical Expertise: Skilled in implementing and operating Systems Application and Processing (SAP) and Enterprise Resource Planning (ERP) in manufacturing environments. Proficient in using Just In Time/Vendor Managed Inventory (JIT/VMI) systems to ensure inventories are stocked to support manufacturing. Skilled in use of Manufacturing Resource Planning (MRP).

Computer Proficiencies: Microsoft products, Internet research.

Communication Skills: Mature values and polished professional image coupled with excellent oral and written communication skills. Outstanding interpersonal skills, demonstrating customer service orientation and team leadership.

> "Another important piece of information is any records on Volunteer/Community Activities additional duty. For example, our base keeps track of all volunteer hours and placements. So if the volunteer or community activity is relevant to the occupational area they are pursuing they can also add this experience to their Federal resume".
>
> —*Emili Morales-Kuchler-GS-09, Employment & Transition Program Community Readiness Technician, Spangdahlem Air Base, Germany*

 15 Sample Military Federal Resumes on the CD-ROM

57

Current job-related certificates and licenses:

Sample:
Federal Aviation Administration Certified Single Engine Commercial, Instrument Helicopter Pilot

Job-related honors, awards, and special accomplishments:

Sample:
Army Meritorious Service (1 Oak Leaf), Army Commendation Medal (3 Oak Leafs)
Army Achievement Medal (2 Oak Leafs), National Defense Medal (1 Oak Leaf)
Armed Forces Reserve Medal, Overseas Training Ribbon
Army Service Ribbon, GWOT Service Medal
Kosovo Campaign Medal, Indiana Commendation Medal
Army Reserve Component Achievement Medal

History of the SF-171, OF-612, Federal Resume Facts

For nearly 40 years, the only application accepted by the Federal government was the Standard Form 171 (SF-171). In 1995, the SF-171 was discontinued, and the government began accepting the Optional Form 612 (OF-612) or a Federal resume. The Federal resume (different from a private industry resume) includes all of the mandatory compliance details that are in the OF-612 and the SF-171. Though the forms are still accepted, we recommend using a Federal resume—it's much more flexible and user-friendly. If an announcement states that you can submit "a resume, OF-612, SF-171 or any other format you choose," then you can submit a Federal-style resume as described in this chapter.

IMPORTANT: When you submit your Military Federal Resume, you do NOT also have to submit the OF-612. You can submit the resume only, as long as it has all of the information described in this chapter and similar to the samples in this book.

Summary

Now that you have created your basic resume and outlined your employment chronology, education, certification and awards, you are ready to learn more about Federal job announcements. In Step 4, we'll look at Federal job titles and position descriptions and how to correlate your experience and interests to them. Later in Step 7, we'll return to writing a resume focused on key words in vacancy announcements.

Step 4   Analyzing Where You Fit in Federal Government
Which Federal jobs are right for you? What salary is right for you?

Step 4: Analyzing Where you Fit in Federal Government

Which Federal jobs are right for you? What salary is right for you?

Which Federal jobs are right for you?

Once you understand a few basics about Federal employment, you will feel more comfortable with your Federal job search.

First of all, it's great to know that the government is hiring! There are numerous opportunities in defense, homeland security, intelligence, law enforcement, and other Federal agencies where you can use your skills and knowledge gained in the military. This step will assist you in identifying and locating those jobs for which you qualify at the right salary. Further, you will be able to effectively search for and analyze jobs on www.usajobs.gov and other Federal employment websites.

Due to the large number of retiring personnel within the baby boom generation, there is an expected "human capital crisis" in the Federal government. Approximately 50% of the 1.8 million government employees are eligible to retire within the next five years. That astounding fact means that jobs and opportunities are available for YOU!

How much money do you want to make?

How do you qualify for a certain Federal salary? Learn how to analyze your own education and experience to determine how you can qualify for a certain salary. Study the three different Federal pay systems so that you can understand government pay.

Three Federal Pay Systems

A. Pay Bands – this brand new pay system for Federal employees is incorporated in DoD's National Service Personnel System, but is also used in other organizations.
B. General Schedule, or GS, for professional, administrative, technical, clerical (white-collar) positions.
C. Federal Wage System, or FWS, for trade or craft (blue-collar) positions.

A. PAY BANDS—A GROWING ALTERNATIVE TO THE GENERAL SCHEDULE

This new pay system is currently being used by Department of Homeland Security, DoD agencies, a few pilot agencies, and potentially may spread to the entire Federal government!

Many agencies have found the current GS grade system too rigid for recruitment and promotion, and have created more flexible pay and grading systems within their own organization. For instance, within the GS system, an employee must work in a particular grade for one full year before promotion eligibility. Also, managers do have limited flexibility to offer exceptional candidates higher beginning salaries.

Pay banding groups occupations with similar job characteristics together, and merges two, three, or more GS grades into a single "pay band." For example take a job that previously was announced at the GS-9 level, with promotion potential to GS-12. Under the GS grading system, the vacancy would show a pay range of $38,500 to $49,000, and advancement beyond GS-9 would be subject to promotion rules including one year time in grade at each level. Under pay banding, the announcement could show a position the pay for which spans GS grades 9 through 12, and the pay range would be $38,500 through 70,500. Initial salary placement would depend on qualifications and advancement within that range would be determined by performance without the time-in-grade restriction.

Another advantage of Pay Band is that managers can promote individuals within the band based on performance. Pay banding systems rely heavily on performance to determine pay and placement within the band. Having broad bands reduces the need for competitive promotions and gives managers more authority to effectively address human resources needs.

Pay Band agencies do not use the GS, WG or GG acronym before the grade or salary. Each agency has its own unique acronym Pay Band salaries.

How do you know where you fit in the Pay Band Salary? You can look at the following sources to determine your pay, grade and how your qualifications convert into a specific salary or pay.

> ### On the CD-ROM: More Resources for Federal Job Descriptions
> ⊙ Classification Standard Sample and Website
> ⊙ Qualification Standard Sample and Website
> ⊙ Many vacancy announcements analyzed and interpreted

B. GENERAL SCHEDULE (GS)–HIGHLIGHTS

General Schedule jobs encompass professional, administrative, clerical, and technical occupations. The GS has 15 grades, each representing a progressively more responsible level of work difficulty and responsibility. Each grade has 10 steps.

GS is a national pay system, but all national rates are increased by locality pay adjustments. A GS-9, Step 1 employee in Des Moines, IA is paid less than the same employee in San Francisco, CA, due to the increased cost of living.

Salary increase **within** a grade is based on a combination of performance and time in the grade. Career movement **between grades** is through promotion.

C. FEDERAL WAGE SYSTEM (FWS)–HIGHLIGHTS

Pay is set in the Federal Wage System by locality. There are more than 250 local wage areas covering both appropriated fund and non-appropriated fund jobs (non-appropriated jobs are NOT paid by a Congressional budget, but rather by the agency's own earnings).

There are separate grading systems and wage scales for non-supervisory employees (WG), leaders (WL) and supervisors (WS). Each grade has 5 pay steps: Step 2 of each grade is set at the full prevailing private industry rate for similar work in the local area; Step 5 is set 12 percent above the prevailing rate.

Movement **within** a grade is based on performance and time in grade. Movement **between** grades is based on promotion.

SALARY TABLE 2005 - General Schedule*
SALARY TABLE 2005-GS
Incorporating The 2.50% General Schedule Increase
Effective January 2005
Annual Rates by Grade and Step

GRADE	STEP 1	STEP 2	STEP 3	STEP 4	STEP 5	STEP 6	STEP 7	STEP 8	STEP 9	STEP 10
1	16016	16550	17083	17613	18146	18459	18984	19515	19537	20036
2	18007	18435	19031	19537	19755	20336	20917	21498	22079	22660
3	19647	20302	20957	21612	22267	22922	23577	24232	24887	25542
4	22056	22791	23526	24261	24996	25731	26466	27201	27936	28671
5	24677	25500	26323	27146	27969	28792	29615	30438	31261	32084
6	27507	28424	29341	30258	31175	32092	33009	33926	34843	35760
7	30567	31586	32605	33624	34643	35662	36681	37700	38719	39738
8	33852	34980	36108	37236	38364	39492	40620	41748	42876	44004
9	37390	38636	39882	41128	42374	43620	44866	46112	47358	48604
10	41175	42548	43921	45294	46667	48040	49413	50786	52159	53532
11	45239	46747	48255	49763	51271	52779	54287	55795	57303	58811
12	54221	56028	57835	59642	61449	63256	65063	66870	68677	70484
13	64478	66627	68776	70925	73074	75223	77372	79521	81670	83819
14	76193	78733	81273	83813	86353	88893	91433	93973	96513	99053
15	89625	92613	95601	98589	101577	104565	107553	110541	113529	116517

*Does not include locality pay for various cities in the U.S.

WHAT IS THE FEDERAL JOB SALARY OR GRADE FOR WHICH YOU BEST QUALIFY?

Here's a Quick Chart to compare your current military rank to an equivalency chart showing Federal grade and salary. While the following chart offers a quick guide, agency HR specialists will use the qualifications standards, which focus on qualifications, work experience, training and education to determine your grade eligibility rather than the rank-to-grade method. Note: Describing the usefulness of this chart is on page 65.

Quick Guide – Military to Federal Equivalency Chart

Federal Civilian Grade—General Schedule	Federal Civilian Grade—Wage System	Military—Commissioned Officer (Army/Air Force/ UMSC, then Navy/Coast Guard ranks)	Military— Warrant Officer	Military--Enlisted
GS-01				E-1
GS-02				E-3
GS-03	WG 1-8			E-4
GS-04	WG 9-11			E-4
GS-05	WL 1-5			E-5
GS-06	WS 1-7			E-6
GS-07		O-1 Second Lieutenant or Ensign	WO-1	
GS-08				E-7
GS-09	WG 12-15	O-2 First Lieutenant of Lieutenant (Junior Grade)	CWO-2	
GS-10	WS 8-13			E-8
	WL 6-14			
GS-11		O-3 Captain or Lieutenant	CWO-3	E-9
GS-12		O-4 Major or Lieutenant Commander	CWO-4	
GS-13	WS 14-19	O-4 or 5 Lieutenant Colonel/ Major or Commander/Lieutenant Commander	CWO-5	
GS-14	WL-15	O-5 Lieutenant Colonel or Commander		
GS-15		O-6 Colonel or Captain		
SES or equivalent		O-10 General or Admiral O-9 Lieutenant General or Vice Admiral O-8 Major General or Rear Admiral (Upper Half) O-7 Brigadier General or Rear Admiral (Lower Half)		

The Military to Federal Equivalency Chart

This chart does not work if your rank does not reflect the quality or level of the work you were performing. Let's say you are currently an E-4. If your military work is professional, then the chart suggests that you can be considered for GS-5 jobs. But maybe your E-4 service was spent aboard a ship maintaining and repairing marine equipment such as propulsion equipment, lifeboat davits, anchor handling gear, or maybe even missile tube equipment. This is traditional craft, trades, and labor (blue-collar) work that falls into the wage system. Our equivalency chart would suggest you could qualify for a non-supervisory job as high as WG-11, or perhaps a wage leader job as high as WL-5. These may be useful rules of thumb, but they are only that. Agencies do not use an equivalency chart to determine your qualifications for a particular job. This chart is just a starting point for you to analyze various military ranks with Federal job grades and salaries.

SOURCES OF INFORMATION TO HELP YOU DETERMINE YOUR FUTURE SALARY

Federal Vacancy Announcements

Your BEST SOURCE for determining the salary for a prospective Federal job is the Federal vacancy announcement's QUALIFICATIONS section. This method is faster and easier, and far more accurate than consulting the Classification Standards or the Qualifications Standards. The vacancy announcement's qualifications section will tell you exactly what specialized experience, education, training or years of experience are required to qualify for the position. Read the DUTIES in the announcement to decide if you actually want to perform this job for 40+ hours per week!. The vacancy announcement is covered in more depth in Step 5. Again, this is your BEST SOURCE OF INFORMATION ABOUT A SPECIFIC JOB'S, GRADES, DUTIES AND QUALIFICATIONS!

Qualifications Standards

The Office of Personnel Management has written Qualifications Standards for most Federal jobs. These are available in the Qualifications Standards for occupational series (or job title) and show the details required for each position. Federal agencies are required to apply these standards during the hiring process. In addition, Qualifications Standards measure how people qualify; Classification Standards determine job grades.

Classification Standards for Federal Jobs

Position Classification Standards are similar to the Qualifications Standards. This source is primarily used by human resources specialists and outlines exactly what is required in a certain job at a certain grade level. The classification standards are used to classify a job. The HR specialist can determine the correct title, occupational series, and grade for each unique set of duties. As a jobseeker, reading the classification standards will give you a detailed picture of what is required at each successive grade level. You can also get a sense of how best to target your resume for your grade.

Finding a Federal Job That is Right for You

We analyzed 14 common military-to-Federal job series, 200 MOS and 48 vacancy announcements to help you recognize Federal jobs that may fit your experience and training. We compared the qualifications for these military jobs to government jobs in our exclusive "Find Your Federal Job Chart™" and included the position descriptions.

FEDERAL JOB SERIES ANALYZED:

- ⊙ **Administrative Occupations**
- ⊙ **Aviation** or Aviation-Related Career Fields, including Aeronautical Engineering, Engineering Technician, Air Safety, Flight Operations and Air Traffic Control or ATC Support
- ⊙ **Biological Laboratory** and Animal Health Laboratory Services Occupations
- ⊙ Criminal Investigation Occupations
- ⊙ **Electronics** Career fields including: Engineering, Engineering Technician, Production Control, Training, and Electronics Mechanic
- ⊙ **General Administrative** career field, including: Program Support or General Administration work in almost any conceivable federal work setting
- ⊙ **Human Resources Management** career field, including specialist and support positions working in both civilian and military personnel specialties
- ⊙ **Law Enforcement** occupations and possibly combat arms specialties for lower graded openings
- ⊙ **Logistics**, including Logistical Support, General Supply and Inventory Management
- ⊙ **Intelligence Analyst** - Primary and duty specialties that provide a background in analyzing information and reaching conclusions based on the analysis, or education that substitutes for this kind of experience.
- ⊙ Related **Military Equipment Repair**, including Heavy Mobile Equipment Repairer, HVAC Equipment Mechanic
- ⊙ **Security Specialist** - Security/Safety Carrier field, including jobs in the Department of Homeland Security.
- ⊙ **Training and General Education** Career Field – Training Specialist, Supervisory Training Specialist, Law Enforcement Specialist (Training)
- ⊙ **Property Disposal Clerk and Management** - Various occupations that provide a background in managing and disposing of property
- ⊙ **Program & Management Analyst** – Virtually any staff planning experience would qualify for this broad occupational field which includes analytical training and writing

ABOUT THE FIND YOUR FEDERAL JOB CHART™ —on the CD-ROM

The Find Your Federal Job ChartTM which is on the next 9 pages is also on the CD-ROM! You will find 48 LINKED actual vacancy announcements (closing dates are not current, but the announcements are real). You will also find the short narrative descriptions about each position linked in the Excel sheet. To find more current announcements similar to these go to *www.usajobs.gov* and the DOD agency websites.

FIND YOUR FEDERAL JOB CHART™

Fields of Military Training & Experience	MOS	Related Federal Civilian Work Fields or Occupations	Examples of Federal Agencies Hiring for Jobs like these
Administrative Occupations	**ENLISTED ONLY**		Virtually every Federal civilian organization has office clerical and technical jobs. We identify only a few of the many possibilities in this example For many jobs in this broad field, education beyond high school counts less than related work experience to qualify for the jobs. Thus, the experience you gained in the service of your country may make you eligible to continue that service in a new office clerical or technical support capacity.
	Army--71L	Misc. Clerk and Assistant, GS-0303	
	Air Force--3A000, 3A051	Office Automation Clerical and	
	Coast Guard--60	Assistance, GS- 0326	
	Marine Corps--0151	Clerk-Typist, GS-0322	
	Navy--YN, SN 9750	Correspondence Clerk, GS-0309	
		Work Unit Supervising, GS-0313	
		Secretary, GS-0318	
Aviation Or Aviation-related Career Fields Including Aeronautical Engineering, Engineering Technicians, Air Safety, Flight Operations, And Air Traffic Control Or Atc Support	**ENLISTED**		
	Army--15Q, 93C, 71L	Air Traffic Assistance, GS-2154,	Department of the Air Force
	Air Force--1C1xx, 3AOxx;	Flight Operations Clerk, GS-0303	Department of the Army
	Coast Guard--591, 360	Flight Operations Records Assistant,	
	Marine Corps--7257, 0151, 9935	GS-0303	
	Navy--ET1570; AC(numerous possible)		
	9566, SN9750, YN		
	All services--mechanics with experience	Aviation Safety Inspection, GS-1825	Federal Aviation Administration
	in avionics, powerplants, or airframes		
	for aircraft over 12,500 pounds gross		
	weight at takeoff		
	OFFICER AND WARRANT OFFICER		
	Army--21A, 21D	Aerospace Engineer, GS-0861	Department of the Air Force
	Air Force--62E1A, 62E1B, 62E3A,	Aircraft Maintenance Management,	Department of the Army
	62E3B, 32Exx	GS- 1601	Department of the Navy
	Coast Guard--61, 55, 56	Army Training Instructor (Aviation),	
	Marine Corps--1120, 1330, 6005, 9620	GS-1712	
	Navy--150, 151, 152, 510, 653,		
	Secondary MOS 54xx, 1101,		
	DMOS (possible) 8002, 8004, 4205, 4230,		
	4305, 4310, 9442		
	NOTE: Engineering jobs have a positive		
	education requirement.		

Fields of Military Training & Experience	MOS	Related Federal Civilian Work Fields or Occupations	Examples of Federal Agencies Hiring for Jobs like these
	ENLISTED ONLY		Department of Veterans Affairs
Biomedical Laboratory And Animal Health Laboratory Services Occupations	Army--91K, 91R, 91T	Biological Science Laboratory	Department of the Army
	Air Force--4T051, 4T052, 4T090	Technician, GS -0404	Department of the Air Force
	Coast Guard--Unknown	Medical Technician, GS-0645	Department of the Navy
	Marine Corps--See below (Navy)	Medical Technical Assistant, GS-0650	USDA, Agricultural Research Service
	Navy--M, HM8506	Animal Health Technician, GS-0704	DHHS, Indian Health Service
Criminal Investigation Occupations	**ENLISTED**	Criminal Investigator, GS-1811	Department of Justice--
	Army--95D	(Usually has a duty title of "Special	Federal Bureau of Investigation
	Air Force--7S091, 7S031, 7S071,	Agent.")	Bureau of Alcohol, Tobacco, Firearms,
	7S091, 7S000	Securities Compliance Examining,	and Explosives
	Coast Guard--401	GS-1831	Drug Enforcemeny Administration
	Marine Corps--5821, 5822	General Investigations, Inspection,	Department of Homeland Security--
	Navy-- MA2002	and Compliance, GS-1801	Customs and Border Patrol
			Immigration and Customs Enforcement
	OFFICER & WARRANT OFFICER		Secret Service
	Army--31A, 311A		Department of the Treasury--
	Air Force--31P1, 31P3, 31P4, 85G0		Internal Revenue Service
	Coast Guard--09, 024		Every department, Office of Inspector
	Marine Corps--5805, 5803		General
	Navy--649y, 749y		Securities and Exchange Commission

ON THE CD-ROM
SAMPLE OF ANNOUNCEMENT SUMMARY AND NARRATIVE:

Department of the Army, **Criminal Investigator**, GS-1811-05/07/09, $26,699 - $52,591 Annual.

A surprisingly large number of agencies employ criminal investigators. Your likelihood of being hired for these law enforcement jobs improves if you have directly related experience or a college degree. Many agencies like to hire experienced individuals who also have degrees, but usually recruit such candidates at the GS-9 level or above. A year of relevant experience as an E-4 may qualify you for the GS-5 level, while a year as an O-1, W-1 or E-7 may qualify you for the GS-7.

This particular vacancy seems to have no promotion potential beyond GS-9, but many jobs in this occupation go to GS-12 or even 13 without competition. Criminal investigators often are required to sign mobility agreements as a condition of employment, and there is a maximum age restriction for employment. Keep in mind that most criminal investigators are paid 125% of their grade and step (as compensation for the requirement to be available for unscheduled extra hours of work). Other federal investigator occupations do not regularly receive this additional pay.

FIND YOUR FEDERAL JOB CHART™

Fields of Military Training & Experience	MOS	Related Federal Civilian Work Fields or Occupations	Examples of Federal Agencies Hiring for Jobs like these
	ENLISTED		
	Army--35F, 35H, 35Y, 39B	Electronics Mechanic, WG-2604	Department of the Air Force
	Air Force--multiple specialties in the 2A		
	and 2P career fields.		
	Coast Guard--None noted		
	Marine Corps--2871, 2874, 2881		
	Navy--AT6650, AT6658, AT6704, AT6705,		
	AT6718, ET1589		
Electronics Career Fields Including Engineering, Engineering Technician, Production Control, Training, And Electronics Mechanic	**OFFICER & WARRANT OFFICER**		
	Army--918B, 918E	Electronics Engineer, GS-0855	Department of the Air Force
	Air Force--62E1E, 62E3E	Electronics Technician, GS-0856	Department of the Army
	Coast Guard--58, 013	Training Instructor (Electronics),	Department of the Navy
	Marine Corps--9624	GS-1712	Marine Corps
	Navy--618, 628, 718, 728, numerous		Department of Defense
	DMOS working in electronics		Federal Aviation Administration
	NOTE: Engineering jobs have a positive		National Institute of Standards and
	education requirement.		Technology
			National Oceanic and Atmospheric
			Administration
			USDA Rural Utilities Service
	ENLISTED		
	DoD does not identify any specific enlisted MOS comparable to this career field. Many senior NCOs and Petty Officers should have work experience that qualifies them for some specialist jobs in this broad field, but you will have to review individual vacancy announcements to determine your likelihood of qualifying for a particular job. Far more enlisted personnel should have work experience that qualifies them for assistant jobs in this broad career field.	Various Titles, GS-0301, e.g., "Mission Support Specialist" Various Titles, GS-0303, e.g., "Mission Support Assistant" and "Program Support Assistant"	Many departments and agencies use the GS-0301 and -0303 occupational series, which are reserved for administrative jobs that do not fit any other specific series. Department of Homeland Security particulary uses these series to hire for many jobs.
General Administration Career Field, Including Program Support Or General Administration Work In Almost Any Conceivable Work Setting	**OFFICER AND WARRANT OFFICER**		
	Army--None specified		
	Air Force--88AO, 97EO		
	Coast Guard--01, 08, 20, 25		
	Marine Corps-0810		
	Navy--110y, 641y, Possible multiple DMOS,		
	Warrant Officer 741y		

Fields of Military Training & Experience	MOS	Related Federal Civilian Work Fields or Occupations	Examples of Federal Agencies Hiring for Jobs like these
	ENLISTED		
	Army--75B, 75F, 75H	Human Resources Assistant, GS-0203	All departments and agencies employ HR assistants. The military departments also employ HR assistants who focus on military personnel matters.
	Air Force--3S0xx, SU0xx	Human Resources Assistant (Military),	
	Coast Guard--381	GS-0203	
	Marine Corps--8534		
	Navy--PN		
	OFFICER AND WARRANT OFFICER		
Human Resources Management Career Field, Including Specialist And Support Positions Working In Both Civilian And Military Personnel Specialities	Army--42B, 43A, 50A, Warrant Officer 420A	Human Resources Specialist, GS-0201	All departments and agencies employ HR assistants. The military departments also employ HR assistants who focus on military personnel matters.
	Air Force--30C0, 36P1	Human Resources Specialist (Military),	
	Coast Guard--10, 11, 12, 14, 16, 17,	GS-0201	
	Warrant Officer 018		
	Marine Corps--0170, 9640, 9815		
	Navy--120y, Secondary MOS 3130,		
	DMOS 30xx, 31xx, 32xx, 39xx		
	Note: Espceially at the lower grades,		
	it is possible to enter this career field		
	without specialized experience by		
	meeeting the qualifications based on		
	education. Specialized experience is often		
	essential to compete successfully for jobs		
	above GS-5 or GS-7.		
	ENLISTED	Police Officer, GS-0083	Dept. of Veterans Affairs
	Army--95B, 11B, 11C, 11Z	U.S. Marshall, GS-0082	Department of Homeland Security
	Air Force--3P000, 3P091	Game Law Enforcement, GS-1812	Customs & Border Protection
	Coast Guard--741	Customs Patrol Officer, GS-1884	Immigration & Customs Enforcement
	Marine Corps--5811, 5812, 5813,	Border Patrol Agent, GS-1896	Secret Service
	5814, 5819, 0311, 03xx	Investigator, GS-1810	Department of the Interior, Fish &
	Navy--MA, MA2002	Alcohol, Tobacco and Firearms	Wildlife Service
Law Enforcement Occupations (And Possibly Combat Arms Specialties For Lower Graded Openings)		Inspection, GS-1854	Postal Service
	OFFICER & WARRANT OFFICER	Compliance Inspection and Support,	Tennessee Valley Authority
	Army--31A, 311A	GS-1802	Defense Security Service
	Air Force--31P1, 31P3, 31P4. 85G0		Department of Justice
	Coast Guard--09, 024		Bureau of Prisons
	Marine Corps--5803, 5804, 5805		Bureau of Alcohol, Tobacco, Firearms,
	Navy--649y, 749y, DMOS 2750,		and Explosives
	2771, 2775, 2780, 2790, 3412		Department of State

FIND YOUR FEDERAL JOB CHART™

Fields of Military Training & Experience	MOS	Related Federal Civilian Work Fields or Occupations	Examples of Federal Agencies Hiring for Jobs like these
	ENLISTED		
	Army--92A, 71L	General Supply, GS-2001	Department of Defense
	Air Force--2G0xx, 2S0xx, 3A0xx,	Inventory Management, GS-2010	Department ofg the Air Force
	Coast Guard--420, 360	Logistics Support Assistant, GS-0303	Department of the Army
	Marine Corps--0411, 0431, 0491, 3043,		Department of the Air Force
	3044, 0151		Coast Guard
	Navy--9549, AK, AN9750, SK28xx, 9566,		General Services Administration
	SN9750, YN		Virtually every department and large
			independent agency of the Federal
			Government
Logistics, Including Logistical Support, General Supply And Inventory Management			
	OFFICER & WARRANT OFFICER		
	Army--90A, 92A,	Logistics Management Specialist,	Department of Defense
	Air Force--20C0, 20c0x, 21R1, 21R3,	GS-0346	Department ofg the Air Force
	21R4	General Supply, GS-2001	Department of the Army
	Coast Guard--020	Inventory Management, GS-2010	Department of the Air Force
	Marine Corps--0402, 0430		Coast Guard
	Navy--310y905, 310y906, 310y908,		General Services Administration
	310y943, 651y905, 651y906, 651y908,		Virtually every department and large
	651y943, 751y, 751y905, 751y906,		independent agency of the Federal
	751y908, Secondary MOS 1302,		Government
	many possible DMOS		
	SENIOR NCO	Intelligence Specialist, GS-0132	Department of Defense
	Army--18F, 98Z, 97G, 96Z, 97Z		Defense Intelligence Agency
	Air Force--1N000, 1N171, 1N191,		Defense Counterintelligence Field
	1N071, 1N091		Activity
	Coast Guard--411		Army
	Marine Corps--2691, 0291, 0211		Air Force
	Navy--IS		Navy
			Department of Homeland Security
Primary And Duty Specialties That Provide A Background In Analyzing Information And Reaching Conclusions Based On The Analyses, Or Education That Substitutes For This Kind Of Experience	**OFFICER & WARRANT OFFICER**		Departmental Headquarters
	Army--35E; 351B		Customs and Border Protection
	Air Force--71S1, 71S3, 71S4		Immigration and Customs Enforcement
	Coast Guard--Unknown		Transportation Security Administration
	Marine Corps--0210, 0215		Department of Justice
	Navy--DMOS 2748, 9517, 9616,		Federal Bureau of Investigation
	9617, 9781		Drug Enforcement Administration
			Bureau of Alcohol, Tobacco, Firearms,
			and Explosives
			Nuclear Regulatory Commission

FIND YOUR FEDERAL JOB CHART™

Fields of Military Training & Experience	MOS	Related Federal Civilian Work Fields or Occupations	Examples of Federal Agencies Hiring for Jobs like these
Related Military Equipment Repair	**ENLISTED ONLY**	Heavy Mobile Equipment Repairer,	Department of Defense,
	Army--62B	WG-5803-08	Defense Logistics Agency
	Air Force--2T351		Department of the Army
	Coast Guard--None		Department of the Air Force
	Marine Corps--1341, 1349		Department of the Navy
	Navy--CM		U.S. Marine Corps
	ENLISTED ONLY	Air Conditioning Equipment	Department of Defense,
	Army--51K	Mechanic, WG-5306-10	Defense Logistics Agency
	Air Force--3E151, 3E171, 3E191		Department of the Army
	Coast Guard--702		Department of the Air Force
	Marine Corps--1161, 1169		Department of the Navy
	Navy--MM4291, UT6104, UT6105		U.S. Marine Corps
			Department of Veterans Affairs
Security/safety Career Field, Including Jobs In The Department Of Homeland Security That Are Directly Involved In Security Of Our Nation	**ENLISTED**		Transportation Security Administration
	Army--51M, 75B, 75F, 75H	Security Screener, GS-0019	DoD and all military departments
	Air Force--1S0xx, 3E7xx, 3S0xx	Fire Fighter, GS-0081	Department of Agriculture
	Coast Guard--210, 381	Security Assistant, GS-0086	Department of Homeland Security
	Marine Corps--9954, 9956, 7051, 8811, 8534		Many other departments and agencies
	Navy--9595, SW6021, PN		
	All services--Persons whose MOS has		
	provided training in observation and		
	analytical skills while performing routine		
	and repetitive work, sometimes under		
	considerable pressure. This may include		
	some combat arms MOS.		
	OFFICER AND WARRANT OFFICER	Security Specialist, GS-0080	
	Army--31A, Warrant Officer 311A		
	Air Force--31P1, 31P2, 31P3		
	Coast Guard-09, Warrant Oficer 024		
	Marine Corps--5803, 5804, 5805		
	Navy--649y, Warrant Officer 749y,		
	DMOS 2750, 2771, 2775, 2780, 2790		

FIND YOUR FEDERAL JOB CHART™

Fields of MilitaryTraining & Experience	MOS	Related Federal Civilian Work Fields or Occupations	Examples of Federal Agencies Hiring for Jobs like these
Training And General Education Career Field. This Is A Particularly Difficult Area To Analyze Because In Almost Every Instance The Agency Is Looking For Someone Who Has A Combination Of Subject Matter Expertise And Training Or Education Development And/or Presentation Skills. Vacancy Announcements Must Be Carefullly Reviewed To Determine Which Skills Are Paramount And What Subject Matter Expertise Is Necessary. Many Senior Ncos And Petty Officers And Many Commissioned And Warrant Officers Will Qualify For Individual Jobs, But This Is Never A Sure Thing. Examine The Vacancy Announcements Very Closely To Judge Your Qualifications For Any Job In This Broad Field	**ENLISTED**	Training Specialist, GS-1712	Department of Homeland Security
	DoD does not identify any specific enlisted	Supervisory Training Specialist, GS-1712	Department of Agriculture
	MOS comparable to this career field. See	Law Enforcement Specialist (Training),	Other Departments and Agencies
	comments above.	GS-1801	
	Officer and Warrant Officer		
	While DoD does identify a number of		
	commissioned officer MOS that could		
	qualify for education and training jobs,		
	we do not identify any here because of		
	the importance of subject matter expertise		
	when qualifying for these jobs. See		
	comments above.		
Various Occupations That Provide A Background In Managing And Disposing Of Property, Or, At Entry Grades For The Specialist Jobs, A Degree That Meets Educational Requirements That May Substitute For Experience	**ENLISTED**	Propety Disposal Clerical and	Department of Defense,
	Army--92A, 92Y	Technical --GS-1107	Defense Logistics Agency
	Air Force--2G000, 2G071, 2G091,	(May be a better fit for enlisted)	Department of the Army
	2S000, 2S051, 2S071, 2S090		Department of the Air Force
	Coast Guard--420		Department of the Navy
	Marine Corps--0411, 0431, 0491		U.S. Marine Corps
	Navy--9549, SK2819		General Services Administration
	OFFICE & WARRANT OFFICER	Property Disposal Management,	
	Army--92F, 920A, 920B	GS-1104	
	Air Force--21R(x), 21R(xx)	(Good fit for offices and warrant	
	Coast Guard--33, 34	offices; may be a fit for some senior	
	Marine Corps--3002, 3010	NCOs)	
	Navy--310y		

Fields of Military Training & Experience	MOS	Related Federal Civilian Work Fields or Occupations	Examples of Federal Agencies Hiring for Jobs like these
Virtually Any Staff Planning Experience Should Help Qualify For This Broad Occupational Field. A Degree That Includes Analytical Training And Writing Will Also Help Meet Alternate Education Requirements	**ENLISTED**	Program & Management Analyst,	Virtually every department and independent agency uses this particular title and series. The duties of jobs in this series vary tremendously. Some focus on internal management issues; others focus on how and how well programs meet their goals.
	Army--71L	GS-0343	
	Air Force--3U000. 3U071, 3U091,		
	3A000, 3A071, 3A091,		
	Coast Guard--Unknown		
	Marine Corps--0171, 0193, 9935		
	Navy--Unknown		
	Officer & Warrant Officer		
	All MOS		

FEDERAL JOBS FOR FORMER MILITARY –
48 Vacancy Announcements and Federal Jobs are Analyzed and Interpreted

On the next 15 pages, you can read summaries of Federal jobs and vacancy announcements that will be of special interest to military personnel. The entire announcements can be found on the CD-ROM. The closing dates of some announcements will be past, but you can find other similar announcements on www.usajobs.gov.

These jobs could be of interest to military personnel who have specialized experience in the 14 career areas listed on page 66. Federal HRM Expert Harry C. Redd has researched these announcements and interpreted the following information for you:

- Agency, Job title and salary
- Recommendations for matching military rank to competitive federal grade
- How you could qualify for a certain grade level based on experience
- How your relevant military experiences could relate to the federal job skills needed

Why you should read these announcements:
To learn about federal job titles, specialized skills, qualifications, typical grades and salaries. To learn about federal vacancy announcements and how they give you extensive information about the jobs. The better you understand the announcements, the better your resume will match the required qualifications and the more successful you will be with receiving interviews and job offers.

ADMINISTRATIVE, SECRETARIAL AND ASSISTANT OPPORTUNITIES
Federal Job Series: 310, 303, 3188

Department of the Army, **USAR Unit Administrator**, GS-0303-5/07. Salary: $27,966 - $45,032 Annual
This is an example of a job well suited to the many service members who honed their administrative skills while in uniform. It also represents an opportunity to remain actively involved in the uniformed service (in this case the Army reserve) since it requires concurrent service in the Reserve while employed as a civilian. Recruitment is at GS-5, 6, or 7, with promotion potential to GS-7. Qualifying for GS-5 means a year of experience equal to GS-4. A year of relevant experience as an E-4 probably will meet this requirement. Note that there is a link in this announcement to the qualifications standard.

Department of Agriculture, Agricultural Marketing Service, **Agricultural Marketing Assistant (Office Automation)**, GS-0303-05/06.
There are plenty of jobs outside the Defense and Homeland Security departments. If you're from agricultural America and want to return to your roots, this may be the kind of job you should seek. It is also the kind of job for which many spouses of separating military personnel might qualify as well. To meet the GS-5 offering, you need a year of relevant experience equal to GS-4. A year of experience as an E-4 may meet that requirement.

Department of the Navy, Navy Field Offices, **Secretary (Office Automation)**, GS-318-05. SALARY RANGE: 26484 - 36681
In the civil service a secretary is a personal assistant to an individual (or sometimes to a small staff) and is the principal clerical or administrative support employee for the unit. In other words, a secretary can be a pretty powerful position. Being the principal assistant to a unit head or other manager offers a lot of opportunity to learn about the organization and to market yourself as well. If your administrative or clerical background in one of the armed forces has prepared you properly, these are very good jobs to pursue. The same is true for spouses of service members. For those with the skills, look for the GS-318 series. While this particular vacancy goes only to GS-5, some jobs in this series can reach GS-8 or higher.

AVIATION OPPORTUNITIES
Federal Job Series: 0343

Department of Transportation, Federal Aviation Administration, **Aviation Safety Inspector**, FG-1825-9/12, Salary: $37,390 – 70,484
These jobs are ideal for members of all of the armed forces who have worked as mechanics in avionics, powerplants, or airframes for aircraft over 12,500 pounds gross weight at takeoff. Some specialties in this broad occupational field require FAA licenses; all require substantial experience and may require supervisory experience. There are even specialties that require a commercial airline pilot's license and extensive flying experience.

Separating mid-level and senior enlisted specialists and noncommissioned officers/petty officers who have worked in the aviation field may want to consider these jobs as a way to build on the experience and skills the gained while in uniform. Flight rated commissioned and warrant officers may want to consider openings for specialties that require their pilot skills. The fact that the announcement is open continuously for one year suggests both that there are numerous jobs Nationwide and that FAA does not find it easy to fill these positions.

The "FG" pay plan is unique to the FAA. The pay rates for the FG grades (9, 11, 12) are roughly comparable to the same GS grades. Promotion beyond FG-12 will only be possible through competing for higher jobs, probably in the supervisory and managerial ranks.

Department Of The Air Force, Air Force Personnel Center, **Air Traffic Assistant**, GS-2154-09. Salary: $41,772.00 - $54,300.00
This is an example of a nice paying job in the aviation support career field that would allow service members to trade successfully on their military experience. All of the uniformed services have jobs that perform work similar to the duties of this one. Furthermore, this particular announcement says that the job is closed except to persons with status, including Army civilian employees serviced by Ft. Stewart, but the announcement then also states that applications will be accepted from veterans eligible under the Veterans Employment Opportunity Act, which means veterans, even without qualifying for veterans preference, can apply for this job while the general public cannot.

Department of The Air Force, Air Force Reserve, Headquarters, **Operations Flight Technician**, GS-0303-07. Salary: $24,677.00 - $39,738.00
This another example of a job in the aviation support field that would allow separating enlisted personnel who have worked in support of military aviation to use the experience they gained in uniform to work as federal civilians. We chose this example simply to help show the range of civilian jobs the Federal Government has in the aviation field. We found several other GS-303 announcements for jobs working in support of the aviation career field, and all were at the GS-7 grade level. They may be ideal opportunities for persons whose work experience has been around the aviation field but has focused largely on general office skills. You must be in the Air Force Reserves for this position.

BIO MEDICAL TECHNICIAN OPPORTUNIITES
Federal Job Series: 0404, 0645, 0704

Department of the Navy, Naval Medical Command, **Biological Science Medical Technician**, GS-0404-6/7, vacancy announcement number NW4-0404 -DE. Salary: $30,947.00 - 44,706.00 USD Annually
This example is typical of jobs which appeal to separating service members with laboratory research technician training and experience. The GS-6 opening requires a year of relevant

experience equal to GS-5. A year of laboratory technician experience as an E-5 might qualify you for GS-6. Similarly, a year of relevant experience as an E-6 might qualify you for GS-7.

Department of Health and Human Services, Indian Health Service, **Medical Technician**, GS-0645-4/7. SALARY RANGE: $23,863.00 - 33,071.00 USD per year
While another technical job, this differs from the biological science medical technician job listed above because this one involves working with patients in a hospital laboratory setting. This kind of work is ideal for individuals who have gained experience and training in military medical technician jobs, and the grade range advertised suggests that experienced individuals from E-4 to E-7 could compete successfully for the job.

Department of Agriculture, Animal and Plant Health Inspection Service, **Animal Health Technician**, GS-0704-5/9. SALARY RANGE: $26699 - 52591
This is another technical job family that some separating service members might find within their reach. The work helps protect our country against outbreaks of disease that might result from sick animals in the food chain. There is also a component of the job that involves observing or monitoring individuals who are working on a fee or contract basis. This part of the Department of Agriculture is a first-responder agency helping protect the United States against both intentional and accidental outbreaks of disease. To qualify at the lowest level for this particular announcement one would have to have at least a year of relevant experience as an E-4, while qualifying for the highest grade would likely require at least a year of relevant experience as an E-7, W-2, or O-2.

CRIMINAL INVESTIGATION AND LAW ENFORCEMENT OPPORTUNITIES
Federal Job Series: 0083, 1810, 1811, 1801, 1802

Department of Veterans Affairs, Veterans Health Administration, **Police Officer**, GS-0083-05/06. 26,699.00 - 38,694.00 USD per year
This is an example of a federal law enforcement job for which many service members could qualify. Unlike criminal investigators, this occupation does not require a college degree. It is a good occupational choice for enlisted personnel with service experience in law enforcement work. It has an entry-level grade and is therefore also appropriate for lower ranked combat arms enlisted personnel. There are supervisory positions at higher grades which can be pursued after gaining work experience.

DOD, Defense Security Service, **Investigator**, GS-1810-05/07, promotion potential to GS-12. SALARY: - $26,699.00 - $33,071.00
This is another example of federal civilian investigative work that might be a good fit for both junior officers and somewhat senior enlisted personnel with some law enforcement work or investigations experience or training. A degree is not required for this job, although a college degree can qualify an individual without directly related experience for the entry-level GS-5 grade. One year of relevant

experience equivalent to the GS-4 level will qualify you for this level—meaning that a year or relevant experience as an E-4 or PO-3 may represent qualifying experience. The career path for this particular vacancy is to GS-12, which has a very competitive salary. Work in the GS-1810 occupation is not the same as criminal investigation (these investigators do not carry guns or enforce criminal laws) but the investigative skills are closely related.

Department of Justice, U.S. Marshals Service, **Detention Enforcement Officer**, GS-1802-6/7. Salary: $34724-$47402
This work involves control and transport of prisoners and detainees. In order to qualify for the GS-6 level, applicants need at least one year of experience equal to GS-5. Relevant experience as an E5 or PO-2 might make you competitive. While combat arms personnel may not have enough qualifying experience to apply for these jobs at the GS-6 or 7 level, you might want to look for such jobs at lower grades, where less experience is required. The physical requirements of jobs in this series are a good match for your training in the combat arms.

Department of the Army, **Criminal Investigator**, GS-1811-05/07/09, $26,699 - $52,591 Annual
A surprisingly large number of agencies employ criminal investigators. Your likelihood of being hired for these law enforcement jobs improves if you have directly related experience or a college degree. Many agencies like to hire experienced individuals who also have degrees, but usually recruit such candidates at the GS-9 level or above. A year of relevant experience as an E-4 may qualify you for the GS-5 level, while a year as an O-1, W-1 or E-7 may qualify you for the GS-7.

This particular vacancy seems to have no promotion potential beyond GS-9, but many jobs in this occupation go to GS-12 or even 13 without competition. Criminal investigators often are required to sign mobility agreements as a condition of employment, and there is a maximum age restriction for employment. Keep in mind that most criminal investigators are paid 125% of their grade and step (as compensation for the requirement to be available for unscheduled extra hours of work). Other federal investigator occupations do not regularly receive this additional pay.

Department of Justice, Bureau of Alcohol, Tobacco, Firearms, and Explosives (ATF), **Industry Operations Investigator**, GS-1801-09 (promotion potential to GS-12). Salary: $26,699 - $52,591 Annual
This is another kind of investigator job chosen to show that you don't have to be a criminal investigator to contribute to the war against crime in the U.S. This particular announcement is being used to fill jobs through a program called the Federal Career Intern Program. This program is increasingly popular. To qualify for the GS-9 level, you need one year of relevant experience at the GS-7 level, which probably means a year of experience as an O-1 W-1, or E-7.

Department of Homeland Security, United States Secret Service, **Criminal Investigator**, GS-1811-05/09, Promotion Potential to GS-13, vacancy announcement number Special Agent. Salary: $36,478.00 - $47,422.00 per year, plus applicable locality adjustment.

This example highlights the promotion potential that can exist even when being hired at GS-5 or GS-7. At the Resume Place, we have encountered many enlisted personnel who "shot too high" when they applied and ended up being found "ineligible" by the agency with the vacancy. Remember that civil service rules require that you have 1 year of experience at the next lower civilian grade. And then remember that criminal investigators are paid 125% of their pay rate. It may be better to seek and accept a lower initial grade to get the job, especially if the job subsequently offers noncompetitive growth to GS-13 as this one does. Remember to focus on your long term and immediate goals.

Department of the Navy, Navy Field Offices, **Criminal Investigator**, GS-1811-5/15. Salary: $39,613 - $71,678 per year
This broad spectrum announcement, used by Navy to develop and maintain an inventory of qualified applicants to meet what appears to be a large and continuing need for criminal investigators, offers employment opportunities for service members whose experience was at almost every pay level from E-4 through O-5. It represents the kind of job opportunity that exists if you are willing to look for it. These jobs certainly are worth working hard to find.

ELECTRONICS OPPORTUNITIES
Federal Job Series: WG 2604, GG 0855 and 0856, GS 1712

Department of the Air Force, Air Force Personnel Center, **Electronics Mechanic**, WG-2604-10/10. Salary: $36836 per year - $42971 per year
We selected this position to show the kinds of skilled electronics mechanics jobs that are available and the relatively high salaries they command. This job and ones like it are ideal for well trained, highly motivated senior enlisted specialists who are leaving the armed forces and want to continue to serve their country. While the vacancy announcement specifies one position, further reading shows that this is an "open continuous" announcement that may be used to fill multiple vacancies. There is a lesson in that revelation—read the announcement if the job interests you. What looks like a single vacancy may in fact be one of many!

Department of the Navy. Office of the Secretary of the Navy (covers Navy and Marine Corps positions), **Electronics Engineer**, GG-0855-05/13. Salary: $32,084.00 - 97,213.00 per year
This is just one of many examples of electronics engineer vacancy announcements we found. We chose to include it because it shows the typical range of grades for which these jobs are recruited, and because this is an "open continuous" announcement aimed at filling multiple jobs as the need arises. We found numerous other announcements from all of the military departments, from DoD agencies, and from civilian agencies such as FAA, National Institute for Standards and Technology, and USDA Rural Utilities Service. Some of the higher graded announcements (up to GS-15 equivalent) we found were for jobs in civilian agencies, so qualified persons looking for higher paying jobs should not ignore civilian agencies when searching for jobs!

Electronics Engineer positions have a positive education requirement, so they may be more appropriate search targets for officers leaving the service than for most enlisted personnel. However, if you possess the education then you should definitely consider jobs in this high-demand occupational field.

Department of the Army, USAJFK Special Warfare Center & School, **Training Instructor (Communications)**, GS-1712-09. Salary: $41,772 - $54,300 Annual
Given the armed forces' emphasis on training, and the number of instructors/trainers the forces develop, this vacancy announcement points to another way to use military experience in the civilian employment world. Note that this job requires a combination of knowledge and skills in developing instructional goals and methods, ability to present instruction, and subject matter knowledge in electronics. There is a positive education requirement for this occupational series, but experience may be substituted for it. This raises the strong possibility that not only officers and warrant officers, but also senior enlisted specialists, NCOs and Petty Officers may be qualified for these jobs. One reason for including this announcement is to remind readers that many different occupational series (and job titles) may lead to rewarding federal civilian careers using training experiences from the military.

Department of Justice, Bureau of Prisons/Federal Prison System, **Electronics Technician**, GS-0856-11/11. Salary: $52,780 - $68,615 per year
While we found electronics technician vacancy announcements from all of the military departments, we chose this civilian agency announcement to help remind readers that lots of Federal departments and agencies have need for the skills you developed while serving in the armed forces. Keep your search broad and increase your opportunities to find the ideal job!

These jobs require experience more than education, and therefore are good targets for senior enlisted specialists, NCOs and Petty Officers who have worked in the electronics field. Note that the job has physical demands—something most separating service members won't find daunting!

GENERAL ADMINISTRATION OPPORTUNITIES
Federal Career Series: 0301

Department Of Homeland Security, Immigration and Customs Enforcement,
Mission Support Specialist, GS-0301-05/09, $28,620.00 - $56,371.00 per Annum
As you will see when you search USAJobs, DHS uses this "301" occupational series a lot. Numerous job titles are associated with it. What these jobs all have in common is that they require experience or education in general office administration, akin to an office manager. Many service members have received training and gained experience that would make them good candidates for these jobs. When you search them out, look at the grades they are filling and what the promotion potential is. We noted that some of these jobs (such as this one) go to GS-12, while others are limited to GS-09 only.

Department Of Homeland Security, Citizenship and Immigration Services,
Mission Support Specialist (HRM), GS-0301-09/11, $44,756.00 - $70,397.00 per Annum
Your area of emphasis will be human resources management. This position involves a variety of administrative and management services essential to the operations of the office (including, but not limited to, management and information systems, telecommunications, budget, finance, procurement, human resources, training, logistics, property, space, records and files, printing and graphics, mail, travel, and office equipment) and serve as an advisor to management on assigned administrative matters. In addition, you will conduct or participate in the evaluation of administrative programs, systems and methods and identify ways to improve the efficiency and effectiveness of these services at the local level. You will also represent the office in dealings with vendors and organizations within the agency that have primary responsibility for these services. Many enlisted service members separating from the armed forces have the requisite support experience to be successful candidates for this and similar support jobs. Our point is simple: focus on the diverse experiences you have had in the military that supports the mission and you will demonstrate your knowledge, skills and abilities.

HUMAN RESOURCE MANAGEMENT OPPORTUNITIES
Federal Career Series: 0203, 0201

Department Of Homeland Security, US Coast Guard,
Human Resources Assistant (Military OA), GS-0203-07, $35,452.00 - $46,088.00
Here is a job working in support of homeland security that requires a background in office automation and knowledge of federal civilian HR practices and procedures. Senior enlisted specialists may meet the requirements for this job, especially since the evaluation criteria do not specifically say the experience has to be in Federal civilian HR—just in HR. This is a merit promotion announcement, so the job is not open to the general public. Being a former or separating member of the armed forces is a distinct advantage, but will not convey additional points for veteran's preference. Spell out your qualifications very clearly!

Department of the Navy, Commander, Navy Installations, Naval Operations
Human Resources Assistant, GS-0201-09, $44,001.00 - $57,197.00
Employees in these jobs provide expert civilian human resources management advice and assistance to managers, supervisors, and employees in their agencies. When competing for jobs in this field above the entry (GS-5 and -7) levels, applicants must have progressively greater directly related experience or education beyond the bachelor's degree level. Experience gained as a military personnel officer or in related military fields may meet the qualifications requirements; be sure to document your education and experience carefully so the agency may properly assess your qualifications. Almost every Federal agency has positions in this occupational field. Once hired by a Federal agency, there are lots of HR openings for which you can compete for both promotion and lateral movement.

Department of The Army, Joint Activities
Human Resources Specialist (Military), GS-0201-11, $50,541.00 - $65,704.00
This position works directly to maintain a segment of the Army's enlisted personnel program. Similar to Workforce Planning in the military, you would work with management on directorate missions regarding their quality responsibilities, control systems and problem areas. You would recommend a formal corrective action process regarding the recurring deficiencies and systemic problems identified through evaluations. It differs from the GS-0201 position in the previous announcement because this one focuses directly on military human resources matters. Jobs such as this offer good transition possibilities to senior NCOs and Petty Officers, Warrant Officers, and commissioned officers with experience in Military Personnel Management. Remember, however, that because this is a civil service position, applicants are subject to "time in grade" requirements, so it will be important to show how your work experience equates to at least 1 year of experience equal to GS-9 to compete for this G-11 opening.

LOGISTICS AND SUPPLY OPPORTUNITIES
Federal Job Series: 0346, 2010, 2001, 303

Department of the Air Force, Air Force Reserve, Headquarters, **Logistics Management Specialist**, GS-0346-09/11. Salary: $37,390.00 - 58,811.00 Annually
Note that this is a continuously open announcement and that applicants must be willing and able to join the Air Force Reserve. We found many logistics management specialist vacancy announcements; clearly this is a field where lots of job opportunities exist.
All of the military departments are hiring in this field, and there are opportunities for all levels of skill and experience. If you are willing to look outside the military departments, you will find civilian agencies also need good employees with skill in this area. We found a high graded (GS-13/14) announcement in Department of Energy. If you have good experience in this field, your job opportunities today as a Federal civilian look awfully good.

Department of the Navy, Commander in Chief of the US Atlantic Fleet, **Logistics Management Specialist/Officer**, GS-0346-9/11. Salary: $41,772.00 - 65,704.00 USD per year (depends on location and individual job)
This is a specialized position which provides academic and operational training for members of carrier battle groups as well as personnel from other warfare disciplines involved in integrated strike and air superiority operations. Responsible for acquisition and logistic support involved in the delivery and off load of targets and target construction material as appropriated from the Defense reutilization and Marketing Office (DRMO). This position serves as a liaison with representatives of Fleet Commands, Joint Forces Command (JFCOM), other services, multiple agencies, contractors, and field activities regarding infrastructure target/systems, airspace issues/ requirements, and programs to ensure continuous program execution and support.

Department of Defense, Office of the Secretary of Defense, **Professor of Life Cycle Logistics Management**, AD-0346. Salary: $64,067-113,070 per year
This announcement is for a professor position at the Defense Acquisition University, which ought to stress the importance DoD puts on work in the logistics field. Pay for this job is administratively determined, and in this case roughly approximates the pay rates for GS grades 12 -15. This is a great opportunity for more senior officers with extensive experience in life cycle management. This announcement is further evidence of the importance the Department of Defense places on logistics management experience.

Defense Logistics Agency, **Inventory Management Specialist**, GS-2010-12. Salary: $63,260.00 - 82,234.00 USD per year
We included this announcement to show the variety of occupations in the broad logistics field. The military trains many people in inventory management; and the skills and knowledge gained while in uniform can serve to qualify some of those individuals for Federal civilian jobs. This specialist position supports the requirements of the Armed Forces and other federal activities and agencies worldwide. Jobs in this field are good targets for senior enlisted specialists, NCOs and Petty Officers as well as commissioned and warrant officers. Good experience can carry you well in his career field.

Department of Defense, Defense Logistics Agency, **General Supply Specialist**, GS-2001-09/11. Salary: $41,772.00 - 65,704.00 per year
General supply specialist is another job area many separating service members should explore. The experience you gained in the general supply field should be valuable in you job search. While this particular vacancy announcement is for a job at a Defense Logistics Agency facility, you will find similar jobs throughout the Federal Government. Depending on the grade level being filled, jobs in this career field may be well suited for service members at the senior enlisted ranks, warrant officers, and commissioned officers. Experience is important for jobs in this field. This announcement is very interesting because of this information which is important when writing your federal resume. Be sure to include these skills in your resume!

Desired Skills:

Weight	Description
High	Policy Development
High	Policy Interpretatn
High	System Tracking
High	Material Control
High	Receiving
High	Transportat'n Modes

High	Training Experience
High	Conduct Studies
High	Supply Distribution
High	L Distr
High	L DSS

Department of Defense, Defense Education Activity, **Logistics Support Assistant**, GS-303-07. Salary: $34,149 - $44,395 per yea

This announcement shows that not every position working in the logistics field requires extensive experience in logistics management. This is a well-paying clerical support job providing logistical support for the dependent school system at a major USMC facility.   Note that the vacancy announcement says this announcement may be used to fill either a permanent or temporary position. Be sure which you are applying for and be clear on which you are willing to accept!

Many enlisted service members separating from the armed forces have the requisite support experience to be successful candidates for this and similar support jobs. Our point is simple: focus on what you know and look for good Federal civilian jobs that allow your knowledge, skills, and abilities to shine.

INTELLIGENCE SPECIALIST OPPORTUNITIES
Federal Job Series: 0123

Department of Homeland Security, Transportation Security Administration, **Intelligence Operations Specialist**, SV-132-H, I or J. SV-132-H, I, or J
Annual Salary Range - SV-H $44,400 - $68,800
Annual Salary Range - SV-I $54,100 - $83,900
Annual Salary Range - SV-J $66,000 - $102,300
Intelligence specialist jobs seem to be a fit for many military primary or duty occupational specialties. In this particular example an alternate pay system is used. SV-H has a pay range equivalent to GS-12, the next two grades are equivalent to GS-13 and GS-14. These jobs pay really well. It also means more officers than NCOs will qualify for this particular announcement, since qualifying for SV-H (or GS-12) requires 1 year at the next lower level, (or GS-11). It is very likely that you would need a year of relevant experience as an E-9, W-2, or O-3 to meet that requirement. The good news, however, is that other announcements for this particular (GS-0132) series can focus on hiring at GS-9 or lower, meaning that many experienced enlisted personnel should be viable candidates for them.

Department of the Army, **Intelligence Specialist** (GMI Analyst), GG-0132-9/11/12/13 (Annual Salary Range - SV-H $44,400 - $68,800; SV-I $54,100 - $83,900; SV-J $66,000 - $102,300). This example shows a lower hiring grade than the preceding example, meaning a wider range of active duty service members might qualify for this job after leaving the service. In this particular case hiring begins at GS-9, meaning qualified applicants need at least 1 year of qualifying experience at the GS-7 level. It is likely that a year of relevant experience as an E-7, O-1, or W-1 would meet this requirement. This example also tops out a grade lower than the preceding TSA example.

EQUIPMENT OPERATOR AND MECHANIC
Federal Job Series: WG 5803, 5306

Department of the Navy, U.S. Marine Corps, **Heavy Mobile Equipment Repairer**, WG-5803-08. Salary: $37,390 – 70,484

Many service members learn trades and crafts skills while on active duty. Often, those skills translate into equivalent federal civilian jobs in the Federal Wage System. This is an example of such a job. If you learned how to repair heavy mobile equipment in the military, you can do the same work as a civilian. And unlike your peers who seek GS jobs, there is no requirement that you have a year in grade at the next lower federal grade. If you can do the job, you can be hired.

Department of the Navy, Navy Field Offices, **Air Conditioning Equipment Mechanic**, WG-5306-10. Salary: $37,390 – 70,484

If you learned the skill of repairing air conditioning equipment while in the military, this may be just the federal job for you. Note there are multiple vacancies and they are in Europe. If you want to live overseas and be employed by the U.S. Government, this is one way to do it.

Department of the Air Force, **Air Conditioning Equipment Mechanic**, WG-5306-10. Salary: $37,390 – 70,484

We included this example just to prove that more than one employer uses civilian air conditioning mechanics, and to show that not all such jobs are overseas. If you have learned and practiced the skill, this could be your federal civilian job.

SECURITY AND SAFETY OPPORTUNITIES
Federal Career Series: 0019, 0080, 0081, 0086

Department of Homeland Security, Transportation Security Administration, **Transportation Security Screener**, SV-0019, Pay Band D, $23,600-$35,400
This is a physically demanding job involving strenuous physical effort and long periods of standing. It requires shift work and may involve overtime. It requires a courteous and professional demeanor at all times, and the ability to make effective judgments in both routine and crisis situations. In short, this job may be ideal for many separating service members. Women

leaving the military may find these jobs attractive because this is an occupation where preference may be given to women in hiring under certain circumstances.

Department Of The Army, Army Installation Management Agency, **Firefighter**,
GS-0081-6/6, $31,903.00 - $41,474.00 per Annum
All of the armed forces have trained fire fighters, making these jobs a natural for those who wish to continue in that field while working for their country as civilians. Fire fighters are subject to demanding physical requirements, and there is a maximum age for entering this occupation. If you are qualified for jobs such as these and are interesting in continuing in this kind of work, be sure to carefully read and completely follow the requirements contained in the vacancy announcement. Don't let inattention to administrative requirements keep you from getting the job you want!

Department Of The Army, Army Intelligence and Security Command
Security Assistant, GG-0086, $35,452.00 - $46,088.00 per Annum
Many separating service members may have gained the knowledge needed to successfully compete for security assistant jobs. And their work experience may well have already gained them the security clearances needed for these jobs, which would work to their advantage when competing for these jobs. This job and ones like it represent a way to continue to protect our country's security after shedding the uniform.

Department of the Navy, (NAWCAD)
Security Specialist, GS-0080- 9/11/12, $43,365 - $81,747 per Annum
This particular position focuses on many areas of security managing all Sensitive Compartmented Information (SCI) billets. Other security specialist positions may focus on other areas. They all share in common a need for progressively responsible specialized experience in security operations and protocols specific to the area of security on which they focus. The number of such positions may be surprising, and there should be a lot of separating service members who can compete successfully for them Just be sure to check the requirements carefully and present yourself well. Also look carefully at what the position requires, such as in this case, where random drug testing and travel one to five nights per month are clearly part of the job.

TRAINING AND EDUCATION OPPORTUNITIES
Federal Career Series: 1712, 1801

The armed services have thousands of skilled trainers who spend years developing skilled soldiers, sailors, marines, airmen/airwomen, and coast guardsmen/women. Federal agencies also have a substantial need for individuals who can train or develop employees in the civilian workforce. Nonetheless, it is a frustrating experience to find good matches between the civilian employee needs of Federal agencies and the experiences that service members have gained during their military service. To a large degree, this is because the civilian jobs often require specific subject matter knowledge in combination with the education or training skills. Often, the subject matter knowledge is paramount for job title purposes, making searches that focus on training or education skills hard. Below we show some of the possible job titles you might find during your search for jobs that would make good use of the training and education skill the military gave you—as long as you also have the requisite subject matter knowledge.

Department of the Navy, Naval Criminal Investigative Service Training Department, at the Federal Law Enforcement Training Center, Glynco, Georgia.
Training Instructor (Law Enforcement), GS-1712-11/13, $50,541.00 - $93,643.00
This training instructor will teach courses for specific subject matter, which involve highly complex law enforcement techniques, operations, and issues. Training is an important element of military service, and instructors are needed at FLETC. This work involves course development, lesson plans, practical application sessions and much more.
Notice the differences in the position and specialized experiences needed for the grade levels:
GS-11: Experience teaching to adult learners in a Law Enforcement training Academy environment. Experience with power point presentations and excel spread sheets in the classroom.
GS-12: Plans, develops own lesson plans, student texts, test questions and related classroom material and uses diverse instructional methods in order to present federal law enforcement subjects in classrooms and during practical application sessions.
GS-13: Provide resource expertise in the area of his/her specialty, determines the need for research in their assigned field of expertise and assures that results are incorporated into classroom presentations. Participates in AD HOC Committees made up of representatives of the Federal Law Enforcement community and other agencies concerned with training policies and academic requirements. Makes decisions, proposals and/or recommendations significantly changing, interpreting or developing NCIS training programs.

Department Of Homeland Security, Federal Law Enforcement Training Center,
Law Enforcement Specialist (Instructor), GS-1801-13, $72,035.00 - $93,643.00
This is an example of a training job where the subject matter expertise is paramount. Without the necessary law enforcement experience, someone simply could not do the job. Note that this is a time-limited (term) job initially for a period not to exceed 13 months, but may be extended for up to 4 years. Be aware of such conditions before you apply for any job! Undoubtedly there are separated and separating service members who could qualify for this job, but the numbers are probably small. The employing agency recognizes that the recruitment pool may be small—note the paragraph about Federal civilian retirees being eligible for appointment without having to offset their salary by the amount of their pension. For really hard to fill jobs, this is a new recruiting advantage given to some Federal agencies.

PROPERTY DISPOSAL SPECIALIST
Federal Job Series: 1104, 1107

Department of the Army. Joint Services & Activities Supported by the Office of the Secretary of the Army, **Property Disposal Specialist** (Utilization), NH-1104-02. Salary: $37,390 – 70,484
Managing a program to dispose of property is important whether the manager is in uniform or civilian clothes. Note that the part of Army announcing this vacancy is under an alternate personnel system and that the announced grade is "02." In reality, this is a pay band that includes GS grades 5-11. Once hired, advancement through the pay range (bottom of GS-5 to top of GS-11) is determined by individual performance. This is a good job for someone who has at least one year of experience in property disposal (or perhaps property management) at or above E-5, or who had a bachelors degree.

Department of the Navy, Navy Field Offices, **Property Disposal Clerk**, GS-1107-04/07. Salary: $37,390 – 70,484
For service members with clerical experience who are separating at E-4, this is an example of a kind of work you might seek as a federal civilian employee. You do not need specialized experience to qualify for GS-4. You will need specialized experience to qualify for the job as a GS-5 or higher   Most likely the year of specialized experience could still be as an E-4 to qualify for GS-5.

PROGRAM AND MANAGEMENT ANALYSIS OPPORTUNITIES
Federal Job Series: 0343

This and the next 4 examples were chosen to demonstrate the many possibilities associated with the GS-0343 occupation. You will find these jobs in almost every government organization, and you will find the range of their duties to be astounding. This is an occupation where subject matter experience is less important than experience in analyzing and making judgments. We believe that many duties military personnel experience in staff planning and operations jobs may provide the kind of experience that will qualify applicants for this broad occupation.

Department of Health and Human Services, National Institutes of Health, **Management Analyst**, GS-0343-9/11/12. Salary: $41815 - 78826
This particular announcement is looking for someone whose focus will be on analyzing and reporting on internal management activities and their effectiveness. To qualify at the lowest level would require a year of relevant experience at the GS-7 level, which probably means a year of experience as an E-6, O-1 or W-1 will meet the requirement. Alternatively, a person can qualify for GS-9 with a masters degree.

Department of Homeland Security, U.S. Secret Service, **Program Analyst**, GS-343-9/11/12/13. Salary: $41,815 - $93,742 P.A

Here is a job which supports protecting our nation without requiring direct law enforcement activities. This job focuses on planning, developing, and coordinating management techniques and methods that support protective, administrative, and investigative missions. Hiring is at a high enough grade that anyone below E-6, O-1, or W-1 probably would not qualify on the basis of military experience alone. The potential to advance without competition to GS-13 after being hired is very good.

Department of Justice, Drug Enforcement Administration, **Program Analyst**, GS-0343-9/11/12/13. Salary: $41,815 - $93,742 P.A.
A Program Analyst with the D.E.A. also has an opportunity to protect our country without being on the front lines. The announcement requests the same kind or experience requirements as the preceding example and also offers GS-13 potential without further competition. Again, this is a good kind of work for junior officers and senior NCOs.

Department of Homeland Security, Transportation Security Administration, **Program Analyst** (Readiness Standards and Evaluation), SV-0343-F. Salary: $41,815.00 - $93,742.00 Annual
This announcement is for a job under an alternate personnel system. Within TSA, pay range F is equivalent to GS-5/7/9, so this announcement should appeal to potential applicants whose qualifying experience is at or above E-5, or possess a bachelors degree.

Merit Systems Protection Board, Office of Policy and Evaluation, **Program Analyst**, GS-0343-13/14. SV-0343-F Annual Salary Range - $31,100 - $46,700
We included this example to reinforce how broadly this particular occupation is applied in federal agencies. This announcement is looking for someone at a very high starting grade, meaning that the agency wants a very experienced analyst. This is the kind of job where your military experience would need to be deep, and at least a year of it would most likely have to have been at or above the O-4 or W-4 level just to qualify for the lower of the two announced grades.

OTHER SOURCES FOR DETERMINING YOUR AGENCY AND JOB TITLE

List of Federal Agencies – They're all hiring!
You can either target specific agencies with specialized missions, or you can take a look at the complete list of agencies on the CD-ROM.

List of Occupational Series / Jobs in Government – On the CD-ROM
This list breaks down the Federal job titles into Occupational Series or Families of Jobs. Below we provide a brief overview of the Federal government's approach to organizing its civilian jobs by occupational groups and individual series. Knowing your best Federal job title could help you with *www.usajobs.gov* research. Some Federal jobs are NOT listed in this chart. The Department of Homeland Security has created many new job titles that are not on this list.

ANALYZE WHERE YOU FIT

4

Summary

Understanding the jobs that are most relevant to your past experience and how to qualify for certain salaries can be complicated. Now that you have a better idea about government job titles and your salary/grade/pay band levels, you can begin searching for vacancy announcements that match your requirements. When you find a couple of job announcements that are of real interest—and for which you believe you are qualified—you can focus your resume with lessons from Step 7.

Step 5   Understanding Federal Vacancy Announcements
Learn how to analyze Federal job announcements for mission, qualifications and keywords

Step 5: Understanding Federal Vacancy Announcements
Learn how to analyze Federal job announcements for mission, qualifications and keywords

Researching and analyzing Federal vacancy announcements is important for two reasons: the first is to locate significant Federal job opportunities; the second is to identify keywords to include in your resume. When you are ready to focus your resume as described in Step 7, you will return to the vacancy announcement and add keywords from the "duties" and "qualifications" sections.

Learn how to understand and analyze Federal job vacancy announcements

Before you can find the best vacancy announcements for your skills and interests, it is helpful to understand what is in the vacancy announcement that is important to your job search. At first glance, Federal job announcements seem lengthy and arduous to read. Take the time, however, to glean the information the Federal human resources staff is conveying. **My experience has shown that when jobseekers become more familiar with vacancy announcements and "how to apply" instructions, they apply more frequently for jobs.** In this step you will gain understanding of Federal vacancy announcements and the information you need to be a competitive jobseeker.

TWO TYPES OF JOB ANNOUNCEMENTS

Job Announcements with specific closing dates: These announcements are for positions that are being specifically recruited for. The timing for responses could be as little as a couple of days or as long as several weeks. Agencies set these deadlines based on their experience with the relevant job markets.

Open Inventory / Standing Registers / Database Announcements: These are announcements for jobs that are continually being recruited for or when a future need is anticipated. The closing date could be the distant future, or there may be none at all. The names of qualified applicants are stored in a database, and HR staff will search the database when a supervisor requests a person meeting the job's requirements. Timing for filling jobs covered by this kind of announcement is unknown, so you may be in for a long wait if you respond to one. But you could be pleasantly surprised too by the speed with which the agency offers you a job. What is certain is that if you do not have your resume in the database, you won't be considered at all.

HOW TO READ AND UNDERSTAND A FEDERAL JOB VACANCY ANNOUNCEMENT:

Let's look at one vacancy announcement for the most important features of information that will affect your job search. We will use a Homeland Security Department, Customs and Border Patrol announcement for MISSION SUPPORT SPECIALIST (TRAINING) for our analysis.

93

MISSION SUPPORT SPECIALIST (TRAINING)	
SALARY RANGE: 26,699.00 - 76,261.00 USD per year	OPEN PERIOD: Friday, June 03, 2005 to Friday, June 17, 2005
SERIES & GRADE: GS-0301-11/12	POSITION INFORMATION: Full Time Career/Career Conditional
PROMOTION POTENTIAL: 13	DUTY LOCATIONS: 1 vacancy - Washington, DC
WHO MAY BE CONSIDERED:	
Status Candidates (Merit Promotion Elig)	

Title of Job and Grade

Consider the job title - does it sound interesting? Mission Support Specialist (Training) could be a great job if you were a Mission Support Specialist Trainer while in the military. However, be sure to read the duties section to understand the job clearly. This announcement is for a Series 0301, Grade 11/12 with promotion potential to GS-13. This is an announcement with career advancement opportunities!

Geographic Location

The position is in Washington, DC. Be sure to check whether you can apply if you live outside this geographic area, and if relocation expenses will be paid. This announcement states this on the third page: 12. *Relocation expenses will NOT be paid for anyone selected for this position.*

Closing Date

This announcement closes on June 17th, 2005. Closing dates vary widely but are essential to know! Current openings have closing dates in the vicinity of 5 days to 4 weeks. These are jobs that are open and ready to be filled. Open Inventory or Database Announcement closing dates may be 2 to 4 years in the future. These organizations are building resume databases for future job searches. All announcements are valid however, and you should submit resumes to a variety of types.

Who Can Apply

Are you in the "area of consideration?" Look first for announcements that say "Open to all U.S. citizens." Subject to a few restrictions (citizenship and sometimes age), these jobs are open to all qualified applicants. If you are currently in the military, are a veteran, or previously worked for the Federal government, you can also look for jobs that allow "status candidates," or current employees to apply.

As Veterans, you can probably apply for jobs that are "Open to Anyone", and jobs that are "Open to Status" candidates because of your preference. Study Step 2 from this book to see if you can apply to all government jobs.

Knowledge, Skills, and Abilities

Check to see if KSA narratives are required, and if they need to be written separately or incorporated into the text of your resume.

How to Apply

This description of "how to apply" seems long, but what they are saying here is that you apply through the online resume builder. They are making it clear what they do NOT accept. This is a Defense Finance and Accounting Service Delegated Examining Unit (DEU) job announcement. Best advice: just follow the directions here.

MISSION SUPPORT SPECIALIST

You may submit an online application for this position by selecting the 'Apply Online' button at the bottom of this announcement or by connecting to
http://www.dod.mil/dfas/careers/nonstatus/ca_ns_deuVerify.htm/

You must submit your application so that it will be received by the closing date of the announcement.

When using the DFAS DEU Job Kit, the appropriate geographic location code for this position is "8840." Please follow the instructions in the DFAS DEU Job Kit for the proper placement of this code in your resume. When using the on-line resume builder, click on the box for "Washington, D.C."

The DFAS DEU does not accept SF-171s, OF-612s or other types of application submissions. Only resumes submitted via the DFAS DEU on-line resume builder located at www.dod.mil/dfas/careers/nonstatus/ or resumes formatted and submitted in compliance with instructions contained in the most current DFAS DEU Job Kit will be accepted. Incomplete or improperly formatted resumes will not be processed. Applicants who wish to apply by hardcopy or e-mail may obtain a copy of the DEU Job Kit from the website listed above or by calling the DFAS DEU at (816) 926-1522. The DFAS DEU TDD number for the hearing impaired is (816) 926-3215.

Use of a postage-paid government agency envelopes to file job applications is a violation of Federal laws and regulations. Applications submitted in postage-paid government envelopes **will not be accepted.** Electronic resumes must be received by 11:00 p.m., eastern standard time on the closing date in order to be considered. If submitting a hard copy resume, it must be received in this office by 4:00 p.m. central time on the closing date.

No additional documentation will be accepted with the resume. Applicants will be contacted if additional documentation is needed.

Duties

This Mission Trainer is going to be very busy managing the entire training operation, as well as conducting training (the last sentence). The description of duties is written based on the vacancy's position description. This section includes numerous "keywords" that you should include in your Federal resume (we have boldfaced the keywords here). More on Keywords in Step 7!

MAJOR DUTIES:

You will **coordinate** and perform a wide variety of **administrative and management services** essential to the **operations** of the office (including, but not limited to, **management and information systems, telecommunications, budget, finance, procurement, human resources, training, logistics, property, space, records and files, printing and graphics, mail, travel, and office equipment**) and serve as an **advisor** to **management** on assigned administrative matters. In addition, you will conduct or participate in the **evaluation** of administrative programs, systems and methods and identify ways to **improve the efficiency** and **effectiveness** of these services at the local level. You will also **represent** the office in dealings with **vendors** and **organizations** within the agency that have primary responsibility for these services.

Your area of emphasis will be **training**. As such, you will be responsible for providing management assistance in all areas of training. This includes **determining training needs; scheduling and coordinating training sessions**; dealing with **vendors**; arranging the availability of **training locations and equipment**; and **designing training programs** tailored to meet the demands of the organization. You will also **develop training lessons and plans**, inform staff of upcoming training and **serve as the office advisor** on training issues. In addition, you will **conduct training activities, document training in an automated system, provide feedback** to **high level management** to acquire necessary training support resources and **manage all training aids, devices and equipment**.

Qualifications

Are you qualified? If so, then this is a good announcement for you. This section is important to understand for the success of your application. If you want to earn the salary of a GS-11, read the qualifications required for this grade. There are some excellent keywords and descriptions in this section that could help you write a better resume. The qualifications are usually based on experience, education and training or a combination of experience and education. It's interesting to see the difference in qualifications between the 11 and the 12. If you want to be considered for both grades, be sure to cover the qualifications for both.

QUALIFICATIONS REQUIRED:

GS-11: You qualify at the GS-11 level if you possess one year of specialized experience that equipped you with the skills needed to perform the job duties. This experience must have been equivalent to at least the GS-9 grade level. Examples include coordinating and monitoring a variety of training projects (e.g., the preparation of training requests and individual development plans, the execution of a portion of a mission support plan); identifying and recommending solutions to a wide range of training problems; analyzing training data from a variety of sources to develop trends, patterns, profiles, estimates, and studies (e.g., input on succession planning studies); preparing preliminary and finished reports and documents on training matters (e.g., local operating procedures to implement or ensure compliance with new or changed training requirements); and representing the office in dealings with vendors and personnel from training organizations.

-OR-

You may substitute a doctoral degree or three full years of progressively higher-level graduate education leading to such a degree in a qualifying field for experience at the GS-11 grade level. This education must have been obtained from an accredited college or university and demonstrate the skills necessary to do the work of the position. (A course of study in business administration, public administration, and related fields is qualifying.) Check with your school to determine how many credit hours comprise three years of graduate study. If that information is not available, use 54 semester or 81 quarters hours.

Combining experience and Education: Appropriate combinations of successfully completed post-high school education and experience also may be used to meet total qualification requirements for the GS-11 grade level. Refer to www.cbp.gov for information on how to combine experience and education.

GS-12: You qualify at the GS-12 level if you possess one year of specialized experience that equipped you with the skills needed to perform the job duties. This experience must have been equivalent to at least the GS-11 grade level. Examples include applying (and modifying, if necessary) established practices to specific training problems which involve many variables; conducting independent evaluations on training functions and preparing study findings, recommendations, and reports (e.g., training plans); providing advice on a variety of training programs and procedures; making agreements and commitments on training matters at meetings and during telephone discussions in accordance with previously received instructions; and performing liaison functions with training organizations, including effectively presenting the organization's needs and establishing harmonious working relations with counterparts.

REQUIREMENTS

U.S. Citizenship: Candidates must be United States citizens and present proof of citizenship, if selected.

Background/Security Investigation: You will need to successfully complete a background security investigation before you can be appointed into this position.

How you will be evaluated

This section is very insightful and interesting because you can actually see how they will score your application. Notice that they will add up the answers to your occupational questionnaire for this particular announcement (each announcement and agency might be different). Any points for Veterans' Preference will be applied. Your application score will be based on how well your knowledge, skills and abilities (as demonstrated in your resume and in the answers to your questions) match the required skills for the position.

HOW YOU WILL BE EVALUATED:
Once the occupational questionnaire and resume (and any applicable supporting document, such as DD-214, transcripts, etc.) is received a numeric rating is assigned based on your responses to the questionnaire. The score is a measure of the degree to which your background matches the knowledge, skills and abilities required of this position. Please follow all instructions carefully. Errors or omissions may affect your rating.

VETERANS PREFERENCE: Five points may be added to the eligible ratings of veterans who: Entered the military service prior to October 14, 1976; served on active duty during the Gulf War between August 2, 1990 and January 2, 1992, regardless of where the person served; or, served in a military action for which they received a campaign badge or expeditionary medal. Medal holders and Gulf War veterans must have served continuously for at least 24 months or the full period for which called or ordered to active duty. Ten points may be granted to the eligible ratings of disabled veterans; Purple Heart recipients; spouses or mothers of a 100 percent disabled veteran; or the widows, widowers, or mothers of a deceased veteran.

Finding Keywords and Skills in the Vacancy Announcement

Once you have found a vacancy announcement and read through it sufficiently to determine your interest and eligibility, it is time to analyze the announcement for keywords. This step is crucial! Without identifying the keywords, you cannot customize your application materials to the announcement. This is where you will market yourself to the Human Resources personnel and help them understand why you should be hired for the job.

Highlight the important skills and duties in the announcement. Read both the "duties" and the "qualifications" sections. Look at the following announcement samples and the words that are highlighted. If you can include these words (or some of them) in your resume as skills or experience, your package will stand out when the HR staff member reviews the applications. These three announcements have a wide range of grade level and salary offerings so that there is room for advancement. Training is expected and experience will be gained in the lower grades. You can enter these positions at any of the grades listed. These announcements with multiple grade offerings are a good source for positions offering career opportunity in government.

EXAMPLE 1 – Department of the Army

INTELLIGENCE SPECIALIST (OPERATIONS SUPPORT), JOINT ACTIVITIES

Additional Duty Location Info: 1 vacancy - FL - Miami

SALARY RANGE: 43,660.00 - 82,304.00 USD per year	**OPEN PERIOD:** Monday, July 18, 2005 to Monday, August 01, 2005
SERIES & GRADE: GG-0132-9/12	**POSITION INFORMATION:** - This is a Permanent position. -- Full Time
PROMOTION POTENTIAL: 11/12	**DUTY LOCATIONS:** 1 vacancy - FL - Miami

WHO MAY BE CONSIDERED:

Applications will be accepted from United States citizens and nationals.

MAJOR DUTIES:

You will be the Intelligence Directorates focal point for **intelligence budget, manpower and personnel management.**

Provide **technical advice, review, evaluate, coordinate, develop and present briefings on manpower, personnel & budget requirements, allocations and authorizations.**

You will develop/manage the **program budget**; prepare/submit intelligence initiatives and resource input.

Assess the adequacy of **resource programming** and recommend solutions.

Administer the **manpower program**; analyze **intelligence organizational structures**, functional alignments, command relationships, manpower requirements, utilization, and position grade structure requirements.

Provide technical advice/guidance;

Conduct studies of intelligence mission/workload changes involving multi-disciplined intelligence missions, functions & organizations.

Coordinate with the **staff to identify/recommend solutions** to unusual personnel related issues. This position requires knowledge of the **Intelligence disciplines and analysis**.

About the Position: The incumbent will work for the Director of the Plans Division, at Headquarters, United States Southern Command (USSOUTHCOM) in the Intelligence Directorate, Plans Division in Miami, Florida with normal working conditions and atmosphere. We are located in building 8401, NW 53rd Terrace, Miami, Florida.

EXAMPLE 2 – Federal Bureau of Investigation

INVESTIGATIVE SUPPORT SPECIALIST GS 1801-5/7/9/11 (EX)

SALARY RANGE: 30,789.00 - 73,378.00 USD per year	**OPEN PERIOD:** Thursday, July 14, 2005 to Wednesday, July 27, 2005
SERIES & GRADE: GS-1801-05/11	**POSITION INFORMATION:** Excepted Service Appointment This position will be filled on a full-time, permanent basis.
	DUTY LOCATIONS: 1 vacancy - Houston, TX

WHO MAY BE CONSIDERED:

This announcement is open to all qualified applicants who reside within the Houston, Texas commuting area.

This position is being advertised concurrently under Merit Promotion procedures in Announcement Number HO-2005-0072. Candidates who wish to be considered under both External and Merit Promotion procedures must apply to both announcements. This position is also being advertised concurrently to FBI employees in all locations under Announcement Number HO-2005-0073.

JOB SUMMARY:

The FBI is like no other career choice you've explored. It's challenging, compelling, and important. Whatever your background or expertise, you will find an FBI future exceptionally rewarding because the work you perform will have a daily impact on the nation's security and the quality-of-life for all U.S. citizens.

Location: Houston, Texas

Working Hours: 8:15 - a.m. - 5:00 p.m.

Salary:
GS-5: $30,789.00 $40,031.00
GS-7: $38,138.00 $49,581.00
GS-9: $46,652.00 $60,643.00
GS-11: $56,445.00 $73,378.00

Relocation Expenses will be borne by the selectee, except employees returning from Legat assignment.

Area Information: Houston is the fourth largest city in the United States, with a population of 3.4 million people, and is the ninth largest field office in the FBI. Houston offers moderately priced housing, and numerous cultural and intellectual opportunities. There is no state income tax in Texas, and economic indicators are positive.

EXAMPLE 2 – (CONTINUED)

KEY REQUIREMENTS:

- U.S. Citizenship Required.
- The selectee must be able to obtain a Top Secret clearance.

MAJOR DUTIES:

GS 5: Performs **research and analysis functions** relative to the least complex investigative case leads for the purpose of facilitating overall investigative efforts of the office.

Assists **Special Agents and/or higher level specialists in the research** and **analysis** of the more routine leads emanating from **on-going investigative cases**. Participates in the **documentation** of basic **research results**, receiving guidance and assistance from higher level analyst or Special Agent personnel.

GS 7:   Provides **essential investigative support** towards the Bureau's overall **investigative mission** by processing a variety of criminal and general (i.e. security, applicant, civil, etc.) investigative leads and portions of conventional investigative cases, barring any known or suspected indication of physical danger.

Receives assignments in terms of investigative leads and segments of more routine investigative cases emanating from officially assigned cases assigned to Special Agent personnel.

Utilizes manual and automated information resources, determine most viable sources of information and conducts research of varied information.

Prepares synopsis of research findings in proper format to be included for use in official investigative case documentation findings.

Prepares routine subpoenas and participates in personally serving same to individuals identified. Receives and/or participates in handling telephonic and face-to-face complaints from outside sources and the general public.

EXAMPLE 2 – (CONTINUED)

MAJOR DUTIES (CONTINUED):

GS 9: Provides **vital investigative support** towards the Bureau's overall investigative mission by processing a full range and variety of criminal and general (i.e. security, applicant, civil, etc.) investigative leads and cases from inception to completion, barring any known indication of serious physical danger.

Responsible for **serving subpoenas**, maintaining and developing a wide range of diverse liaison contacts and sources.

Independently determines **necessary principal and supplemental leads** for research and analysis. **Receives general investigative cases,** being assigned as the "case Agent", to process from inception to completion.

Prepares graphic aids regarding research findings, such as assessments of property boundaries. Prepares detailed synopsis of research findings in final form to represent or supplement official investigative case document results.

Orally or in writing, sets out additional leads for coverage by other field offices and/or FBIHQ and/or advises case agent personnel of suggested investigative trails.

Initiates and prepares subpoenas, personally serves majority of these subpoenas.

Provides significant advice and guidance to Agent personnel requiring subpoena(s) issued in connection with on-going cases.

On recurring rotational basis, handles telephonic and face-to-face complaints from outside sources and the general public. May be called upon to **testify** in a court of law as to content of information obtained manner of obtainment, and chain of custody of evidence.

GS 11: **Provides invaluable investigative support** towards the Bureau's overall investigative mission by processing a variety of **intricate and multifarious criminal and general (i.e. security, applicant, civil) investigative cases and leads.**

Serves subpoenas; maintaining and developing a vast cache diverse liaison contacts.

Receives portions of cases, and/or disjointed leads emanating from investigative cases officially assigned to Special Agent personnel.

Independently **determines necessary principle, supplemental and previously neglected leads for research and analysis. Conducts extensive research, analyzes all information found.**

Prepares graphic aids regarding research findings, such as assessments of property boundaries.

EXAMPLE 3 – U.S. Army

DEPARTMENT OF THE ARMY

Vacancy Announcement Number: WTEJ04951531

OPEN DATE: July 01, 20xx; Closing Date: July 30, 20xx	**POSITION:** - Electronics Engineer, GG-0855-5/07/09/11/12
SALARY: $31,302 - $76,261 ANNUAL	**PLACE OF WORK:** Assistant Secretary of the Army, Threat Simulation Management Office, Redstone Arsenal, AL - Duty Station: Fort Bliss, TX
POSITION STATUS: This is a full-time permanent position	**NUMBER OF VACANCIES:** 1

MAJOR DUTIES:

Serve as an electronics engineer involved in the intelligence design, development and lifecycle production and deployment of hardware threat systems for the Army Threat Simulator Program with particular emphasis on electronic subsystems.

Assignments include several **Air Defense related areas such as early warning radars, fire control radars, IR systems, C3 systems, anti-aircraft artillery directors and jammer systems.**

Technology areas represented by these air defense categories include **radar transmitters, receivers, signal processing, moving target indicators, data display systems, mobile system design, packaging techniques, system life cycle engineering system test procedures and system instrumentation.**

Define specifications for these systems, initiate procurement actions and exercise technical supervision of assigned development problems.

This is a developmental position; full performance is a GG-12.

QUALIFICATIONS CONTINUED ON NEXT PAGE

EXAMPLE 3 – (CONTINUED)

QUALIFICATIONS:
- GS-05: 4 year course of study leading to a bachelor's degree directly related to this occupation.
- GS-07: Bachelor's degree directly related to this occupation and 1 year of experience directly related to this occupation equivalent to at least the next lower grade level, or 1 year of graduate level education, or superior academic achievement.
- GS-09: Bachelor's degree directly related to this occupation and 1 year of experience directly related to this occupation equivalent to at least the next lower grade level, or 2 years of progressively higher level graduate education leading to a master's degree or equivalent graduate degree.
- GS-11: Bachelor's degree directly related to this occupation and 1 year of experience directly related to this occupation equivalent to the next lower grade level, or 3 years of progressively higher level graduate education leading to a Ph.D. degree or equivalent doctoral degree.
- GS-12 and above: Bachelor's degree directly related to this occupation and 1 year of experience directly related to this occupation equivalent to the next lower grade level.
- The experience described in your resume will be evaluated as related to the qualifications, knowledge, skills and abilities required for this job.
- One year of experience in the same or similar work equivalent to at least the next lower grade or level requiring application of the knowledge, skills, and abilities of the position being filled.

Summary

Searching for Federal job vacancy announcements is challenging; however, it is critical to the success of your job search campaign to find the best announcements for you and to analyze those announcements for keywords. Using those keywords in a relevant context in your Federal resume is critical. Take your time and make sure you find job announcements that are appropriate for your salary, location and experience level. The next step will show you where to find these announcements and the websites and databases where you can submit your application for Federal jobs.

Step 6   Search for Federal Jobs

Introduction to Federal job listings, websites and search techniques

Step 6: Search for Federal Jobs
Introduction to Federal job listings, websites and search techniques

Now that you better understand vacancy announcements, can interpret salary or grade information, and have collected a few target job titles, you may begin your search for suitable jobs on www.usajobs.gov and other agency websites.

On the following pages we've taken an in-depth look at a range of popular job sites. These include independent agency websites and commercial automated systems used to recruit job candidates.

> *www.USAJobs.gov*
> *Question-Driven Systems, including QuickHire*
> *Resumix – Keywords Systems*
> *www.donhr.navy.mil*
> *www.cpol.army.mil*
> *http://www.afpc.randolph.af.mil/*
> *www.dla.mil*
> *www.nsa.gov*

For a more comprehensive list of Federal employment websites and databases, refer to the Quick Guide at the end of this chapter.

IMPORTANT "HOW TO APPLY" JOB TIP FOR FEDERAL JOBS:

Applying for Federal jobs on any of the websites in this chapter or any agency will probably involve 2 or 3 or 4 steps for on-line applications. Each agency announcement will have different instructions, but they are basically these:

a. Complete a Profile or Registration on-line
b. Copy and paste your resume in their Resume Builder or form
c. Then you could be required to answer Questions, submit narrative essays, or fill out a Supplemental Data Sheet
d. Then you might find instructions to fax DD 214, transcripts and other documents. Watch the timeframe for faxing!

Much more on "How to Apply" in Step 9.

Major Job Search Sites and Advanced Search Techniques

USAJOBS: USAJOBS.GOV
One of the five most popular career job sites on the internet!

www.usajobs.gov

To find vacancy announcements for jobs for which you are qualified or would be interested in, we recommended three search techniques involving just three to four criteria selections. Most likely, this will produce many interesting results.

SEARCH TECHNIQUE 1 – **GEOGRAPHIC**

Start at *www.usajobs.gov* and select the SEARCH link
Geographic Search – the entire state where you live
Agencies – SELECT ALL
Job Title - SELECT ALL
Click on YES if you have been in the military, or click NO to read announcements that are open to people who have not worked in government before.

All of the jobs in your selected state or city will appear. Scroll through them carefully as they may not be in alphabetical order. There will be a variety of jobs, grade levels, and titles. If you are qualified for a GS-7/9, you may scroll directly to these positions. Consider all job titles; a government job title doesn't tell the whole story!

SEARCH TECHNIQUE 2 – **AGENCY**

> From the *www.usajobs.gov* home page, again select the SEARCH link
> Agency Search - SELECT AN AGENCY
> Locations - SELECT ALL
> Jobs - SELECT ALL
> Click on YES if you have been in military or government, or click on NO if not.

For example, a search for all National Institutes of Health jobs, U.S.-wide, will display all available jobs nationwide. This type of search provides the broadest variety of job titles within the agency that you can find. Scroll through them all, even if there are 10 screens. Look for the grade level that is right for you.

SEARCH TECHNIQUE 3 – **JOB TITLE**

> From the *www.usajobs.gov* home page, again select the SEARCH link
> Job title – SELECT A SPECIFIC TITLE
> Location - SELECT GEOGRAPHIC LOCATION

AVUECENTRAL RECRUITING SYSTEM:
www.avuecentral.com

Avuecentral.com is a question-driven system developed and maintained by AvueCentral, a private industry company holding contracts with a number of Federal agencies. AvueCentral posts Federal vacancy announcements, and receives and assesses job applications for the Federal government on their website (www.avuecentral.com). Agencies that use avuecentral.com place their job announcements here as well as on the OPM website (www.usajobs.opm.gov). Avuecentral.com is a free, easy-to-use website.

www.avuecentral.com

Announcements	Specific – good list of duties
Closing Dates	Current listings and open inventory
Resume Builder	10 screens, copy and paste
Job Duties / Length	6,000 characters
Registration / Profile	Yes

QUESTION DRIVEN ON-LINE APPLICATIONS:

For example: *www.hhs.gov* and *www.epa.gov* – two of QuickHire, Monster Government Solution Recruitment Federal Agencies.

Department of Health and Human Services is one of approximately 120 federal agencies who are using the QuickHire or Monster Government Solutions System for receiving and managing applications from federal job applicants. This application system involves a Registration with electronic resume copy and paste (16,000 characters). It also requires applicants to answer Questions and submit Short and Long Essays.

Department of Health and Human
Services QuickHire Registration Page
https://jobs.quickhire.com/scripts/hhs.exe

Environmental Protection Agency
Browse and Registration Page
http://www.epa.gov/ezhire/

Announcements	Both descriptive and a few generic
Closing Dates	Current listings and a few open inventory
Resume Builder	One online field, copy and paste
Job Duties Length	16,000 characters – entire resume
Registration / Profile	Questions Yes
Questions	Yes – look for these!
Essays	Yes – Just like KSAs!

DONHR - U.S. NAVY HUMAN RESOURCES:
www.donhr.navy.mil

The U.S. Navy and Marine Corps have their own website on which you can post your resume. You may copy and paste your resume into their online builder, then search for announcements that match your qualifications. Go to the "Jobs, Jobs, Jobs" page to search for civilian job vacancies by geographic area, salary or job title.

NOTE: DON announcements are not particularly descriptive. They may have "generic" job descriptions instead of specific "duties," like other announcements. These are "Open Inventory" or database announcements.

U.S. Navy Civilian Hiring and Recruitment Tool
https://chart.donhr.navy.mil

Agencies Served	U.S. Navy and U.S. Marines
Announcements	Generic – short descriptions of duties
Closing Dates	Current listings and Open Inventory (mostly)
Resume Builder	8 Screens, copy and paste
Job Duties Length	6,000 characters
Registration / Profile	Questions Yes
Supplemental Data Sheet	Yes
How to Apply	Self-Nominate after resume is in database
Track & Follow-up	Not easy, no automated system

DEFENSE LOGISTICS AGENCY:
www.dla.mil

The Defense Logistics Agency (DLA) is a U.S. Department of Defense (DoD) agency. The DLA website is unique because it allows you to receive a list of your keywords and skills by email after you submit your electronic resume to the database. This is a very helpful feature!

www.dla.mil

Agencies Served	Defense Logistics Agency
	Defense Contract Management Agency
	Defense Contract Management Agency Int'l
	Defense Supply Systems
	Defense Distribution Center
	Defense Logistics Information Center
	Defense Reutilization Marketing Center
	Defense Human Resources Center
Announcements	Both descriptive and generic
Closing Date	Current listings and Open Inventory
Resume Builder	8 Screens, copy and paste

CPOL - U.S. ARMY CIVILIAN PERSONNEL ON-LINE:
www.cpol.army.mil and *http://acpol.army.mil/employment/*

Although the U.S. Army posts its civilian vacancies on the USAJobs website, if you would like to be considered for a civilian position at any Army duty location, you MUST locate the vacancy announcements here and post your resume into the Army's resume builder. If you are interested in civilian positions with the U.S. Army, you might save time by going directly to this website to find the announcements and apply for the jobs.

The Army Civilian Resume Builder and ANSWER Tool
(Applicant Notification System Web-Enabled Response)
https://cpolst.belvoir.army.mil/public/resumebuilder/builder/index.jsp

Agencies Served	U.S. Army military bases and agencies worldwide
Announcements	Both descriptive and generic
Closing Dates	Current listings and Open Inventory
Resume Builder	EXCELLENT – one field – copy and paste!
Registration / Profile	Questions Yes
Supplemental Data Sheet	Yes
Job-Specific Questions	No
Track & Follow-up	ANSWER system – track your job offers in a great database – Great system!

AFPC - U.S. AIR FORCE CIVILIAN EMPLOYMENT:
http://www.afpc.randolph.af.mil

You can find specific jobs with closing dates on this website. There is a resume builder on this website also with its own database. You may submit your resume and select your job announcements.

Air Force Resume Writer
https://ww2.afpc.randolph.af.mil/resweb/resume/resume.htm

Agencies Served	U.S. Air Force civilian jobs worldwide
Announcements	Excellent keywords and descriptions
Closing Dates	Current listings and Open Inventory
Resume Builder	Easy to use – copy and paste
Registration / Profile	Questions Yes
Supplemental Data Sheet	Yes
Job-Specific Questions	No
Track & Follow-up	Yes, a system to check status online

NATIONAL SECURITY AGENCY:
www.nsa.gov

The National Security Agency is always hiring. Just submit your resume to their database and wait for a response. You cannot follow up on your resume submission, however.

www.nsa.gov

Agencies Served	National Security Agency
Announcements	Careers and jobs are both descriptive and generic
Closing Dates	Database collection
Resume Builder	12 screens, copy and paste
Job Duties Length	3,000 characters
Registration / Profile Questions	Yes
Supplemental Data Sheet	No
How to Apply	Submit your resume and profile to database
	Check your target jobs on the shopping cart
Track & Follow-up	No system for applicant; wait for HR contact

QUICK GUIDE
TO THE MOST POPULAR FEDERAL JOB LISTING WEBSITES
FOR FORMER MILITARY PERSONNEL

www.usajobs.gov
The official Office of Personnel Management's website of Federal job listings. You can create an individual profile to receive vacancy announcements by email. BEWARE: If you only use the email announcement system with specific job titles, you could be missing some jobs with titles that are new or unusual. It's best to search usajobs.gov once per week, as well as sign up for the email service.

www.avuecentral.com
A commercial website with as many job listings as *www.usajobs.gov*. You may submit your resume into their resume builder and apply for jobs at approximately 15 agencies, including FEMA, civilian U.S. Coast Guard, and some Department of Homeland Security.

www.fedjobs.com
A commercial website where you can read vacancy announcements and, for a small fee, sign up for an email service that will send you full vacancy announcements based on your criteria.

www.Federaljobsearch.com
A commercial website where you can read vacancy announcements and, for a small fee, sign up for an email service that will send you full vacancy announcements based on your criteria.

SELECTED AGENCY WEBSITES WHERE AGENCY JOB ANNOUNCEMENTS, REGISTRATION, PROFILE, RESUME BUILDER, SUPPLEMENTAL STATEMENTS AND/OR SPECIFIC JOB-RELATED QUESTIONS MAY BE FOUND:

Civilian Army positions: *www.cpol.army.mil*
Civilian Navy and Marines positions: *www.donhr.navy.mil*
Air Force Personnel Center: *http://www.afpc.randolph.af.mil/*
U.S. Coast Guard   *http://www.uscg.mil/hq/cgpc/cpm/jobs/vacancy.htm*

Defense Logistics Agency: *www.dla.mil*
Federal Bureau of Investigation: *www.fbijobs.com*
National Security Agency: *www.nsa.gov*
Central Intelligence Agency: *www.cia.gov*

SEARCH THE WEBSITES OF EXCEPTED SERVICE DEPARTMENTS AND AGENCIES AND INTERNATIONAL ORGANIZATIONS:

The following agencies do not always list their jobs on *www.usajobs.gov*. Since they are not part of the competitive service, they are not required to list all of their jobs or internships on OPM's website. If you are interested in these agencies, you should look directly on their websites:

GENERAL AGENCIES:

Federal Reserve System, Board of Governors
Defense Intelligence Agency
Federal Bureau of Investigation
Agency for International Development
U.S. Nuclear Regulatory Commission
Postal Service
United States Mission to the United Nations

Central Intelligence Agency
U.S. Department of State
Government Accountability Office
National Security Agency
Post Rates Commission
Tennessee Valley Authority

Department of Veterans Affairs, Health Services and Research Administration:

Physicians, Dentists, Nurses, Nurse Anesthetists, Physicians' Assistants, Podiatrists, Optometrists, Expanded-function Dental Auxiliaries, Occupational Therapists, Pharmacists, Licensed Practical/Vocational Nurses, Physical Therapists and Certified/Registered Respiratory Therapists.

JUDICIAL BRANCH
LEGISLATIVE BRANCH

PUBLIC INTERNATIONAL ORGANIZATIONS:

International Monetary Fund
United Nations Children's Fund
United Nations Institute
United Nations Secretariat

Pan American Health Organization
United Nations Development Program
United Nations Population Fund
World Bank, IFC and MIGA

Summary

The more familiar you are with vacancy announcements, the more successful you will be in finding interesting and suitable announcements, writing a competitive resume, and accurately completing the "how to apply" instructions. It's ideal to look for job announcements at least once a week and examine the "qualifications", "duties" and "how to apply" sections carefully. Good luck with your quest! As promised, in Step 7 we will return to your basic resume and learn how to focus it toward job announcements with keywords, skills and qualifications.

Step 7   Focus Your Military Federal Resume

Sell yourself with your accomplishments, keywords, projects and specialized experience

Step 7: Focus Your Military Federal Resume
Sell yourself with your accomplishments, keywords, projects and specialized experience

Writing your Military Federal Resume is one of the most important documents you may write in your career. The art and science of writing this resume is twofold: it must be written specifically toward the job you are seeking; and must be formatted correctly. Central to this of course, is applying for jobs that you are truly qualified for. If you achieve all this, you will have job interviews and offers!

This chapter will show you several ways to add specialized Federal job description content, keywords, accomplishments, projects and military training and awards that will achieve the results you are seeking.

The Civilian Resume vs. the Military Federal Resume

Military terminology has historically been changed in civilian resumes to reflect its targeted audience, in most cases private industry, government contract and even Federal agencies. Today human resources recruiters want to read about your tangible military experiences. Supervisors are actively seeking military personnel to work as civilians in support of defense operations, the war fighters wherever they are, and the Veterans' Administration serving the military bases and personnel worldwide. The government needs ex-military personnel like you who understand the unique needs of active duty military personnel and operations.

Nine Ways to Focus Your Resume and Get Noticed!

Look at the sample electronic resumes in this chapter and notice the keywords, military details, headlines, accomplishments, core competencies, and special electronic formatting solutions. These details are the key to an outstanding application!

1. Use keywords and language from the announcement in your paper and electronic resumes.
2. Maintain military details! Your Military Federal Resume will include information such as rank, service name, base or post locations, operation names in which you served, relevant experiences with numbers and details, specific training course titles, accomplishments and quotes, and more.
3. Use headlines for paper resumes (*HOT, NEW TIP!*) to create visual interest and highlight your most impressive qualifications and skills.
4. Feature accomplishments, i.e. projects with details, specific results with supporting information that demonstrate specialized experience.
5. Include important core competencies for value-added experience.
6. Write a comprehensive summary of qualifications at the top of your resume.
7. Retain your best Military Federal Resume on your database. Copy and paste additional versions for several occupational series.
8. Learn electronic resume tips to create a first-rate database application.
9. Include other qualifications, including awards, certifications, specialized training, community service, and education.

Let's look more closely at these 9 important Military Federal Resume writing lessons:

1. **INCLUDE KEY WORDS AND LANGUAGE FROM THE ANNOUNCEMENT IN YOUR PAPER AND ELECTRONIC RESUMES.**

   These important keywords and content are located in the duties, qualifications and often other paragraphs of the announcement. As stated in Step 5, Analyzing Vacancy Announcements and Keywords, every resume sample in this book and CD-ROM will include important keywords and skills for the targeted job announcement. For many automated resume management systems, keywords and skills are integral to a successful application. We have carefully researched and analyzed the electronic resume samples included in this book. To illustrate how important keywords are, if you do NOT include relevant keywords in your electronic resume, your resume may not be found in the database. Keywords are important for automated resume systems, as well as for the HR Specialists who read resume descriptions to ensure qualifications for the job.

2. **MAINTAIN MILITARY DETAILS!**

   Since the government is looking for former military personnel with relevant, significant and specialized skills, by all means maintain military descriptions of projects, training, operations, challenges and programs in your resume. Refer to the Comparison Chart – Military Federal Resume vs. Civilian Resume in Chapter 3, page 44 for a review of the difference between the military Federal and civilian resume.

3. **USE HEADLINES TO CREATE VISUAL INTEREST AND HIGHLIGHT YOUR MOST IMPRESSIVE QUALIFICATIONS AND SKILLS.**

   Headlines are a hot, new concept in resume formatting! Just use all caps for a five- or six-word phrase or introduction to your job description, rather than the generic "noun" method. Use creative verbs and language to "tell a story" of your experiences and projects. Make it interesting. These visual/verbal upgrades will keep the reader engaged for a few seconds longer, and may result in further consideration of your application!

   Sample Work Experience with noun format vs. headline format:

   02/2003 to 05/2004; 44 hrs/wk, PERSONNEL MANAGER, MANAGEMENT SUPPORT BRANCH (CW4), United States Army Reserve, Headquarters, 63d Regional Readiness Command, Los Alamitos, CA 90720

   Noun format:
   MILITARY RECRUITER …

   Headline format:
   MANAGED HISTORIC RECRUITMENT OF ACTIVE DUTY / DIRECTED HUMAN RESOURCE

122

OPERATIONS. Administered military personnel services for Command Special Actions for one of the largest Army Reserve Commands in the U.S. Working under strict 2-week deadline, planned, designed, and implemented active duty recruitment notices. Notified recruits in writing and over the phone.

Basic format:
PERSONNEL MANAGEMENT …

Headline format:
WROTE NEW PERSONNEL REGULATIONS; IMPLEMENTED NEW PROCEDURES TO ACHIEVE LARGE CALL-UP DEMAND. Initiated and recommended guidance and policy to best resolve complex and sensitive issues. Wrote instructions to announce and employ procedures.

Noun format:
CONGRESSIONAL RESEARCH AND CASE MANAGER …

Headline format:
RESEARCHED SENSITIVE, IMPORTANT CONGRESSIONAL / WHITE HOUSE INQUIRIES. Case Manager for inquiries from Army Office of Chief Legislative Liaison concerning Reservist actions and events involving diverse set of performance issues.

Noun format:
LINE OF DUTY INVESTIGATOR …

Headline format:
MANAGED MORE THAN __ LINE OF DUTY INVESTIGATIONS DURING THE COURSE OF ONE YEAR. Coordinated initiation, completion, and approval of formal and informal LOD investigations. Ensured accurate documentation and validation of service connected injuries, diseases, or deaths.

Noun format:
RECRUITER, COMMAND SELECTION BOARD …

Headline format:
DIRECTED RECRUITMENT AND SELECTION OF ___ SENIOR OFFICERS IN ___ MONTHS. Coordinated senior officer Command Selection Boards. Produced semi-annual requirements based on available command personnel. Wrote and distributed vacancy announcements and application instructions.

4. FEATURE ACCOMPLISHMENTS, I.E. PROJECTS WITH DETAILS, SPECIFIC RESULTS WITH SUPPORTING INFORMATION THAT DEMONSTRATE SPECIALIZED EXPERIENCE.

The Office of Personnel Management instructions for writing the Federal resume (OF-510) state these two simple words for writing the Work Experience section of your resume: Duties and Accomplishments. The duties are covered with keywords and content. Include accomplishments in your resume to make it unique to you.

Your accomplishments speak directly to the hiring manager about your personal experiences. Hopefully, your words will impress hiring managers enough so that they will want to interview you and seriously consider you as an employee in their offices. Accomplishments demonstrate what you have DONE in the past and what you are CAPABLE of in the future. Your examples should be specific - include project title, task name or situation, your actions, important challenges you overcame, and the results with supporting information.

MORE ON PROJECT DESCRIPTIONS

Be sure to read Step 8, KSA Writing. You will learn much more about the importance of and how to write effective project descriptions for KSAs and your electronic resume. Many announcements DO NOT require KSAs, only a resume, in which case your significant projects must be covered in the resume!

Sample Accomplishments:

Example 1

As CRASH EVALUATOR AND TRAINING CONSULTANT, personally reviewed incidents of helicopters being shot down or crashing. To decrease number of occurrences and ensure safety of personnel, recommended to Army Chief of Staff to deploy a training team to analyze conditions and develop specific training tasks for inclusion in stateside training prior to deployment. **Developed a separate training and validation plan** for helicopter units after arrival in Iraq but prior to employment in combat. Successfully **put into operation** processes and procedures that were adopted as standard Army training.

Example 2
Special Assignment: Managed and redesigned the training program for the conversion of an artillery unit to a transportation unit in 1999. The planned 3-year training program was not effectively implemented prior to mobilization of the unit. Under immediate deployment deadline, developed a comprehensive training strategy on basic and advanced combat tasks at the mobilization station. Created reports and briefings to keep Army leadership informed of training issues, teams, and policies on a daily basis. **Results**: Successfully trained and deployed more than 3,500 ready combat soldiers over a period of one year.

Example 3
- Successfully managed one of the largest logistical movements in the shortest period of time in the history of the U.S. military.
- Relocated 1,800 personnel from 19 states to international sites with full accommodations and material required for safety and performance of services.
- Recognized for outstanding logistical insight, planning, and efficiency to meet or exceed the demands of U.S. Government customers providing services in international countries.

5. INCLUDE IMPORTANT CORE COMPETENCIES FOR VALUE-ADDED EXPERIENCE.

Core competencies are the "value-added" skills that Federal HR specialists and hiring managers recognize in resumes. In your military work you have demonstrated outstanding teamwork, resourcefulness, diplomacy, leadership, creativity, bravery (risk-taking), determination, perseverance, strategic thinking, the ability to plan, coordinate, organize, meet deadlines and work under pressure.

You will learn how these core competencies are blended into the work experience and other qualifications sections of your resume. You can read core competencies from the Veteran's Administration, Marine Corps and Office of Personnel Management's Executive Core Qualifications on the CD-ROM about this book. Include these important leadership and managerial competencies in your resume and KSAs.

 Important Federal Core Competencies are listed on the CD-ROM

6. WRITE A COMPREHENSIVE SUMMARY OF QUALIFICATIONS AT THE TOP OF YOUR RESUME.

A Summary of Qualifications is a synopsis of your most important career experiences. An abstract of approximately 350 words, it is your "elevator speech" on paper that will impress the reader with your highest level experiences. Some resume builders do not have a field for the summary, but others have. The Army has a new resume builder in which you can copy and paste an entire resume into one online field. This is a convenient, flexible format. As of now, the space for a summary for Navy, USMC and AF is the Summary of Qualifications at the end of the Resume Builder.

Wherever you place the summary, it is an important resume section because it is an excellent opportunity to engage the reader, highlight important keywords and skills, and unite your entire military career picture into a compelling, action-oriented paragraph.

Tips for writing an optimal Summary of Qualifications:
1. Analyze the announcement "duties and qualifications" section.
2. Write your summary based on the targeted knowledge, skills, abilities, and duties of the position sought.
3. Include your leading skills and experiences.
4. Strive to make your summary a "page-turner" introduction.
5. Your goal is to impress the hiring official to want to meet you, set up an interview, and/or consider you for his or her team.

The following Summary of Qualifications examples can be used at the beginning or end of the resume depending on the resume builder format.

Example 1
- Results-oriented Human Resources professional with proven career as head of staffing, retention, and development of more than 34,000 highly-skilled information technology and telecommunications workers.
- Exceptional leadership and team-building skills. Excel at motivating teams to overachieve.
- Versatile and proactive problem-solver with high level of integrity.
- Successful supervisor, managing, monitoring, coordinating work and mentoring up to 156 employees.
- Mature values, coupled with excellent written, oral communication skills and a polished professional image.
- Proficient in use of Microsoft products, military personnel management databases, and conducting Internet research.

Example 2
Summary of Qualifications: Managed operations, personnel, and resources of large-scale organizations and projects. Executive management professional, able to identify trends, develop teams, and determine modus operandi to implement strategic plans. Frontline professional with proven background in managing and implementing high dollar projects. Establish and ensure sound operations, quality assurance, and quality control. Leadership ability to optimize team production and maximize group motivation through synergy, empowerment, and open communications. Exemplary public relations and public speaking abilities.

Professional Knowledge, Skills, and Abilities: Knowledge of Federal procurement laws, rules, and regulations gained in work for master's degree, supplemented with reading of Federal Acquisition Regulations and Defense Acquisition Regulations, and self-paced studies from DoD websites. Utilize weighted matrices, linear regressions, PERT, and other decision-making formats to arrive at the "best" supplier, offering most value added. Utilize Request for Quotes (RFQs) and Requests for Information (RFIs) for bid proposals on standard contracts.

Oral Communications Skills: Negotiated contracts involving subcontracting and third party installments. Frequently incorporated time leveraging, setting concessions for job to be completed on time and at a reduced cost. Liaison for military, Federal, and municipal agencies during Combined Federal Campaign and United Way for the City of San Antonio. Led team that raised more than $1M in a two-month period.

7. **RETAIN YOUR BEST MILITARY FEDERAL RESUME ON YOUR DATABASE. COPY AND PASTE ADDITIONAL VERSIONS FOR SEVERAL OCCUPATIONAL SERIES.** With most of the resume builder applications, you can submit only one resume at a time. If you submit for a management analyst position one week, you should be careful to revise your resume toward an administrative officer position the next week. You don't know when HR recruiters will search for candidates in the database. Your ONE resume should cover keywords and skills for both series if possible. The way to cover two or three sets of skills and keywords is to analyze the vacancy announcements for your target jobs. Make a list of keywords and get them in the resume the best way possible.

8. **LEARN ELECTRONIC RESUME TIPS TO CREATE A FIRST-RATE DATABASE APPLICATION.**

Do's & Don'ts for Resumix and Other Electronic Formats

DO -
Compile & Research
- Locate all of your written career documents, such as resumes, SF-171s and position descriptions.
- Research keywords, skills, and industry language.
- Consider your experience, skills and career interests.
- Determine your salary requirements and qualifications.
- Schedule time to research, write, and edit. Regard this as a career management project.

Focus your Resume Content
- Write one resume that will include keywords from all of your career objectives
- Emphasize the last 10 years of experience
- Write your best attempt, then edit again – twice!
- Find an editor or additional person to review your resume

Include your Accomplishments

- For each of your past jobs relevant to the position being sought, include one to three of your greatest accomplishments with details. Remember to make every effort to grab your reader's attention!

Formatting and Readability

- IMPORTANT: Compose and edit your resume in a word processing program, then copy and paste your resume text into the online form or resume builder.
- Adhere to the page length instructions or character limitations for each agency. TIP: If you are writing a 5-page resume, include your most recent information within the first 3 pages.
- Use easy-to-read type fonts, such as Times Roman or Arial.
- Use readable font sizes: 11 or 12 point type.
- Maintain at least one-inch margins around the copy.
- Use ALL CAPS, bold, italics, or bold italics for highlighting job titles or other important point. Do not overuse these effects though.
- Insert white space to improve readability, such as a double space between paragraphs.

Remember your passwords and usernames
Study, read, and follow the examples in this book and on the CD-ROM

DON'T -

- Use oversize paragraphs (paragraph length approximately 8-10 lines).
- Write long-winded, run-on sentences. Keep sentence length concise and easy to read (7 to 14 words per sentence).
- Use third person verbs, for instance "directs and coordinates" Use present tense verbs for your current position, "plan, direct, and coordinate." For past positions use "planned, directed, and coordinated."
- Copy and paste your position description language or evaluations direct and uncut into your resume.
- Overuse acronyms; aim for as few as possible. If you do use acronyms, spell out the words followed by the acronym in parenthesis. Example: Department of Defense (DoD). Thereafter you may use the acronym alone.

9. **INCLUDE OTHER QUALIFICATIONS, INCLUDING AWARDS, CERTIFICATIONS, SPECIALIZED TRAINING, COMMUNITY SERVICE, AND EDUCATION.**

Your awards from the military are impressive and well-deserved. Certifications are critical for many positions. Specialized training is expensive and important. Community service demonstrates many skills and competencies for leadership, communications and service. Education may be essential to your qualifications for the job. All of the samples in the Appendix and on the CD will include these sections.

Sample Military Federal Resumes

SAMPLE 1. MILITARY FEDERAL RESUME – LTC, LOGISTICS OR PROGRAM MANAGER, U.S. ARMY NATIONAL GUARD

This Military Federal Resume includes keywords, accomplishments and headlines which are relevant to the target position and important to the hiring supervisor. This resume reads like a history lesson from Kosovo. Defense managers (who are probably former military) and other managers who are in the war fighter support business will appreciate and be impressed with the full details of this manager's logistical challenges. They will remember Kosovo, the historically-significant, fast-track deployment of the National Guard, and the sheer numbers of personnel and materiel that moved quickly to support the war.

> *Note 1:* **RANK:**
> The Military Federal Resume will include the rank, if the rank of the military person is in line with the applicant's job objective. This person is an LTC, 0-5. He is seeking a GS-12/13 position. He will accept a GS-11, if a good opportunity comes along to get into government. Therefore this rank is in line with his target grade level. This will let the Human Resources Specialist know very quickly in his evaluation that he has the experience for the GS-12/13 position.

Target Positions: Logistics Management, Transportation Management, Program & Management Analyst, Administrative Officer
Future Customer Base: War fighters, Defense employees and agencies, military base commands
Future Mission Interest: War Fighter Support Operations; Logistics, Project Management, Defense-related work
Target Grade: GS 12/13 positions
Format: Resumix format (an electronic resume format) for DoD applications
Resume Notes: The notes interpret the strategy for writing each section

01/2004 to Present; 40 hrs/wk; Ohio Army National Guard, LOGISTICS OFFICER (Lieutenant Colonel, O-5) (Note 1), G-4 KFOR 6A, HQ, 37th Armored Brigade, Camp Bondsteel, Kosovo APO, AE 09340; Supervisor, Colonel Adam Gray, DSN phone: 555-785-7332; Commercial phone: 1-011-49-666777-485-7229 (may contact).

Mobilized in support of Global War on Terrorism.

NATIONAL GUARD TO KOSOVO: Primary logistics Senior Staff Officer directing the Call to Active Duty and logistical transportation of 1,800 Army National Guard troops from 19 states to Kosovo for Operation Enduring Freedom in just 6 months.

> *Note 2:* **OPERATION ENDURING FREEDOM:**
> The name of the war is easy to recognize and sets the context for this significant logistical experience using the same language that is used in the Washington Post and other national media.

DIRECTED LOGISTICS MANAGEMENT OPERATIONS FOR THE LARGEST CALL TO ACTIVE DUTY IN NATIONAL GUARD HISTORY: Planned and directed logistics operations to achieve support of a supply chain of 1,800 personnel from 19 states deployed to Kosovo. Evaluated and implemented all aspects of logistics assistance mission activities. Integrated logistics, including financial, transportation (air, rail, vehicle, convoy, commercial air), road network planning, and supply chain support for an 1,800 personnel task force from 19 states deployed to Kosovo. Developed logistics operations to support task force operations, equipment, personnel, and foreign nation and host nation requirements.

> *Note 3:* **NATIONAL GUARD TO KOSOVO:**
> This is a National Guard to Kosovo "story." This resume is readable, compelling, and understandable. It sets the context for the experiences that are described later in more detail.

Ensure logistics of moving clothing and equipment that exceeded normal mobilization issues in order to increase the soldiers' comfort and effectiveness. Directed purchases of all items and supplies for meals, lodging, laundry, maintenance, and general support while en route and upon arrival.

> *Note 4:* **LOGISTICS MANAGEMENT OPERATIONS:**
> This is the premiere skill that this candidate can offer any hiring agency. It is nicely featured in the top half of page one of the resume. Nobody can miss this skill set because of the placement and description of his logistics management work.

MANAGED DEPLOYMENT WITH PROJECT MANAGEMENT SOFTWARE: Use the Army Time Phased Force Deployment system and the Joint Operations Planning and Executive System to manage the project timeline within a period of just 6 months.

> *Note 5:* **SOFTWARE:**
> Most managers use some kind of software or database to manage information. This is excellent experience that will be used again and again, probably not the "Army Time Phased" system, but one that has similar features and purposes.

COORDINATED OPERATIONS WITH CONTRACTORS, U.S. ARMY EUROPE AND TASK FORCE LEADERSHIP: Developed reports for U.S. Army Europe and Task Force leadership for use in operational planning and decision-making. Coordinated with contractor for current and future support operations. Provided status information to upper management. Expedited requests, cancellations, shipment changes, and general logistics information to Command group and subordinate units.

SUPERVISED A CULTURALLY DIVERSE TEAM: The team was comprised of 7 officers and 11 enlisted (E-5–E-8) logisticians and administrative personnel. Trained employees on technical regulations, processes, policies, and procedures. Set priorities and assigned tasks. Guided employees to resolve difficult technical issues. Mentored employees toward effective and rewarding careers. Coached employees in customer service techniques. Promoted cooperative working relationships and fostered cohesive team work. Monitored and evaluated performance. Implemented or recommended corrective actions, when necessary. Recognized outstanding performance of staff in areas of multi-tasking, deadline management, problem-solving and teamwork.

> *Note 6:* **SUPERVISION:**
> This is a very important, detailed paragraph that will be recognizable to any employer. Not only does he supervise, but he trains, assigns tasks, guides, mentors, coaches, and recognizes success.

ACCOMPLISHMENTS: QUICK MOVEMENT OF SOLDIERS IN 47 UNITS TO GERMANY, THEN KOSOVO. Successfully developed and managed the Base Support Plan, Transportation Plan, and Operation Needs Statements to safely and expeditiously support the movement and living and working needs of 1,800 soldiers within 47 separate units, spread across 19 states. Logistically moved soldiers to the mobilization station, deploying them on to Germany, and subsequently on to Kosovo.

> *Note 7:* **ACCOMPLISHMENTS:**
> This is a critical paragraph with RESULTS of efforts, ideas, plans, deadlines and leadership capabilities. This paragraph is one of the most important paragraphs in this resume!

01/2002 to 12/2003; 40 hrs/wk; United States Army, STAFF OFFICER (Lieutenant Colonel, O-5), Army Operations Center, Pentagon, Washington, D.C. 22209
Supervisor: Colonel David Scott, 722-999-7722 (may contact).

Mobilized in support of Global War on Terrorism.

PENTAGON CRISIS ACTION TEAM STAFF OFFICER: Managed daily communications to produce most accurate and timely information on Army Training Policy and Programs to the Secretary of the Army, Army Chief of Staff, and all other senior Army leadership. Developed and presented written and verbal briefings. Prepared correspondence for senior Army leadership to use in congressional testimony and policy decisions. Tracked and coordinated with U.S. Army Pacific Command and Safety Center on current operations and events and briefed senior Army leaders.

DIRECTED AND PLANNED MOBILIZATION TRAINING TO MEET DEPLOYMENT DEMAND. Staff Action Officer at Headquarters Department of the Army. Identified issues, developed and implemented curriculum to meet training needs involved in mobilizing and deploying Army units involved in Global War on Terrorism. Identified training units and issued orders for units to join mobilization stations in Afghanistan and Iraq. Trained soldiers on all institutional and qualification-type training. Received requests and implemented additional training for subordinate units at mobilization stations.

ACCOMPLISHMENTS: RECOMMENDED A NEW TRAINING AND VALIDATION PLAN UPON ARRIVAL IN IRAQ TO IMPROVE SAFETY AND REDUCE CRASHES. As Crash Evaluator and Training Consultant, personally reviewed incidents of helicopters being shot down or crashing. To decrease number of occurrences and ensure safety of personnel, recommended to Army Chief of Staff to deploy a training team to analyze conditions and develop specific training tasks for inclusion in stateside training prior to deployment. Developed a separate training and validation plan for training helicopter units after arrival in Iraq but prior to employment in combat. Successfully developed processes and procedures that were adopted as standard Army training.

SPECIAL ASSIGNMENT: PLANNED A NEW TRAINING PROGRAM FOR TRANSPORTATION UNIT. Artillery unit was converted to a transportation unit in 1999. The planned 3-year training program was not effectively implemented prior to mobilization of the unit. Developed a comprehensive training strategy to train units on basic tasks and advanced combat tasks at the mobilization station so they could be deployed. Developed reports and briefings to keep Army leadership informed of training issues, teams, and policies on a daily basis.

Military Federal Resume Templates are on the CD-ROM

All of these samples are on the CD-ROM in Microsoft Word. They will be easy to use as a Template to write your own Military Federal Resume.

SAMPLE 2. CIVILIAN OR GOVERNMENT CONTRACTOR RESUME – LTC, LOGISTICS OR PROGRAM MANAGER, U.S. ARMY NATIONAL GUARD

The Civilian Resume leaves out the details of technical military experience:

Target Positions: Logistics Management, Transportation Management, Program & Management Analyst, Administrative Officer
Future Customer Base: Commercial, retail, industrial, possibly some government
Future Mission Interest: Commercial transportation, logistics management, supervision
Target Salary: $75-85K
Format: Electronic format (an electronic resume format) for corporate databases
Resume Notes: Interpret the strategy for writing each section.

The Military to Civilian Translated language includes:
- National Guard as a major U.S. Government customer
- Kosovo is now an international site (country specifics are left out) and senior officers are now called senior managers.
- The following words are left out or changed: soldiers, units, officers, enlisted, U.S. Army Europe and Task Force, Command, subordinate, personnel, Base Support Plan, deploy, expedite, Army Time Phased Force Deployment system and the Joint Operations Planning and Executive System, mobilization, Call to Active Duty for Reservists in National Guard History.

01/2004 to Present; 40 hrs/wk; Ohio Army National Guard, LOGISTICS MANAGER. Supervisor, Adam Gray, Commercial phone: 1-011-49-666777-485-7229 (may contact).

LOGISTICS MANAGEMENT OPERATIONS: Planned and directed logistics operations for a large movement of personnel and materiel to an international site in support of the Nation's Security. Senior planner for all aspects of logistics planning, including: financial, transportation (air, rail, vehicle, convoy, commercial air), road network planning, and supply services support for 1,800 personnel from 19 states assigned to international sites. Developed on-site accommodations logistics for operations management, equipment, personnel, and foreign country requirements.

PROJECT MANAGEMENT SOFTWARE: Managed this large, record-breaking, 6-month logistical project effectively through the highly-skilled use of project management software, similar to Microsoft Project Management.

PROGRAM MANAGEMENT / ADMINISTRATION: Developed reports for corporate-level senior decision-makers for operational planning and decision making. Oversaw contractor performance providing on-site management and support services. Expedited specialized requests, cancellations, shipment changes based on changing customer requirements and situational changes. Developed expertise in devising and creating solutions to first-time logistical solutions. SUPERVISION: Achieved this successful logistical management contract through the leadership and supervision of hard-working, skilled and culturally-diverse team of 18 logisticians and administrative personnel. Trained employees on technical regulations, processes, policies, and procedures. Set priorities and assigned tasks. Guided employees to resolve difficult technical issues. Mentored employees toward effective and rewarding careers. Coached employees in customer service and safety techniques. Promoted cooperative working relationships and fostered cohesive team work. Monitored and evaluated performance. Implemented or recommended corrective actions, when necessary. Recognized outstanding performance of staff in areas of multi-tasking, deadline management, creative problem-solving and teamwork.

ACCOMPLISHMENTS: Successfully managed one of the largest logistical movements in the shortest period of time in the history of the U.S. Military. Relocated 1,800 personnel from 19 states to international sites with full accommodations and materiel required for safety and performance of services. Recognized for outstanding logistical planning, efficiency, and logistical insight to meet the demands of U.S. Government customers providing services in international countries.

> "I like this resume format, the use of all caps for the job titles tells the reader they have a new chapter in the applicant's life to read and use of the shaded box to identify the applicant gets your attention up-front. It tells the story that will meet the applicant's objectives.
>
> —*Fred W. Freeman, Colonel, USAF (retired)*

SAMPLE 3. MILITARY FEDERAL RESUME – MSG, OPERATIONS, U.S. ARMY

Target Positions: Administrative Officer, Program Manager, Trainer, Human Resources Specialist
Future Customer Base: Law Enforcement, Security, Homeland Security, Immigration & Border Patrol
Future Mission Interest: Government Programs, Homeland Security
Target Grade/Salary: GS 9 through 11 positions; $48K minimum
Format: Electronic format

10/2000 to present. 40 hours per week; OPERATIONS OFFICER, MSG. 38th Personnel Services Battalion, APO AE 09139, Bamberg, Germany. Supervisor, CPT John Smith, 49-999-888-2222, $48,000.00 annually.

CHIEF ADVISOR, PROGRAM MANAGER AND ADMINISTRATIVE OFFICER FOR COMMAND PLANS: Chief Advisor to Battalion Operation Manager and Executive Officer for personnel, budget, training, policies, procedures, resources, schools, inspections, travel, manpower needs, security, and correspondence. Evaluate findings and recommendations on efficiency reviews of operations. Develop plans of action and milestones to incorporate needed improvements to correct deficiencies. Arrange and provide briefings on operation requirements. Prepare briefing slides for command visits. Plan and coordinate command inspections.

SUPERVISE THE LARGEST ARMY PERSONNEL SERVICE IN EUROPE: Directly supervise 4 military personnel supporting largest Army Personnel Services organization consisting of 289 soldiers and 93 civilian employees. Provide leadership and manage diverse military personnel programs including leave, awards, personnel requirements, advancement, performance evaluations, educational programs, transfer programs, and personnel assignments.

SUPPORT COMMAND MISSION AND OPERATIONAL TASKINGS: Manage administrative needs relevant to contingency program planning and force modernization, including command mission and function statements, military manning, distribution, classified information, range operations, battalion suspense and operational taskings, and military personnel programs. Plan and coordinate personnel deployments, redeployments. Plan and manage Command's military and civilian TDY travel program, including budget formulation, reports, orders, and arrangements. Oversee battalion's security program, Nuclear Biological Chemical program, communications section, and a $90,000 TDY budget.

Directly support the Executive Officer, Command Sergeant Major, and Commander in obtaining information, tabulating data, composing command level correspondence and summaries. Research, develop, coordinate, and publish command and community policies and review policy guidance. Maintain and track Command Group assignments to ensure timely receipt of actions by units and staff.

135

TRAINING TO MEET CONTINGENCY AND MISSION OBJECTIVES. Supervise quarterly training briefings and manage field training exercises. Liaison for German Partnership unit to plan, execute, conduct, train German and American units on weapons and physical fitness. Plan and coordinate transition-to-war, contingency peacetime missions, force modernization, and wartime emergency planning policies for the battalion. Review policy guidance for the battalion operation branch and recommend changes to exercise, force modernization, and mass casualty plans.

RECOMMEND LONG RANGE TRAINING OBJECTIVES. Based on program evaluations, recommend training objectives in terms of organizational structure, programs, and milestones to meet training and operational resource requirements and objectives. Perform program evaluations to sustain deployment posture and ensure continued support of personnel and units moving through the 98th ASG and 100th ASG. Prepare and review policy letters, SOPs, and propose changes to USAREUR guidelines. Interview unit commanders and first sergeants to gain information about organizational missions, functions, and work procedures.

MANAGE AND ANALZYE MANPOWER TO MEET TRAINING AND BATTALION EXERCISES. Coordinate Command's military manpower management system. Assure FYDP data accurately reflects budgeted end-strength, billet requirements and authorizations, and accuracy of Command's Enlisted Distribution and Verification Report. Prepare and process unit status reports.

SUPERVISE INTERNAL SECURITY FOR EMERGENCY PLANS, EDUCATION, AND INVESTIGATIONS. Supervise Personnel Security Program directing subordinate unit level Security Managers, classified information and materiel control, personnel security, security education, emergency plans, security violations and compromises, classification management, security review of information proposed for public release, security records and foreign travel.

ACCOMPLISHMENTS: Developed a management system that increased efficiency of processing $90,000 in business travel vouchers and achieved 100% accuracy during the annual 2002 audit.

Single-handedly coordinated all Force Protection missions for all subordinate companies in 5 different communities.

Flawlessly planned, executed 5 movements involving a total of 150 personnel to Albania, Macedonia, Kosovo, Turkey, and Iraq. Training and assessing these personnel prior to their movement resulted in all personnel accomplishing their jobs and returning safely home.

Planned, coordinated, trained 260 military personnel in preparation for deployment to Iraq (2003-2004). During 12-month deployment, was tasked twice to deploy a personnel service, casualty and postal team to Najah, Iraq in support of Operation Iraqi Freedom, set up a post office and a Human Resource Center to provide casualty reporting, postal services, and human resources to 2,000 personnel.

SAMPLE 4. MILITARY FEDERAL RESUME – E-6, USMC, ACCOUNTING CHIEF

Target Positions: Budget Technician, Accounting Technician, Specialist
Future Customer Base: Federal or Defense Agencies
Future Mission Interest: Any government agency, Accounting Operations
Target Grade/Salary: GS 7/8 positions; $36K minimum
Format: Electronic format

November 1984 – January 2002, ACCOUNTING CHIEF, E-6, 40+ hrs per week
U.S. Marine Corps, AC/S Comptroller, Bldg 1160, Camp Pendleton, CA 92055-5010
Supervisor: Lt. Col Nathan Kojak (retired); (760) 555-8888; May be contacted.

From 1984 to 2002, was promoted from E-1 to E-6 through series of increasingly responsible assignments. Each level included developing and delivering various training modules, establishing fund administrators, planning, budgeting, auditing fund administrator accounts, and communicating comptroller requirements to organizations within the scope of the comptroller.

LEAD AND SUPERVISOR FOR MILITARY AND CIVILIAN ACCOUNTING TECHNICIANS: Supervised 5-10 military and civilian personnel having a variety of accounting functions. Exercised full supervisory authority and discretion for military personnel; advised managers on civilian employees' performance for annual review. Mentored and counseled civilian employees regarding performance and opportunities for promotion.

ADVISED ON PERSONNEL BUDGETS: Advised senior management concerning $10-20 million in accounting data, including military personnel records and performance reports. Reviewed and analyzed accounting functions. Presented operating budget information in written narratives, briefings and charts/graphics in PowerPoint and Excel.

MANAGED FUNDS ADMINISTRATION AND BUDGET: Applied knowledge of rules, regulations, and government policies to write and edit 30-45 fund administrator requests annually. Analyzed budget data and budget requests. Ensured budgets were processed correctly in accounting system. Advised decision-makers on alternative methods of funding, spending, and accounting of authorized funds. Annually audited, monitored, and analyzed each executed budget for authorized spending.

MANAGED END-OF-YEAR BUDGET AND PERFORMANCE REPORTS: Reviewed fund administrators' performance and advised on reprogramming of funds to support new or revised requirements during the course of the fiscal year. Continually reviewed comptroller programs to ensure data, reports, and staffing were at acceptable levels. Delivered training and supplied appropriate reference materials to correct misunderstandings of accounting systems and procedures.

AUDITED AND ANALYZED FUNDS FOR THE CONTROLLER'S OFFICE: Read and screened classified information and data to evaluate importance to comptroller's office. Coordinated and supervised fund administrator audit teams that conducted reviews to oversee each authorized budget. Maintained and reconciled official accounting records, including official accounting reports after each accounting cycle.

SPECIAL ASSIGNMENT: TRAINER FOR NEW ACCOUNTING SYSTEM. Designed and delivered training, including step-by-step instructions, tested for impromptu application, the application now used as the standard for data retrieval in U.S. Marine Corps accounting system.

KEY ACCOMPLISHMENTS: CONSULTANT FOR AUTOMATED ACCOUNTING SYSTEM. Served as initial point of contact for establishment of an accounting automation system implementation, the Oracle-based SABRS Management Analysis Retrieval Tool System (SMARTS) application. Trained 30-40 personnel prior to launching application on individual computers. Coordinated technical phone assistance and troubleshooting. Modified training module to support specific needs of three major military commands.

Summary

A Defense Finance and Accounting Service Federal manager in the Vendor Pay Business Line said this about job applicants: "People just don't realize the importance of the resume in government. They don't know that the Federal resume is their job application, their examination for qualifications, and sometimes their interview. This resume can make or break their career. They just don't spend enough time thinking about where they are going and what to write on the resume. We need to know more than just the basics to make a decision to hire someone."

Military Federal Resumes are more creative, interesting and targeted than ever before. We hope that you will tell your stories, impress your intended audience, and land interviews because your resume exceeds the competition! Use headlines in your Military Federal Resume to highlight your outstanding skills and competencies, and to demonstrate your dedication to protecting our country and our lives!

GET AN EDITOR, PROOFREADER, OR WRITER IF YOU NEED ONE!
Don't let rusty writing skills keep you from getting a job for which you are clearly well qualified! If writing/editing/grammar is not one of your best skills, find a proofreader or editor to review your resume. Many hiring managers and HR specialists will give less consideration to resumes demonstrating poor writing or grammar skills. This is not the time to cut corners or hastily submit an ill-prepared resume. Your future career is on the line. Get help if you need it!

Step 8   Write Your KSAs
Writing about your Knowledge, Skills and Abilities
based on your best accomplishments and experiences

Step 8: Write Your KSAs
Writing about your Knowledge, Skills and Abilities
based on your best accomplishments and experiences

Writing a notable Knowledge, Skills, and Abilities (KSA) essay as you transition out of the service presents many of the same challenges for anyone writing a KSA, plus a few others.

Just write an interesting and impressive story about your experiences

As with any well crafted KSA, your first goal in answering these essay questions, which are frequently required as part of your Federal application package, should be to develop an interesting "story" that presents your professional qualifications and basically answers the questions posed in the job announcement. At the same time, you will need to demonstrate to what may be an entirely civilian office that you have the experience and technical/managerial qualifications needed for the position.

THINK ABOUT YOUR AUDIENCE –
THE HR SPECIALIST AND SUPERVISOR, WHEN WRITING YOUR KSAS

In many, if not most, cases the first person to review your KSA may be a Human Resources evaluator who will be looking for key phrases in the essay based on the job description, the wording of the KSA question, and possibly some internal checklist developed to rate all applicant KSAs. If you are fortunate to make it through that step, a hiring manager, who may have little experience with the military, will then review your package. If that is not tough enough, your KSAs should also demonstrate a broad knowledge of Federal government initiatives, industry best practices that apply to your area of expertise, and the common issues that often arise in managing any operation or project – even if the KSA does not specifically refer to any of these topics.

Whew! A tough challenge for sure -- but let's follow your military instincts and break the problem down into simpler steps! First, a quick review about how to write a quality KSA.

OTHER SOURCES FOR KSA INFORMATION
Refer to one of the many Resume Place sources for detailed information about writing KSAs in general:

- ⊙ *The Federal Resume Guidebook*, **Chapter 14, "Boosting Your Employment Chances with Great KSAs"**
- ⊙ *Ten Steps to a Federal Job*, **"Step 7: Write Your KSAs and Cover Letter"**
- ⊙ *The Student's Federal Career Guide*, **"Step 7: Write KSAs and Cover Letter"**
- ⊙ *http://www.resume-place.com/services/ksa.html*

A Quick Primer on Writing Great KSAs

What a KSA is NOT: Your KSA should never be a list. The best KSAs tell a story, much in the way you might answer an interviewer or a colleague who asked you a question about one of the toughest projects you ever managed. In answering a question in that setting, you certainly would not just start in listing a long litany of different projects, tasks, or missions that you had led or supported. Most likely, you would first **set the stage:**

> *"Well, one of the toughest projects I ever managed was probably my assignment as the Logistics Officer for the 37th Armored Brigade at Camp Bondsteel in Kosovo ..."*

> *Of course you would really want to impress the interviewer (or your office buddy), so you would probably want to point out just "how tough" the project was!*

> *"We were supporting Operation Enduring Freedom and I was given only SIX MONTHS to transport over 1800 National Guardsmen to Kosovo!"*

> *And then, of course, you would want to point out how your well-thought out plans, your technical know-how, your winning negotiation skills, and your ability to think on your feet had saved the day!*

> *"So the first thing I did was to pull together my team and brainstorm about every step we would need to ...."*

After a full recounting of how you delivered the solution, you might even add in some details about the Transportation Plan and the Base Support Plan you put together, not to mention your Army Commendation Medal and Letter of Appreciation from the General!

What a KSA SHOULD be is a coherent essay that stands on its own and demonstrates the technical, managerial, or project management expertise sought by the hiring agency. It should also say something about you – the employee, the person.

Selecting Good Examples: Before you even think about which examples to use for which KSAs, go through your resume, your personal notes, old Military Personnel Reviews, and routine status reports, and make a list of all of the major projects and operations you participated in, in the last 5-6 years. (This sounds like a good thing to keep updated from now on, doesn't it?) You don't need to have led all of them – even as a participant, you faced interesting challenges.

Make a few notes about each one to help you remember what occurred, and remember that projects that almost failed can be good material for a great story.

NOTES ABOUT EACH PROJECT OR ACCOMPLISHMENT

- ⊙ What was the timeframe?
- ⊙ What assignment were you in?
- ⊙ What did you have to deliver?
- ⊙ What group were you leading?
- ⊙ How did you launch the project?
- ⊙ What were the major steps?
- ⊙ What was the toughest part?
- ⊙ How long did it finally take?
- ⊙ Did you or your team receive any recognition?

Your Core Competencies: Now, think about one more thing – **what was it about you personally that contributed to the success of each project** (or at least rescued it from failure)? Think beyond your technical expertise or Military Occupational Specialty (MOS).

These are called your Core Competencies and a really great KSA will in some fashion illustrate this aspect about you as an employee.

WHAT WAS MOST IMPRESSIVE ABOUT YOUR COMPETENCIES IN THIS PROJECT?

- ⊙ Was it your skills in helping the Command to think through what they really needed?
- ⊙ Was it your ability to get a group of people to work together?
- ⊙ Was it that you were able to negotiate a workable solution with a tough audience?
- ⊙ Was it the fact that you researched, developed, and then communicated a tight project plan and then put in the controls to make it work?
- ⊙ Was it the fact that you kept everyone up the chain of command well informed, even when things were not going well?

 Important Federal Core Competencies are listed on the CD-ROM

Mapping Your Examples to the KSAs: Now, look at the entire list of KSAs for the position you are applying for and try to map which examples could possibly illustrate the skills identified for each KSA. You probably will realize that each of your examples demonstrates multiple skill sets, from the technical competencies requested to the more intangible project management and people skills – but considering the set as a whole will allow you to make the best match.

Ideally, you will want to select TWO examples for each KSA; however this can vary depending on the level of the position, the number of KSAs, and any specific character counts or other directions. With no other specific instructions, a KSA for a mid-to upper-level position should be around one page (a little more is fine for GS-14+) and focus in-depth on two examples. If the job is more junior or if there are a LOT of KSAs (6+), or if the character limits are very tight (under 2000 characters including spaces), you probably can just use one example.

> *Word to the wise: If you are having a very difficult time to come up with examples that illustrate the requested KSAs, take one more moment to reconsider if this job is a good match for your experience. There are plenty of Federal jobs out there that will maximize your military skills and experience – don't waste your time by applying for one where right out of the starting gate, you are not competitive.*

Driving your KSAs with the CCAR

Developing Each Example: OK! So now you have a list of two good examples for each of the KSAs for your package plus some notion of what you want to emphasize about yourself as an employee. Let's focus first on how to write up one good example. Remember your answer to your interviewer about "the toughest project you ever led?" That was actually a good example of what we like to call the CCAR Format. CCAR stands for **Context, Challenge, Actions, Results:**

CCAR Definition

Context –	What was the situation that led to this task?
Challenge –	What was your specific task, how did you get it, what was particularly hard about it?
Actions –	Now provide details about exactly how you set about to complete the task.
Results –	What was the result? Were you successful? Did you get an award? What impact did your project have?

Organizing Your KSA: Again, DON'T START WRITING YET – that's the last step, and if you have prepared well, it won't even be the hardest step. Start by jotting down some informal notes for your first example for each of the CCAR steps. Let's expand that example about when you had only six months to coordinate the military call-up and transport of 1800 troops to Kosovo, and don't worry about writing any pretty sentences at this point:

Context

Just started as the Logistics Officer for the 37th Armored Brigade, Camp Bondsteel, Kosovo, January, 2004, as part of Operation Enduring Freedom.

I had been called up myself as a member of the Ohio National Guard.

I had a team of 7 officers and 11 enlisted (E-5–E-8) logisticians and administrative personnel.

Challenge

I was given 6 months to manage the Call to Active Duty for 1800 Army National Guard troops plus coordinate the logistics and transportation to get them to Kosovo.

This was the largest Call to Active Duty for Reservists in National Guard history.

Actions

Pulled my team together to brainstorm on all aspects of the logistics that would be required – transportation, financial, road network planning, supply chain support.

Researched the regulations, funding, organizational interfaces, host nation requirements, and lessons learned from similar operations.

Developed and presented alternatives to the senior command.

After approval, put together and executed a tight project plan to move people, equipment, and supplies.

Toughest part – negotiating the host nation requirements – involved a lot of negotiation that had to accommodate their local customs.

Results

Developed a Transportation Plan and Base Support Plan

Transported over 150 million square feet of military cargo and 1800 personnel to meet aggressive time and budget constraints.

Received an Army Commendation Medal and Letter of Appreciation from the General.

TAKE NOTE: Once you have a set of notes like this (an outline), actually writing up the example is a piece of cake! Do this for both of your examples – but don't start writing yet!

Putting it All Together

Now, how do we turn these two outlines into one coherent essay? Use the following general outline to put together your KSA. Let's assume for the moment that the actual KSA question is:

KSA sample. Knowledge of a wide range of Federal and agency logistics concepts, principles, and practices.

Introduction – Set the theme. This could very well be something about one of those Core Competencies you picked up on earlier. If in both of your examples, for instance, you started by re-validating the requirements, that would be a great opener:

> One of the constant challenges in almost any major project is knowing where to draw the line. One of the first steps I take in every project is to go back and revalidate the list of requirements. Inevitably, in the middle of this exercise, I always discover some assumptions and unsaid requirements that are out there waiting to pounce.

Background and Training – If you have room, it is often effective right here to mention quickly something about your general background in this area or possibly even some of your training that particularly well-equipped you for the challenges of the projects you are about to recount.

> Throughout my military career, I have led multiple logistics organizations and major projects that required an in-depth knowledge of Federal and agency logistics concepts…..(now name a few). My training in Joint Planning and Joint Operations at the Armed Forces Staff College and the Unit Movement Officer Course well prepared me for the challenges of leading multi-phased logistics projects with stringent performance requirements.

ALWAYS ASK – WHAT WAS THE TOUGHEST PART?

Example 1 – Now *transition* to your first example.

One of the most challenging logistics operations I have led was to plan and execute the transport of 1800 Ohio National Guardsmen to Kosovo in support of Operation Enduring Freedom (now follow your outline to tell the tale)

Example 2 – And *transition* to your second example. Note that transitions are important – you are telling a story so don't just jump from one example to the next.

The experience leading the logistics planning for Operation Enduring Freedom, really paid off in a recent project I led to ….

Closing – Draw some conclusion from what you have learned from this. This should not exactly be a summary. A better close is one that speaks to some insight you have gained from both of these experiences.

Projects rarely fail because of the lack of resources – they generally fail because clear outcomes were not clearly defined or stakeholders were not kept informed about the risks inherent in any major endeavor. While I do my homework to make sure the technical solution is correct, I spend an equal or greater effort on keeping the communications channels open and active.

Addressing a Civilian and/or Non-technical Audience

The Thesis Tale: There is an old joke about the student going on and on trying to explain his thesis to his professor. When the professor finally says, "Just tell me in one sentence what your thesis is about," the student replies, "I don't understand it well enough to explain it in one sentence!"

The point of the Thesis Tale is that if you *really* understand a technical issue *well*, you should be able to succinctly explain it to anyone, even to a non-technical audience. In fact, as you progress up the management chain, that increasingly becomes *the* challenge, and one well worth writing about.

In developing your KSAs, remember that you are addressing an audience that will likely include professionals who are familiar with the military, and many who are not. It will also include reviewers who are technically qualified in the field you are applying for as well as Human Resources recruiters who may have no knowledge at all of your field.

Here are some tips on how to deal with this:

Start with the layman's explanation. Regardless of how technical your write-up may be, always start by explaining the issue in the way you might explain it to a non-technical user or manager. Think about the problem really faced by the organization.

A Recruitment Example: For instance, suppose that as a military recruiter you had to put together a Warrant Officer Program. This is a classic recruitment and marketing example that fully translates to the civilian recruitment world. Rather than emphasizing the military aspects of the task, focus on the impacts to the organization – why was the service having difficulty attracting Warrant Officers? What roles do they play in the military? What marketing approaches did you consider and then successfully employ to raise your recruitment levels?

An Information Technology (IT) Example: If you come from an Information Technology background, rather than starting with the task that you needed to implement a Virtual Server Architecture, start with the fact that the organization had a number of aging servers each dedicated to a different purpose, that it was increasingly costing a lot to manage a disparate set of machines and operating systems, and it was more and more difficult to roll out new capabilities quickly. Now, when you introduce the Virtual Server Architecture, at least provide one sentence that explains how this capability addresses those issues.

Define all acronyms and avoid excessive military terminology. It is important to define every acronym regardless of whether the KSA is technical or not. Even a common term like MAJCOM may be second nature to you but mean absolutely nothing to your reviewer. Substituting Major Command and even avoiding very military terminologies altogether (CONUS, OCONUS, etc.) is a first effective step in "civilianizing" your resume and your KSAs. Have a family member or non-military acquaintance read your write-up and point out the terms and references that would not be easily understandable to a person without a military background.

Include terms from the Job Announcement and KSA Question. This is what the non-technical reviewer will probably be looking for. You don't have to overdo it, but before finalizing your write-up, take one more look at the job description and make sure that you have used similar terminology for the concepts in your KSA. At some point, definitely repeat some small portion of the KSA question itself.

Be specific and provide details. This is necessary to convince the technical reader that you know what you are talking about. Once you have set the stage for the non-technical reader, make sure that you mention the specific equipment, applications, protocols, systems, or standards that were key components in the solution you were implementing or the project you were leading. If you are an IT person, mention the specific software or operating system you were upgrading. If you are a finance person, mention the name of the financial management system you used.

Give every project a name. Even if the project never really had a formal name, make one up. Rather than just saying that you implemented a tracking system for all MIPRs (spell out Military Interdepartmental Purchase Requests!!), tag it as the "MIPR Tracking System." Rather than just saying that you implemented a process to deploy system patches, call it an Enterprise Patch Management System. This gives the impression that you developed something of lasting importance.

RESEARCHING KEY THEMES FOR THE FEDERAL GOVERNMENT AND TARGET AGENCIES.

Another way to impress your KSA reviewer is to speak "their language." Using some of the "lingo" in the job announcement is a first step. More than that, it always pays to take the time to research the agency that you are applying to. Take an in-depth look at their web site, speak with acquaintances who work for the agency, even take the time to call the Human Resources Point of Contact listed with the announcement. As with any job application, "networking" can be one of the best ways to find out what is really important to the hiring manager and to the target agency.

If your resume, your KSAs, and your cover letter mention some of the key themes you discovered about the agency – whether they are concerned about "enterprise architectures," "human capital planning," "Continuity of Operations," or the "War on Terror" – your awareness of these issues will be noticed by the professionals reviewing your application.

KSA Examples

Sample 1

Skill in planning, developing, coordinating and implementing new programs, processes, concepts or procedures.

(Context) In my role as the Chief of Aviation Resource Management with the United States Army at Fort Sam Houston, I worked specifically with quality assurance and quality control in the areas of safety, maintenance, operations, training, logistics, and security for 141 aviation units throughout 21 states. **(Challenge)** To ensure quality in this broad area requires a good information management system. I soon realized the existing system was outdated and that the impact of continuing to use this system would soon have significant negative results. **(Action)** I analyzed the requirements I knew were needed to meet the needs of this vast program. I gathered information on available systems that met these requirements and selected the most cost-efficient system. I developed a management proposal, including a full description of our need and results of continuing with the old system, the new system's capabilities, cost, availability, and the training that would be required to learn the new system. I submitted my proposal to senior management for review and approval. **(Results)** My proposal was so thoroughly written and my knowledge of the program was so well respected, that my proposal was accepted without question. The new information management system was purchased, my employees were trained, and the new system was soon up and running. This all resulted in significant improvements in our ability to manage the quality assurance and quality control program, which ultimately resulted in a more efficient program and a noted cost savings.

(Context) As the Battalion Executive Director for the U.S. Army in Seoul, South Korea, I was the liaison with the South Korean government, working on flight-following procedures for civilian and military flight corridors. I led the flight operations and coordinated all visits by heads of state. **(Challenge)** In this capacity I realized the need to develop a force modernization program that

149

would increase the unit's equipment inventory which would possibly result in an increase in air traffic-following capabilities. **(Action)** I led my unit leaders to research and analyze the current program, paying close attention to processes and procedures being used to follow flights through the corridors. We thoroughly educated ourselves on the existing program and brainstormed and developed a more effective program with improved processes and procedures. **(Results)** Our new program included an increase in equipment inventory that resulted in a 17% increase in air traffic following capabilities.

Sample 2

Ability to represent the activity both within and outside the organization, and to gain support for the program goals.

(Context) As a Recruiter for the Warrant Officer Program and the developer of a winning recruitment program, I continually represented the Army Reserves to a wide variety of groups, individuals, and organizations. Since the purpose of my work was to recruit Warrant Officers, to accomplish this I needed to gain support for the program goals of both the Warrant Officer Program and the Army Reserves. **(Challenge)** This was during a time when many Reserve units were being called up, which caused many of our potential recruits and their families to be concerned about assignments and being sent overseas. I was continually challenged to show the program's benefits to my audiences. **(Action)** To accomplish our recruitment goals and to represent the Army Reserves in the best possible light, I planned, organized, and conducted five community-wide recruiting events to prospective Warrant Officer recruits, their families, and friends. I led my team in presenting oral information briefings with attractively developed multi-media visuals, conducting assessment interviews with interested candidates, and walking them through the application process. **(Result)** Each event was a great success, both in our ability to gain support for the Army Reserves and in our team's ability to achieve our annual recruiting goals.

(Context) As the Personnel Manager for the Management Support Branch of the Army Reserves, I was the Case Manager for official inquiries concerning the actions of reservists and events involving performance issues. **(Challenge)** In this capacity, I conducted investigations that were of a negative nature. This presented me with the challenge of gaining respect and support for the position of my office and the Reserves from those I was interviewing. **(Actions)** I conducted numerous interviews with a variety of subject matter experts both within and outside the Reserves. To represent my organization in the most positive way, I educated myself on the subject of the case and presented myself in a knowledgeable and respectful manner. **(Result)** In every case, I was successful at gathering more than enough information to conduct a solid analysis and compile my findings for submission to headquarters and gained noticeable support for my work, my office, and the Army Reserves. I attribute this success to my ability to represent my organization in a knowledgeable and respectful manner.

Sample 3

Knowledge of a wide range of federal and agency logistics concepts, principles, practices. procedures, and regulations applicable to a full range of logistics management to include cargo and passenger movement, supply chain management, equipment and vehicles management, vehicle maintenance. warehousing, deployment planning and operations, personal property movement, global, fuels and cryogenics, and logistic plans under peacetime and wartime conditions to develop and recommend policies and procedures for the squadron. (Context) As the Primary Logistics Senior Officer for the Ohio Army National Guard's 37th Armored Brigade, I supervised a culturally diverse team of 7 officers and 11 enlisted logisticians and administrative personnel. (Challenge) In this position I was assigned to plan the deployment and direct the logistics for the largest Call to Active Duty in National Guard history. This call-up was of 1,800 Army National Guard troops to Kosovo for Operation Enduring Freedom with only 8 months lead time. Along with accomplishing major planning efforts required by this assignment, I also knew I had to prepare my staff to take on such a substantial call-up. (Actions) I effectively wrote and managed the Base Support Plan, Transportation Plan, and Operation Needs Statements. These documents provided the basis and content for coordinating the logistics operations that would accomplish the movement of cargo, personnel, personal property, equipment and supplies, vehicles, fuels, cryogenics, and necessary warehousing. Along with planning the logistics of this massive movement, I was mindful of the foreign and host nation requirements. I used my knowledge of logistics concepts, Federal and Army regulations, policies, procedures, and practices to train my staff. I developed and recommended policies and policy changes to expedite this call-up. I set priorities, assigned workload, effectively guided my employees to resolve difficult technical issues, and coached them on customer service techniques. I led the integration of logistics, including coordinating all types of transportation, location of warehousing, road network planning, and supply chain management. (Results) This hard work resulted in the safe and expeditious movement of the 1,800 soldiers from 47 separate units, spread across 19 states and all necessary items from the U.S. to Germany, and then on to Kosovo within the allotted time.

For more samples, check out the CD-ROM

Summary

All of this guidance will help whether you are planning to write your KSAs yourself or whether you are interested in hiring a professional to assist you with your final package. If you can identify a good list of examples for your KSAs and develop an in-depth outline for each example, you will dramatically simplify the job (and reduce the time required) for the professional writer.

Remember that no one really understands the projects you will write about as well as you do. The hard part for most of us is to think through how to turn a basic project into an interesting and engaging narrative that makes the reviewer "want to meet you," which after all, is the whole point!

Step 9: Apply for Jobs and Track & Follow-up
How to submit your electronic or paper military Federal resume to agency database

Applying for any Federal job calls for successful accomplishment of the 3 P's – patience, persistence and perspiration! Finding the optimal vacancy announcements for your experience, geographic location and salary preference takes research and time.

You could conceivably find several jobs to apply for each week. With an average of 17,000 jobs listed every day, you could spend 10 hours per week researching the announcements, tweaking your resume, copying and pasting your resume into the various online builders, and tracking and following up on applications. It's a CAMPAIGN!

Federal Job Applications Are Different

The Federal job search culture is different from private sector. The job titles are diverse, the resumes are distinct, there are often essay questions you must answer, there are terms that only the government uses, and the search can take months. At first glance this can be intimidating. Novice Federal jobseekers might try to use materials they have prepared for the private sector, but they won't get far. Worse yet, some might give up or not even try. That's a shame, because once you learn how government hires, it's really not so difficult after all.

The reason the Federal job search process is so complex is that your application package represents an examination (with scoring) of your qualifications. Think about it. In the private sector you submit a cover letter, a bare-bones resume, and perhaps a form or two. Hopefully, you're called in for a screening interview. After that, you might get called back for another one or two interviews that progressively delve deeper into your experience and qualifications.

The Federal job application process involves presenting more about yourself up front: you often answer job-related questions in your profile or registration; you submit a 2-4 page electronic Federal resume; and, you often answer multiple-choice questions and write essays to specific questions. Only then—if at all—do you get to an interview. In this way the Federal government can hire the best qualified people because they are the applicants who made it through the system.

Consider the movement of your resume through the Federal Human Resources Specialist's hands to the Supervisor. Look at the chart on the next page:

FEDERAL HIRING TRAIL – WHAT HAPPENS TO YOUR RESUME

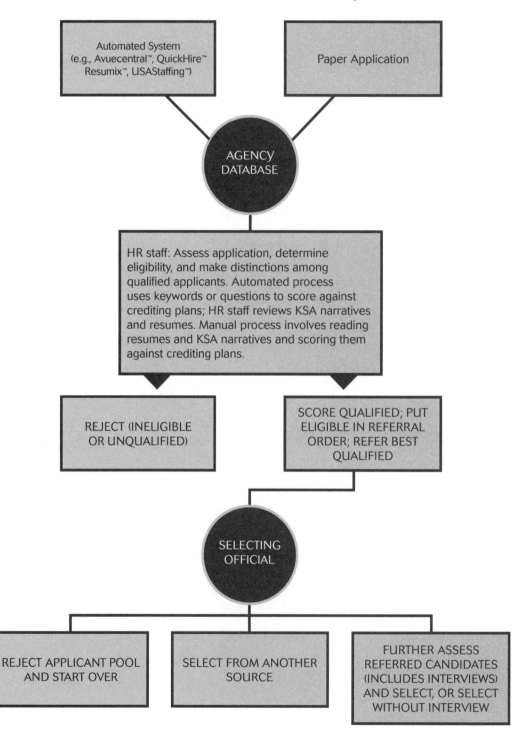

Automated System
(e.g., Avuecentral™, QuickHire™
Resumix™, USAStaffing™)

Paper Application

AGENCY
DATABASE

HR staff: Assess application, determine
eligibility, and make distinctions among
qualified applicants. Automated process
uses keywords or questions to score against
crediting plans; HR staff reviews KSA narratives
and resumes. Manual process involves reading
resumes and KSA narratives and scoring them
against crediting plans.

REJECT (INELIGIBLE
OR UNQUALIFIED)

SCORE QUALIFIED; PUT
ELIGIBLE IN REFERRAL
ORDER; REFER BEST
QUALIFIED

SELECTING
OFFICIAL

REJECT APPLICANT POOL
AND START OVER

SELECT FROM ANOTHER
SOURCE

FURTHER ASSESS
REFERRED CANDIDATES
(INCLUDES INTERVIEWS)
AND SELECT, OR SELECT
WITHOUT INTERVIEW

The most important thing you need to know is...

FOLLOW THE DIRECTIONS! Never deviate from the written instructions for any reason. If they tell you to do something differently, don't do it. Or if you follow their advice, just get their name and telephone number.

NEW RESUME BUILDER COMING TO WWW.USAJOBS.GOV VERY SOON!

OPM is working with Monster Government Solutions to create a new, easier to use *www.usajobs.gov* website. Very soon, you will be able to submit and save 5 DIFFERENT VERSIONS of your Federal resume. And you will be able to submit your resume to *www.usajobs.gov* ONLY, instead of submitting your resume to every single agency's database.

Watch *www.resume-place.com* website for news on the new, easier to apply for website and special insight!

Know the Deadline

Applications for Federal job vacancies will only be accepted while the vacancy is "open" (the exception is for 10-point veterans). Open periods can be as short as a few days or as long as several weeks. They are set by the agencies and represent your window for applying for the job. The closing date is the last day applications will be accepted. It should be clearly indicated on the announcement.

You shouldn't leave your application to the last minute. If you do, be aware that the time of day on the closing day can be important. Many vacancy announcements, especially those on web-based systems, close at midnight on the closing date. Be mindful of how the deadline is expressed. The database for one of the systems many agencies use is maintained in Alexandria, VA, and the closing time is usually expressed in terms of Eastern Time (Standard or Daylight Savings).

Some announcements, especially those emailed or faxed, close at 5:00 PM on the closing date. Each vacancy announcement should tell you the agency's rules. Often supplemental materials, like transcripts, can be submitted shortly after the closing date. **Read the instructions carefully. If you are mailing your application you will want to know if your application must be received or postmarked by the closing date. The difference between these two requirements is huge.** Some vacancy announcements have open periods that are months long, years long, are "open until filled," or are indefinitely open. These are called "inventory-building" announcements and generally are used when an agency expects to fill many jobs over a long period of time. Resumes from qualified applicants are collected in a file, and when a specific job opens up, the file is reviewed. The inventory building announcements are effective for the HR recruiters because the candidates have their resumes posted and ready for review.

Package What They Want

Paper Packages: The appearance of your application is important. If you are sending your materials via U.S. mail, use good quality bond paper. White is the safest paper color, but if you want to be different, use ivory colored paper. Your cover letter, resume, and KSAs should be separate documents. Transcripts can be photocopies and do not need to be official copies. Mail the package in a large envelope so your documents do not have to be folded.

Online Applications: For electronic applications, complete all of the pages and questions. Make sure you complete the submission. Sometimes there are at least 3 steps to applying: Profile / Registration; Resume Builder or Resume Submission; Questions or Essays. Be sure you are not exceeding the maximum number of characters allowed in a web box. There's very little formatting that you can do within web boxes, but make entries as easy to read as possible.

Combination online and fax or mail: If you are asked to apply online, but then fax or mail additional information, make sure you include your SSN, name and announcement number on each paper submitted by mail or fax. You could add a cover letter to the package.

How to apply to agencies using paper applications, mail and fax: Agencies that are still using paper applications will give you a choice of application format. The package is usually mailed, sometimes faxed or hand delivered, rarely emailed. It usually contains the following: Cover letter, Federal Resume, KSAs, supplemental information (like transcripts).

Here's a well written set of instructions for a vacancy announcement:

"Your application will consist of three components. The first component consists of your statement addressing how you meet each of the knowledge, skills or abilities listed for this vacancy. The second component is your Resume. The final component of your application consists of "other" application materials. Examples of these other materials include your college transcripts (if required) and documentation of veteran status (if applicable). Instructions on completing and submitting these items follow."

But the language in a vacancy announcement is usually something like this:

"You may apply using a resume, OF-612 (Optional Application for Federal Employment), or any other written application form."

We recommend that you use the preferred paper format - a Federal resume. Also in the announcement, usually at the end, is the address to which to send your materials, a number to fax it, and perhaps instructions on how to apply with email. If you mail your application, we recommend that you get a return receipt. On the other hand, if you are facing a deadline, faxing and email can deliver your application the same day.

USAJobs is continually improving vacancy announcement instructions and language. Along with other improvements to the format of vacancy announcements, their instructions continue to improve. Currently, you have to read each vacancy announcement very carefully because important information is not presented in a uniform place or manner. The overall goal is to make vacancy announcements more user-friendly, and to reduce the chance that applicants will make mistakes. But even after improvements are made to the announcements, the process will still be complicated and vary among agencies.

HOW TO APPLY TO AGENCIES USING COMMERCIAL AUTOMATED RECRUITMENT SYSTEMS WITH ELECTRONIC RESUME

Federal agencies have choices in how to manage their candidates' resumes and other applications. Most agencies have chosen to use automation to help them, but a few have not. For agencies that do not use automated systems, online application is not possible. Their vacancy announcements will contain instructions concerning submitting applications by mail or other paper delivery system.

Those using automation can choose among developing their own systems, using a system developed by the Office of Personnel Management, or buying or leasing any of several online application systems developed by private companies. Agencies are prohibited from requiring someone to apply electronically, but most agencies with electronic capability will strongly encourage you (and help you if necessary) to submit your application online.

The automated systems that agencies use fall into two broad categories that, for our purposes, we will call "question-driven" and "resume-driven." Here is a run-down on the systems that were in use when we went to press:

QUESTION-DRIVEN SYSTEMS:

This includes the following commercial and government-developed systems presented in alphabetical name order. These are similar but not exactly the same with respect to their look, feel, and job application process. A defining characteristic of this group is that they rely heavily on multiple-choice and "yes-no" questions to make distinctions among job applicants.

QuickHire™ (Owned by Monster.com, Government Solutions) – This system is currently used by about 40 agencies. You will complete a profile, including copying and pasting your resume into one online field; answer more registration questions; then answer more job-related questions which are yes/no and multiple choice. In many instances your answer will trigger a box in which you will be asked to provide a short essay explaining your answer or demonstrating what experience, education, or training you have to support the answer you gave.

9

Resume Tip: QuickHire™ electronic resume online field for copying and pasting your resume allows for 16,000 characters with spaces. This is approximately 5 pages at 11 point type, one inch margins.

USAStaffing™ – This automated system was developed by the Office of Personnel Management. Agencies may purchase the right to use the system themselves, or may contract with staff at OPM to manage the system (conduct the recruiting and prepare the lists of qualified job candidates) for them. You will recognize announcements prepared by this system because of their "Form C" questionnaires, which typically range from 27 to 156 multiple-choice or yes/no questions.

Resume Tip: Use your electronic resume format for this system. You will be copying and pasting the text into the online fields.

Avuecentral™ – This commercial system is used by more than 20 agencies, including the U.S. Forest Service and U.S. Coast Guard. This application is a complex online form, including questions and profile. You can submit your resume one time, then apply to many positions in the database that Avuecentral™ maintains. However, this can only be done for vacancies in agencies using this system.

Resume Tip: Copy and paste your resume builder formatted resume into the AvueCentral™ database.

eRecruit™ – This commercial system is used by NSA, and parts of the Department of Homeland Security. The significant features of this system are its online form screens and questions. Plus it offers a shopping cart for selecting your target careers.

Resume Tip: Follow the instructions to submit your resume. Attach your resume builder formatted resume for the eRecruit™ system.

COPY AND PASTE KEYBOARD SHORTCUTS

You will need to get faster with Copying and Pasting your Template resume into the agency Resume Builders. Try these keyboard shortcuts:

CONTROL A – CREATES EDITED COPY
CONTROL C – COPY
CONTROL V – PASTE
CONTROL Z – IF YOU LOOSE SOMETHING, YOU CAN TYPE CONTROL Z RIGHT AWAY AND GET THE COPY BACK.

RESUME- AND KEYWORD-DRIVEN SYSTEM:

Resumix™ (Owned by Hotjobs.com) – This is the only knowledge-based keyword system used by government agencies. This system is used by NASA and all components of the Department of Defense (including Army, Air Force, and Navy). You submit a resume (called a "resumix" now because of this system) into a complex resume builder, answer personnel questions in a Supplemental Data Sheet, and then self-nominate for specific vacancies. A major distinction between Resumix™ and the question-driven systems is that Resumix™ does not use a series of questions to assess your qualifications. Instead, it applies artificial intelligence to read resumes and distinguishes among applicants through words and phrases included in their resumes.

Resume Tip: Use your electronic resume for the resume builders you will find on the individual Defense agency websites.

HISTORY: THE GENESIS OF RESUME SEARCH ENGINES

Initially, all applicant tracking systems were limited to keyword searches and Boolean logic (nouns connected by specific terms such as AND, OR) to locate candidates. Unfortunately, many qualified candidates were passed by because an applicant was missing a keyword in their resume.

In 1988, Resumix™ was founded. The premise for this product was to apply artificial intelligence to resume searches. The systems read the entire resume and look for content. For example if you used the term ADA in your resume, a keyword search engine will find resumes from programmers (ADA programming language), dentists (American Dental Association) and human resource professionals (Americans with Disability Act). Resumix™ takes ADA into context with other words in a job description to produce matches from the right profession. This system was state-of-the-art for nearly 10 years. The problem is the system has to be taught new terms on a regular basis from well paid "knowledge engineers."

In the late 1990's a new, more cost-effective approach was devised by companies such as Engenium, Burning Glass and Autonomy. The "neural network" search engine was created. A neural network is a powerful data modeling tool. It resembles the human brain in that it acquires knowledge through learning and stores the knowledge. The more the system is used, the smarter it gets. It intelligently reads a complete job description and resume and matches the best candidates in order of probable match. Additionally, this search engine teaches itself, so "knowledge engineers" are not required.

—Jim Lemke, Managing Partner, Hire Solutions
Previous Director of Marketing, Resumix™

9

TRACK AND FOLLOW-UP ON APPLICATIONS

After you have submitted your resumes into the various databases, you CAN track and follow-up with many agencies.

Yes you can. Asking questions, getting information, developing a relationships, getting known are all critical factors in standing out and getting hired. You can track and follow-up on most of your application for federal jobs. Not all, but most. Some of the on-line application systems are extremely automated and are set up so that you will be contacted.

Most vacancy announcements typically include the name of a human resources staff who is responsible for many aspects of the announcement, including collecting the applications. This HR person might have created the vacancy announcement, posted it on USAJOBs and other websites and has frequent communication with the hiring supervisor. They have knowledge of the application process, required information needed, and will soon be accepting all of the applications. They will then coordinate the review of the packages and be part of the rating and ranking process to determine who will get an interview. This HR person is important to you and your future with that agency. Refer back to the Federal Hiring Process chart in Step 6. The process is complex for hiring in government.

Warning, they are busy!
The HR staff members are busy with multiple announcements, various aspects of announcement development, reviewing packages and responding to supervisor needs. Use diplomacy and consideration when contacting them about your package. Your goal is to be helped and remembered favorably!

How long does it take?
The Office of Personnel Management recently wrote a memo asking the agencies to speed up their hiring process to a total of 45 days, from the closing date of the announcement to the interview date. However, the real answer to the question is anywhere from 30 days to 6 months. If you are wondering how they can be so slow and don't they really want to hire good people? The answer is we don't know and yes, they do want to hire the best possible new employees!

Play the Application Game
The best philosophy here is to learn all that you can about the jobs and internships that are excellent for your degree, experience, location, salary and interests. Apply for as many of these applications and internships as you can find. Manage your campaign with dates and editing the packages to focus it slightly. In about 60 days, you will be receiving "hits". The sheer volume of your effort and energy will pay off. Make sure your paper federal resume or electronic version is written with the skills and keywords of your target jobs!

HOW CAN YOU CONTACT THE HR PERSON? RECOMMENDED TELEPHONE SCRIPTS AND EMAIL MESSAGES:

Communicating by Telephone: They probably won't answer the phone, but they are there. They screen their calls. Be ready with a good voicemail. Practice your voicemail message before calling.

Communicating by email: That could be best if they provided an email. They can simply answer a question quickly.

Communicating by fax: Sometimes you only have a fax number. You can write fax inquiries using big type with simple questions.

No contact information: If there is no name or phone, only an address, your only recourse would be to write a letter. If there is not address, only a database, then you can't contact anyone. Just keep submitting and cross your fingers.

SUGGESTED TELEPHONE, EMAIL AND FAX SCRIPTS FOR TRACKING AND FOLLOWING-UP ON EXCELLENT APPLICATIONS:

1st Message – 30 days after the closing date

"Hi, this is John Rodriguez from San Diego, CA. I'm inquiring about my application for Logistics Technician, GS-7, announcement 20205, which I submitted on April 5, 20xx. I'd like to know the status and if the packages are being reviewed soon. Can you please call back, or leave a voicemail at (410) 744 4324."

2nd Message – 2 to 4 weeks after the HR person left a voicemail

"Hi, This John Rodriguez again. Thanks for your voicemail on Monday, April 9th regarding Annct 20205, Logistics Technician. I'm checking again on the status of the review process. I'm still interested in the job, but other opportunities are appearing. I hope that you can make decisions soon and let me know if I going to get an interview. I need a job and I've been looking 6 months. My voicemail again is (410) 744-4324."

3rd Contact – 2 to 4 weeks after the 2nd contact (this time make it by fax or email)

To: Susan Rogers, HR Staff for Announcement 20205, Writer-Editor
From: John Rodriguez, SSN 220-00-0000
Re: Position of Logistics Technician, Announced April 5, 20xx

Hello Ms. Rogers, I'm still hopeful that I'm in the list of Best Qualified Candidates for this position. I've been reading about your agency in the newspaper and see that there are new programs for housing and construction. I would be able to start immediately if I were considered and could land an interview.

9

APPLY FOR JOBS

163

Can you let me know if this position still exists? I am determined to land a federal job and I really like the mission of your agency. I could contribute a lot and be very effective there. Can you please let me know. If another person has been selected, I'd really like to know so that I can pursue other positions.

Thanks so much for your help. I look forward to your call. My phone is (410) 744 4324, you can just leave a message.

YOU GOT REJECTED - 4th Contact – you've been told you're not getting the job – Telephone

Hello, This is John Rodriguez. I got the notice that I am did not get hired for the job. If you had a few minutes, I would really appreciate your help with giving me a reason why I was not selected. I'd really like to work for the government and I felt I was perfectly qualified for that. Job. If you could take a few minutes and call me back or leave a voicemail, I would appreciate knowing what I should change in my resume or my qualifications. Thanks so much for your help. My number is 410 777-7777. Best time to reach me is 8 to 10 am.

YOU'RE GETTING AN INTERVIEW – Congratulations!

Hello, this is John Rodriguez, Thanks so much for the opportunity to interview for this job. I am very pleased! I would like to know if you can give me some insight into the interview system. Will there be one person or a panel interviewing me? Also will the interview follow specific questions? And if so, would I be able to receive these questions ahead of time? I am beginning my research and preparation for the interview now! I look forward to this opportunity. Thanks for any information you can provide!

AFTER THE INTERVIEW – THANK YOU NOTE!

Dear _____:
Thank you so much for your time last Wednesday. I enjoyed meeting you and hearing about your agency. I believe that I would be an asset to your organization and feel clear that I would be able to learn quickly about your mission and programs. I look forward to your decision and hope that I can begin my career at the Office of _____ at Department of _____.
Thank you again,
Sincerely, your name

USEFUL QUESTIONS

1. *Can you clarify something from the announcement for me?*

   If you don't understand exactly what the vacancy announcement requires, ask for a clarification. If the person you're talking to isn't the named contact person, be sure to get his or her name.

2. *Have you received all my materials?*

   Many vacancy announcements require you to submit materials by different methods. For example, you may have to use a USAStaffing online application system where you answer questions on-line and then fax or mail your transcripts. It's a good idea to check to see if all your materials have been received before the closing date.

3. *What is the status of my application?*

   The federal job application process can take a long time. You can call to check on the status of your application, but we suggest you wait about a month after the closing date. You may learn that you did or did not get on the list submitted to the selecting official, or that interviews are being conducted.

4. *How can I improve future applications?*

   This is the most important thing you can ask. If you learn that you didn't get referred for a position, ask the contact person to tell you what you should do to improve future applications. You might learn that you missed a selective factor. You may learn that you weren't qualified for a particular grade. You may learn that you didn't score highly on your KSA's. You may also learn that you scored very well, but were in competition with a very highly qualified group of applicants.

   The HR representative usually will not go into great detail, but may tell you what your overall score was, where your KSA's were weak, and where you ranked among the pool of applicants. If you didn't get the job you were seeking, then talking on the phone with the people who read and scored your materials can be the most valuable five or ten minutes you can spend in this whole process.

> ### COMING SOON! USAJOBS WILL CREATE AN APPLICATION TRACKING SYSTEM.
>
> Some agency application systems, like the Army's system, give users information about the status of their applications. OPM is working on creating a system that gathers from agencies information about the status of applications, and to make that information available to applicants.   But even when this feature comes on line, it's up to you to check on your application's status.

Timing: How long does it take to get hired?

The Office of Personnel Management has recently published a statement requesting that HR offices process applications in 45 days. From the closing date on the announcement until you receive a letter or phone call inviting you to an interview, the time elapsed should be no more than 45 days. Currently, timing for this stage is more like 2 to 4 months. We are hopeful that the review and selection process will get faster. The chart on the following page shows you the flow of your resume from the initial review system to the supervisor who can decide to interview you for the position.

Summary

Don't be discouraged when you see that the "How to Apply" instructions are different for almost every agency. Treat this as a test intended to see if you can apply correctly. With this book and the insights we offer into the various automated systems, you will see that with one good resume and possibly a few KSAs you will be a solid candidate for many announcements.

Step 10   Interview for a Federal Job
Tips for researching, preparation, practice and
confidence building for successful Federal interviews

Step 10: Interview for a Federal Job
Tips for researching, preparation, practice and confidence building for successful Federal interviews

Federal job interviews are different each time

There are many different approaches to interviewing, so this section is intended to help you understand the various methods and to provide some practical tips on preparing!

Managers use many interviewing techniques and processes to develop an understanding of you as a candidate for their position. The interview will depend on the type of position, as well as the information the manager needs to obtain to determine if you are the best "fit" for the position.

Interviews for first-time Federal jobseekers are, in general, not any different from those for current Federal employees. You may be asked about long-term career goals, your interest in the position and the agency, and your long- and short-term educational plans. Be sure that you are comfortable discussing current course work, professors, and what you are learning in a positive mode.

Interviews may be conducted in person, over the phone, and may include an interview panel. Interviews may fall into one of several categories, including:

- Behavioral interviewing
- Technical interviewing
- Competency interviewing
- Combination interviewing
- General interviewing

All of the interview methods listed above call for some preparation on your part. However, you need to understand which type of interview you will be participating in. When you are contacted for the interview, it is appropriate for you to request information regarding the type and method of interviewing that will be conducted.

Let's discuss the different interviewing methods listed above:

Behavioral Interviewing:
An employment interview, situational in nature, is intended to discover how interviewees will respond to different situations.

Technical Interviewing:
Technical interviews are focused on providing the selecting official with additional information regarding the technical or functional skills of the applicant.

Competency Interviewing:

An employment interview in which the competencies, or behaviors have been defined by the organization, and in which applicants are asked questions to determine their possession of the competencies required for the position. These interviews may be also seem like the behavioral interviews described above.

Combination:

The combination interview may involve any of the three interview techniques above, as well as general interview questions.

General Interviewing:

A general interview is based on a variety of questions asked of the applicant, and may cover a variety of issues or concerns. A general interview may also be informal, such as "meeting for coffee" or "let's talk about this."

Interview Tips

Before the Interview

- ⊙ Be prepared!
- ⊙ Check out the website of the agency you're interviewing with and conduct research (size, services, mission, etc.).
- ⊙ Prepare a 1-minute response to the "Tell me about yourself" question.
- ⊙ Know what kind of interview to expect – behavioral, technical, etc. (feel free to ask when scheduling the interview).
- ⊙ Write 5 success stories to answer behavioral interview questions ("Tell me about a time when…" or "Give me an example of a time…").
- ⊙ Prepare answers to the most common interview questions that will present your skills, talents, and accomplishments:
    - Why did you leave or are you leaving your last position?
    - What do you know about our organization?
    - What are your goals/Where do you see yourself in 5 years?
    - What are your strengths and weaknesses?
    - Why would you like to work for this organization?
    - What is your most significant achievement?
    - How would your last boss and colleagues describe you?
    - Why should we hire you?
    - What are your salary expectations?
- ⊙ And remember that nothing will make you look worse than not knowing what you put on your own resume.
- ⊙ Have 10 questions prepared for the interviewer but only ask the ones which were not addressed during your discussion.

- Practice in front of a mirror or with a friend for feedback.
- Have your references' permission. These might be former managers, professors, friends of your family who know you well (but not family members), or people who know you through community service. You want them to be prepared to praise you. It would be beneficial to provide your references with the following information: the job for which you are applying, the name of the organization, and a copy of your resume.

The Interview

- Arrive 10 to 15 minutes early for your interview.
- Carry these items to the interview:
  - A copy of your references (for which you already have permission to contact)
  - Paper on which to take notes
  - Directions to the interview site
- Watch your body language and eye contact. Stand and greet your interviewer with a firm handshake. Crossed-arms appear to be defensive, fidgeting may be construed as nervous, and lack of eye contact may be interpreted as an untrustworthy person. Instead, nod while listening to show you are attentive and alert and most importantly, do not slouch.
- Think before you answer and have a clear understanding of the question, if not, ask for clarification.
- Express yourself clearly and with confidence, however, without conceit. Keep your answers 2 to 3 minutes long.
- Show a sincere interest in the agency and position. (You already know about the organization as you previously conducted your research.)
- Focus on what you can contribute to the organization rather than what the employer can do for you. Don't ask about salary or benefits until the employer brings up this topic.
- Do not place blame on or be negative about past employers.
- End the interview on an assumptive note indicating how you feel you are a good fit for the position at hand and how you can make a contribution to the organization. Ask about the next step, as most offers are not extended on the spot.
- Thank the interviewer and ask for a business card (this will provide you with the necessary contact information).

After the Interview

How do you want to be remembered after the interview? You want to stand out in their memory as a great candidate, personable and with the skills they need. Leave a lasting impression with a friendly handshake and smile.

7 STEPS TO A MEMORABLE INTERVIEW – AND A JOB OFFER

Interview Preparation Tip No. 1 – How do you want to be remembered?

Think about your experiences in terms of what's significant, memorable or interesting. When the manager or managers get together to review the candidates who were interviewed, they will try to remember each of them in some way. You definitely want to be remembered in some way. It could be an experience, skill, story, style, (not your clothes or body language, hopefully), friendliness, attitude, confidence. Think about this.

Interview Preparation Tip No. 2 – Write your Interview Stories.

Write a list of work and non-paid experiences that could be used in a job or informational interview. Be aware that you may not think that certain events are interesting, but others might, so write down all of the possibilities. You can review the list with a friend or partner later to determine which experiences are most interesting. Don't take anything off the list yourself. These "stories" may also be Knowledge, Skills and Abilities statements contained in your Federal application. KSA statements are great practice for interview questions and answers.

Example of types of interesting, successful and memorable experiences:

- ⊙ Leadership - Team Leader or co-team leader for training, emergency preparation, logistics or movement
- ⊙ A success – something you did that saved lives, money, time, improved morale, increased visibility, made something happen
- ⊙ Change – a project you worked on that changed the way things were handled previously. The change resulted in savings of time, effort, money, etc.
- ⊙ Organizational – leadership or active membership in organizations that bring value to a particular audience
- ⊙ New initiatives / ideas – recommended and implemented new ideas
- ⊙ Problem solving – handled, researched and resolved a problem for someone or a group – how did you do it and for whom?

Interview Preparation Tip No. 3 – Practice Speaking your Stories.

After you've written your examples and expanded on them with details, speak your experiences out loud. All speakers and lecturers practice their presentations and briefs before giving them to their audience. Practicing an interview "speech" is just as important. Learn to speak the examples efficiently and with enthusiasm and a smile once in a while if it's appropriate.

- ⊙ Recite your answers in front of a mirror.
- ⊙ Rehearse your response with a friend.
- ⊙ Use a tape recorder and record your answers. Listen to your voice. Are you impressed?
- ⊙ Videotape yourself with someone asking you the questions. Watch the tape. Look for areas to improve and the positive points of your presentation.
- ⊙ Consider delivery style, message, body language and confidence.

Interview Preparation Tip No. 4 – Add the Hiring Agency's Desired Skills, Knowledge and Expertise to your Stories.

Review the vacancy announcement or recruitment advertisement for the job you are seeking. Look for the particular skills they require. Here's some examples:

Team leader, organization, discipline, working across agencies, dependable, analytical, detail-oriented, problem-solving, advisor, technical assistant, support to professionals.

The stories you have written should incorporate these skills. The hiring manager is looking for someone who can "do the job." You want to demonstrate through your examples that you can do the job by integrating the skills they desire into your example. You want to PROVE that you can do the job, not just SAY that you can do the job. That's why it's best to give examples of your skills and experiences, rather than just saying, "I'm a good team member, I always meet my deadlines." Anyone can say that. That statement will not be remembered after a 30-minute interview.

Interview Preparation Tip No. 5 – Get ready to answer interview questions. Be prepared with answers.

At a recent interview training seminar at the National Archives, a supervisor asked that specifics be given regarding Archives Technicians' projects supporting the types of databases, information on the data being managed, customer relationships and other specialized knowledge and procedures that would demonstrate the expertise level of the project – as well as be memorable!

TJ Walker and I used a video camera and interviewed four Archives Technicians in preparation for promotion to Archives Specialist positions. The job is similar, but the casework will be more complex with the promotion.

Sampling of TJ's interview Questions:

- ⊙ Tell me about yourself.
- ⊙ Do you have a memorable example of your work or achievements?
- ⊙ What's the worst part of the job?
- ⊙ What are you most proud of in your career?
- ⊙ What are your greatest strengths?
- ⊙ If you're at a cocktail party what do you talk about?
- ⊙ Do you have any unique talents or specialized knowledge?
- ⊙ Do you have a sense of your weakness as an employee? What are they? What is the effect of your weakness?
- ⊙ How are you different from other applicants for this position?
- ⊙ Why should we hire you?
- ⊙ Anything else we should know about you?
- ⊙ What have you been doing in your current job as a specialist?
- ⊙ Why do you want to be promoted?
- ⊙ What skills do you have that are not being utilized?
- ⊙ What do you mean by that?

Interview Tip No. 5 – Research the Agency or Company Before the Interview

Always research information about the agency or company before the interview. Be prepared to ask questions of the interviewer as well as answer questions. You will probably have an opportunity to ask questions.

Here's a list of places you can go to research companies/agencies:

- ⊙ Website - press releases in particular – this is the latest news of the organization.
- ⊙ Mission Statement - compare their mission statement to your current organization's mission statement. Be prepared to talk about either yours or their mission statement.
- ⊙ About Us – read about the organization set-up, key people, size of the organization and when it was established.
- ⊙ Services / Programs / Mission – what do they do? Who are their major customers? What are their challenges?

Interview Tip No. 6 – Relax, Be Confident, Don't Tense Up Physically

If you are tense, (sitting with your arms tight at your side, shoulders hunched, face downward), the interviewer will not be relaxed either. Practice sitting and talking for the interview.

- Sit on the chair leaning slightly forward – watch the way the interviewer is sitting, but don't look as relaxed as the interviewer. It's better to NOT cross your legs, you can cross your feet. Sit up straight and relax your shoulders.
- Use your hands for the interview. Don't sit on your hands!
- Look at the interviewer when speaking and listening to questions. Very important.
- Smile occasionally but not too much.
- Breath regularly - seriously!
- Listen carefully to the questions. This is more difficult than you think.
- Don't tense up your voice to the point that you do not sound like yourself. (At the National Archives interview class the interview subjects talked differently when the camera was on vs. when the camera was off)
- You will become confident with practice, practice, practice.
- Be confident, but not overly confident. Interviewing is never easy.
- Remember that expert speakers practice, prepare speeches and have coaches. It's okay to walk around the house bragging about yourself.
- You obviously are qualified for the job, or you would not be in the interview. So relax - you can be hired based on your interview!

Interview Tip No. 7 – Know your Message.

- Show the enthusiasm and the skill level that you have.
- Prepare your stories. What happened? Use any knowledge, skills and abilities examples you have written.
- Don't forget the results – talk about the end product!
- Tailor your message for the job.

MEET TJ WALKER, MEDIA AND INTERVIEW TRAINER

These excellent Interview Tips were written by TJ Walker. Mr. Walker is the producer of *www.mediatrainingworldwide.com* and is an expert Interview, Speech, Media and Briefing coach from New York City. TJ trained employees at the National Archives with Kathryn and trains Federal managers in public speaking and training. TJ and Kathryn created an audio tape available at *www.resume-place.com* on How to Handle a Successful Federal Interview.

More Expert Advice

GETTING READY FOR OPEN-ENDED AND BEHAVIORAL QUESTIONS

Quoted From Merit Systems Protection Board Report, The Structured Interview

Managers will ask effective questions. As we've indicated, effective interview questions are based on job analysis to ensure that they are job-related. Effective interview questions are also usually open-ended and behavioral, so that they will elicit useful responses.

Open-ended questions are questions that require the candidate to provide details, and cannot be answered in one word (such as "yes" or "excellent"). Such questions are much more effective than closed-ended questions at developing insight into a candidate's experience and abilities. For example, the closed-ended question, "Can you write effectively?" can be answered with an uninformative "Yes" — a response that sheds little light on the candidate's level of performance in this area. An open-ended question such as, "Describe the types of documents you have written, reviewed, or edited," requires the candidate to provide specifics, and provides much more insight into the candidate's writing accomplishments.

There is a place for the closed-ended question. For example, to learn whether a candidate is willing to travel frequently or can start work on a given date, it is perfectly appropriate to ask a closed-ended question.

Behavioral questions are just that: questions that ask the candidate to describe behaviors — responses, actions, and accomplishments in actual situations. The case for the behavioral question is more subtle than the case for open-ended questions. Although research indicates that both behavioral questions ("What did you do?") and hypothetical questions ("What would you do?") can be effective, many researchers and practitioners generally recommend the behavioral question for two reasons.

First, behavioral questions can provide greater insight into how the candidate will perform on the job, because the best predictor of future behavior is past behavior. Second, behavioral questions may be more reliable than hypothetical questions. Because the response can be verified through reference checks or other means, it is more difficult to fabricate an inaccurate or untruthful answer to a behavioral question than to a hypothetical one.

GENERAL SAMPLE INTERVIEW QUESTIONS

All-inclusive
- Tell me about yourself.
- Why should I hire you?
- What about this job interested you?

Putting You on the Spot
- Why are you leaving your current position?

Difficult Questions
- Can you work under pressure?
- Describe a time when your work performance was poor.
- Describe how you've handled a stressful work situation.
- What are your weaknesses?
- Tell me about your worst boss.

Situational Questions
- Describe a situation where your work or an idea was criticized.
- Describe a difficult problem you've had to deal with.
- Tell me about a time when you had to tolerate people with different backgrounds and interests from your own.
- Tell me about a time when you've been particularly effective in relating with others.
- Most of us can look back on a project or idea we were proud of. Can you describe one of yours that you are particularly proud of?
- Describe a time when you used your public speaking skills.

Miscellaneous
- How long would it take for you to make a meaningful contribution to this department?
- Describe yourself as an employee.
- Describe your management style when dealing with staff and co-workers.
- What do you know about our agency?
- How would you describe your standards of performance?
- Do you prefer working with others or alone?
- Define cooperation.

COMPETENCY-BASED SAMPLE INTERVIEW QUESTIONS

Often an interviewer will ask questions that directly relate to a competency required for the position. Here are some examples.

Attention to Detail
Describe a project you were working on that required attention to detail.

Communication
Describe a time when you had to communicate under difficult circumstances.

Conflict Management
Describe a situation where you found yourself working with someone who didn't like you. How did you handle it?

Continuous Learning
Describe a time when you recognized a problem as an opportunity.

Coping
Describe a situation where your results were not up to your supervisor's expectations. What did you do?

Customer Service
Describe a situation in which you demonstrated an effective customer service skill.

Decision Making
Give an example of how you reached a practical business decision by reviewing all the facts.

Decisiveness
Tell me about a time when you had to stand up for a decision you made even though it made you unpopular.

Leadership
Describe a time when you exhibited participatory management.

Negotiating
Tell me about a time during negotiations when your perceptiveness allowed you to make sense of another person's behavior.

Write your own questions for the interviewers

Samples:
What are the biggest challenges for your agency right now?
Are there any new initiatives or programs that are being set up now?
What are two of the most important competencies you are seeking in this job?
What is the geographic area this position will service?
Is there a large retirement or new recruitment effort going on here?
How would my performance be evaluated?
What professional development is available?
What's next in the hiring and selection process for this job?

Final Words – tell them you want the job

If you think the position would be a great match for your experience and interests, do not hesitate to be enthusiastic. You can make a statement like this one: "I really like the sound of this position. I believe I would be able to lead this team and achieve the objectives that you have outlined here today. I hope that I will be selected for this position. I look forward to the next step. And thank you for the opportunity to interview. It was great to meet you and talk with you about your agency."

Summary

Research, Prepare, Write and Practice, Practice, Practice. If you can use a video camera or recorder to practice speaking your examples and stories, you will feel 100% more confident in an in-person or telephone interview. Role-playing with a coworker or interview coach can help also. If you land the interview, you are almost there. You have hopefully successfully completed the ten steps to transforming your military experience into a competitive Federal resume. Congratulations on all of your effort and time!

Good luck and write to me at *kathryn@resume-place.com* with success stories, challenges and any insight for inclusion in the next edition of this book!

INDEX
Military to Federal Career Guide

TEN STEPS TO TRANSFORMING YOUR MILITARY EXPERIENCE INTO A
COMPETITIVE FEDERAL RESUME

RESUME SAMPLES
Military to Federal Career Guide

TEN STEPS TO TRANSFORMING YOUR MILITARY EXPERIENCE INTO A
COMPETITIVE FEDERAL RESUME

USAJOBS.GOV BUILDER RESUME
8,885 characters (with spaces), 3 pages

Pilot-in-Command, Air Traffic Controller, CW-2
Federal Career Objectives: Pilot, GS-2181-09/11/12
Air Traffic Controller, GS-2152-09/11/12

Anthony Benedetto

CMR 433 Box 222
APO, AE 09182
Evening Phone: 49+999-99-99-999
Day Phone: 49+444-44-14-444
DSN: (333)-333-3333
Email: anthony.benedetto@us.army.mil

Country of citizenship: United States of America
Veterans' Preference: 5-point preference based on active duty in the U.S. Armed Forces
Registered for Selective Service
Contact Current Employer: No

AVAILABILITY

DESIRED LOCATIONS

Job Type:	Permanent	
Work Schedule:	Full Time	
US		

WORK EXPERIENCE U.S. Army, B Company   4/2002 - Present
7-534th Aviation Regiment, CMR 444, APO
AE 09182 US

                                                         Hours per week: 45

Pilot in Command / Flight Lead
PILOT IN COMMAND, ENSURING TECHNICAL AND TACTICAL PROFICIENCY to support real world contingencies worldwide. Maintain highest level of expertise in UH-60L helicopter systems and related flight procedures. Manage, direct, and monitor aircraft and air crews' requirements and mission accomplishments. Monitor co-pilot flying, helicopter systems while navigating and evading enemy threat at night while wearing Night Vision Goggles (NVG). Final decision maker regarding mission execution, accomplishment, and safety.

PRIMARY COMPANY FLIGHT LEAD, plan, brief, and execute variety of difficult missions to standard (within 10 meters of desired location and +/- 30 seconds from designated landing time). Includes air assaults, Long Range Surveillance Detachment insertions, tactical air movements, external and internal cargo transport, and reconnaissance operations in all modes of flight, including day, night, instrument, and NVGs.

Concurrently, receive mission, conduct meetings (in person or phone) with supported unit and design package to best suit the ground commander's intent for overall success. Coordinate and orchestrate ground unit's arrival at battlefield, while synchronizing artillery fire, air attack elements, and other ground forces to result in combined and fluid effort. Ensure complete understanding of overall mission concept by all crew members. Maintain proficiency in air assaults, external loads, Fast Rope Insertion Extraction (FRIES), imbedded Combat Search And Rescue (CSAR) / Personal Recovery, General Support, and VIP Transport.

Maintain proficiency at terrain flight altitudes under day, night, instrument, and NVG flight modes. Use Army Aviation computer programs to conduct planning; or when unavailable, use maps, protractor, and calculator. Conduct Air Movement Briefings to Ground Force Commander and Air Assault Commander using PowerPoint. Conduct detailed, lengthy Air crew Briefings to all the pilots and crew members. Conduct thorough rehearsals with all pilots and ground force key members. Provide training prior to each mission.

SPECIAL ASSIGNMENTS

As Flight Lead for Task Force Storm, briefed and conducted 10-day training of 35 National Guard aviators who are now a part of Task Force Storm in Afghanistan. Unit had no assault-related experience. Efforts resulted in the unit aviators experiencing great success on the war on terror. February 2005

Planned, briefed, and executed marginal Visual Flight Rules (VFR) weather / 0% illumination NVG assault with the 4th Infantry Division with only 5 ½ hours from receiving the mission to H-hour. December 2004

Took over fledgling CSAR training program and developed it into a professional, continuous joint training exercise with the U.S. Air Force's 81st Tactical Fighter Squadron. May 2002

U. S. Army, C Company, 8-101 Aviation Regiment, 101st Airborne Division Ft. Campbell, KY 42223 US   **4/1998 - 4/2002**

Hours per week: 45

Pilot in Command / Flight Lead

ALERTED, ASSEMBLED, UPLOADED, STRATEGICALLY DEPLOYED, AND CONDUCTED MISSIONS within 36-hours as part of Division Ready Force. Performed precise air assault and air movement operations with combined arms team during operations with aligned Infantry Brigade. Maintained highest level of technical and tactical proficiency in all aspects and conditions of helicopter operations, including Day, Night Unaided, and NVG, under visual and instrument flight rules. Able to deploy world wide and land at the objective within 36 hours from notification, which requires last-minute preparation, i.e., packing all equipment, preparing and loading helicopters into cargo planes, and planning the mission while flying en route to an intermediate staging base in the cargo aircraft. Upon arrival, conducted final preparations of mission planning and assisted unloading and building back-up helicopters.

FLIGHT LEAD UNDER DAY, NIGHT, AND NVG CONDITIONS. Conducted and managed planning cells for company and battalion level missions. Performed ongoing training in support of Brigade level units to include NVG operations, instrument flight procedures, external loads, and air assault mission tasks. Managed and reported on overall mission execution and ensured flights reached the objective.

UNIT TRAINER: Trained and mentored aviators and new flight leads in demanding modes of flight. Prepared and instructed company level Survival Evasion Resistance Escape (SERE) training to increase combat readiness.

BATTALION NVG OFFICER / COMPANY NVG CUSTODIAN: Ensured both flight companies in the battalion established and maintained efficient goggle program. Maintained 60 sets of NVGs in compliance with all general Aviation Safety Action Messages. Developed plan to have maximum number of NVGs on hand with less than 10% at scheduled or non-scheduled maintenance. Successfully transferred NVG responsibilities to new custodian with no losses.

COMPANY SUPPLY OFFICER: Managed over $1 million in inventory and unit supply transactions. Managed command's $82 million property book. Updated company shortage annexes and adjusted the commanders' property book, ensuring all hand receipts reflected the property book. Partnered with other shops to correct numerous errors from previous commanders and supply officers. Supervised 6+ lateral transfers of ground NVGs and nearly deleted backlog of NVGs needing transfers to other units.

SPECIAL ASSIGNMENT: Volunteered for JRTC rotation 02-02 and proved versatility as a pilot by performing wide array of missions, including resupply, command and control, and aerial screens. Partnered to train Air Mission Commanders on every mission at JRTC.

ACCOMPLISHMENTS

Demonstrated flight lead abilities during Combined Arms Live Fire Exercise by playing key role in organizing and planning the mission. November 2001

Within one year, went from becoming RL1 to earning D/N/NVG Pilot in Command, flying 350+ hours.

Led company on 4 Brigade level missions.

U.S. Army, D Company 4-58th Aviation Regiment   4/1996 - 4/1998
Grafenwoehr Army Air Field, Grafenwoehr US

Hours per week: 40

Air Traffic Controller

Provided safe, orderly, and expeditious flow of military and civil aircraft within local, controlled airspace. Coordinated with other ATC agencies in handling aircraft en route to further destinations, as well as arriving into local air field. Provided flight following to aircraft near the airspace while on training or real world missions.

SHIFT SUPERVISOR OVER ARMY AIR FIELD TOWER over 4 military and civilian controllers working separate positions. Monitored leave usage to assure appropriate level of staffing. Provided effective training on equipment, regulations, processes, policies, and procedures. Monitored and evaluated performance. Mentored employees. Took or recommended corrective or disciplinary action, when necessary. Coached employees in communication techniques. Resolved technical problems within existing guidelines. Promoted cooperative working relationships among staff to ensure team functioned cohesively.

ACCOMPLISHMENTS
Held Control Tower Operator (CTO) Certificate issued by Federal Aviation Administration. 1997-1998

Rated in one of two Non-Radar Approach Control facilities in the Army.

Rated in Army Aviation Flight Following Service.

EDUCATION

University of Maryland University College

College Park, MD US

Some College Coursework Completed - 5/1997

3 Semester Hours

Tidewater Community College

Fort Story, VA US

Some College Coursework Completed - 5/1996

3 Semester Hours

Churchill County High School

Fallon, NV US

High School or equivalent - 6/1992

JOB RELATED TRAINING

Survival Evasion Resistance Escape (SERE) School; 1999
Warrant Officer Basic Course 99-06; 1999
Warrant Officer Candidate Course; 1998
Primary Leadership Development Course; 1995

ADDITIONAL INFORMATION

MILITARY SERVICE HONORS (14 years active duty)
6 Air Medals, Army Commendation Medal, 3 Army Achievement Medals, Joint Meritorious Unit Award, Army Superior Unit Award, Army Good Conduct Medal, 2 National Defense Service Medals, 2 Armed Forces Expeditionary Medals, Global War on Terrorism Service Medal, NCO Professional Development Ribbon, Army Service Medal, 3 Overseas Ribbons, NATO Medal, Air Assault Badge, Army Senior Aviator Badge.

COMPUTER PROFICIENCIES: Falcon View, Microsoft Word, Excel, PowerPoint, Outlook, Internet navigation

Jeanne R. Grayson

777 Hawkins Avenue
Chicago, IL 44444
Phone: (123) 555-6666   Mobile: (777) 717-8888   Office: (777) 999-4444
E-mail: jrgrayson@email.com

Vacancy Announcement: OSC-05-07, Human Resources Specialist, GS-0201-11/12/13 or
Investigator, GS-1810-11/12/13

Social Security Number: xxx-xx-xxxx
Citizenship: United States
Veterans Preference: 5 points
Security Clearance: Top Secret – SCI Security clearance issued by Department of Defense; held since 1993

SUMMARY OF QUALIFICATIONS

- Results oriented **Criminal Investigator** with extensive experience as a **Human Resources Specialist.**
- Successful career in management and coordination of investigative cases involving **sensitive issues, voluminous records, numerous witnesses, and difficult elements of proof**.
- Dedicated **team member** in investigating aspects of large and complex cases.
- **Mature values**, coupled with **excellent written** and **oral communication skills.** Polished professional image.
- Excellent **listening skills** to **understand issues** and **develop effective solutions**.

PROFESSIONAL EXPERIENCE

U.S. Army Criminal Investigations Division Command	**Protective Services Special Agent**
Protective Services Unit, 777th Military Police Group	**August 2003 – January 2005**
6010 6th Street	$67,000 per year
Fort Benning, GA 33333	40+ hours per week
Supervisor: CW3 Robert Flood, (999) 777-3333; may contact	

Mobilized into active duty in support of Operation Noble Eagle, August 2003 – January 2005.

PLANNED PROTECTIVE SERVICE FOR SENIOR VIPS: Provided personal protection and physical security while in foreign and domestic territories for high level dignitaries, including Secretary and Deputy Secretary of Defense, Chairman and Vice-Chairman of the Joint Chiefs of Staff, Secretary of the Army, Chief of

Staff and Vice Chief of Staff of the Army. Developed detailed and comprehensive operational protection plans, including threat analysis reports, financial requests, man-hour reports, and after-action reports. Installed and monitored electronic surveillance and detection equipment.

MISSION SPECIAL AGENT-IN-CHARGE (MSAC) IN FRIENDLY AND HOSTILE ENVIRONMENTS WORLDWIDE. Team Leader for protective travel missions in friendly and hostile environments. Supervised teams of special agents and foreign counterparts operating worldwide, 24 hours a day. Developed the mission prior to traveling, including collecting intelligence, coordinating mission with host country embassies, briefing and coordinating team members and assigning responsibilities, coordinating travel arrangements, preparing country clearance messages, obtaining weapons clearances, advancing all sites, and assessing security requirements. Entered country prior to team's arrival to manage possible issues and manage security aspect of the mission. Briefed senior leaders, such as dignitaries and staff. Managed the mission to include coordinating local or host nation support, working with interpreters, and maintaining foreign relations. Work was loosely supervised; submitted reports and mission documentation for review.

Worked in civilian clothing that was mission and climate appropriate. Wore protective vests and / or body armor. Carried one or more weapons. Maintained diplomatic passport. Carried international cellular phones and / or satellite phones. Received mission assignments and information via e-mail and secure communication devices. Successfully qualified on assigned weapons quarterly.

Effectively trained 25 assigned agents in mission-appropriate skills and as future MSACs. Monitored and evaluated performance. Mentored and coached agents in protective services operations. Promoted cooperative working relationships among team members. Took corrective and disciplinary action, when necessary. Resolved issues within guidelines. Ensured cohesive team work among staff.

ACTING SECTION SPECIAL AGENT-IN-CHARGE FOR TRAVEL TEAM IN MULTIPLE MISSIONS:
Assigned as manager during supervisor's absence. Received mission information. Generated mission numbers and advised senior command staff. Assigned personnel to missions. Prepared country clearance messages and began travel arrangements. Determined number of support personnel needed and requested fund cites for support personnel. Managed personnel issues. Attended command meetings.

Key Accomplishments

- Although other team members were higher in rank or seniority, was considered most capable to manage mission preparations and perform as **Acting Section Special Agent-in-Charge** of Department of the Army's Travel Team in absence of Special Agent in Charge.
- **Project Manager** for the creation of a new MSAC Checklist designed for new special agents resulting in more consistency in protective service security missions, as well as faster learning curve for a growing Special Agent force.
- Created the first **Support Agent Tracking System**, a Microsoft Access database designed to track personal, professional, and mission information for hundreds of support personnel who were not permanently assigned to Protective Services Unit.

United States Army Reserve	**Criminal Investigative Division Special Agent**
Criminal Investigative Command	**December 1991 – Present**
1401 West Aston Circle	$6,000 per year
Jackson, MI 49202	Part-time; average 35 hrs per month

Supervisor: CW3 Ronald Ludington, (555) 888-2222; may contact

CASE MANAGEMENT: Receive case assignments from Fort Knox, KY. Develop cases and leads using appropriate investigative techniques. Interview numerous witnesses, complainants, victims, suspects, and subjects regarding complex military cases, including difficult elements of proof, sensitive issues, and numerous witnesses. When case elements come together, request supervisory approval and Staff Judge Advocate (SJA) opinion. Work as team with SJA to complete cases.

Prepare well developed reports. Resolve complainants' allegations, when possible. Interview victims on sensitive matters, such as rape and sexual assault and family members of suicide and homicide victims. Gather evidence regarding cases. Take fingerprints. Worked as team member on complex investigations, such as homicide in Germany, variety of sexual assaults, self-mutilation case, suicide at Fort Knox, and numerous traffic fatalities.

MANAGE PHYSICAL SECURITY AND ACCOUNTABILITY OF ALL SENSITIVE ITEMS AND EQUIPMENT, including weapons, badges and credentials. Conduct monthly inspections and inventories. Develop reports and forward information to management.

CONDUCT CRIMINAL INVESTIGATIONS OF OFFENSES in which the U.S. Army has an interest, including interviewing numerous witnesses, conducting undercover operations, performing surveillance, conducting searches, seizing evidence, and VIP security protection. Working with Operations Officer, ensure effectiveness of investigative teams. Assign duties and coordinate logistical support. Train and mentor agents.

CHIEF ADMINISTRATOR / CRIMINAL INFORMATION COORDINATOR / SPECIAL AGENT SUPERVISOR: Manage a variety of assignments to ensure effectiveness of soldiers, including weapons qualifications, physical fitness testing, weight control, evaluation reports, and medical screening. Maintain records in all areas.

Key Accomplishment

- Awarded for 5 years of 100% inventory physical security inspections.

Whitson County Sheriff's Office
2233 Hogeson Road
Whitson, IL 88888
Supervisor: Commander Roger Jones, (777) 999-4444; may contact

Human Resources Generalist
October 1997 – Present
$54,986 per year
40 hours per week

RECRUITMENT / PLACEMENT SPECIALIST, MAINTAINING THE INTEGRITY OF THE HUMAN RESOURCES RECRUITMENT PROGRAM, including applicant screening, interview, and selection process. Ensure strict compliance with the Illinois Commission on Law Enforcement Standards certification guidelines. Initiate and implement strategies to diversify the applicant pool, including locating and attending career fairs, conducting recruitment presentations, and updating Internet job postings. Strategically plan for projected vacancies. Maintain positions control list. Screen resumes and employment applications and conduct pre-employment interviews. Initiate and implement improvements to the applicant selection process and participate in periodic revisions of the employment application. Advise and counsel senior staff conducting senior management interviews. Counsel senior management regarding employee relations issues, explaining related laws and regulations. Review and revise job descriptions. Conduct exit interviews. Prepare yearly statistical reports and provide statistical information to a variety of agencies.

ILLINOIS POLICE CORP SELECTION BOARD MEMBER: National Federal program designed to hire more police officers in over 15 states, with one academy per state. As panel member, reviewed applications, conducted interviews, consulted with other panel members, and advised on selections of police academy candidates for state of Illinois.

TRAINING AND BUDGET COORDINATOR: Manage 5 departmental employee development budgets and a department credit card training expense account, lobby for additional funds, locate and determine most appropriate and cost effective training, schedule training, and annually report use of funds to the state. Balance county's budget against departments' budgets, request adjustments and corrections. Prepare financial reports, request review and submission to the state of reports by county Ways and Means Committee. Prepare reports to obtain state funding of partial reimbursement for police academy participants. Initiate, implement, and maintain employee development database.

PROJECT MANAGER, WHITSON AREA RETRAINING PROGRAM GRANTS: Manage retraining grant with state of Illinois, ensuring adherence to deadlines, attending meetings, and filing financial reports. Schedule training dates, participants, and facilities, and contract with instructors. Develop and file event reports to the state with final financial grant report.

COMMUNITY SERVICE OFFICER / COMMUNICATIONS (911) OPERATOR: Update and maintain automated geographical file to ensure timely emergency response. Compile data and complete monthly statistical reports for eleven townships. Perform timely evaluation of telephone calls, data entry, and dispatch appropriate emergency agency.

Key Accomplishments

- Recognized by Sheriff of Whitson County in Whitson Times for outstanding recruitment efforts that led to full staffing of the Correctional Facility. 2002

Organizational Solutions, Inc.	**Consultant / Owner**
777 Hawkins Avenue	**June 1994 – June 2004**
Chicago, IL 44444	$25 per hour, plus expenses
Supervisor: self-employed	Part-time; average 20 hours per week

CONSULTANT / TRAINER: Consultant for small businesses and home office set-up and implementation. Reorganized, automated, and maintained small businesses and home offices in establishing bookkeeping, filing systems, employee payroll, and payroll taxes. Researched, developed, and presented full office set-up packages, including computer, software, office equipment, office organizational plan, compensation and benefits package. Trained business owners in basic management skills, such as how to interact with employees, conduct meetings, types of benefits to discuss with employees, and management of daily situations, including employee issues, leave, advances, lost / damaged equipment, and performance.

Key Accomplishments

- Managed small one-person business that successfully grew to 15+ employees with expanded service offerings.
- Efforts resulted in client's learning new management techniques and efficiencies, which led to client business expansions and significant savings.

Internet Investigative Services / Colson Enterprises, Inc. **Private Investigator / Owner**
333 Stratton Boulevard, Suite 71 **December 1992 – July 1999**
Chicago, IL 48104 $35-50 per hour, plus expenses
Supervisor: self-employed 45 hours per week

Illinois Private Detective Agency license and Private Security Guard Agency license holder.

BUSINESS OWNER / MANAGER: Marketed and managed investigative firm offering private investigations, contracted security officers, and conducted public record researches and retrieval. Managed bookkeeping, payroll and taxes, and Human Resources related functions.

LEAD PRIVATE INVESTIGATOR PERSONALLY CONDUCTING MULTIPLE DISCRETE INVESTIGATIONS involving employee theft, domestic situations, and locating individuals. Contracted with corporations and law firms to conduct Nationwide Asset Searches, Surveillance Operations, Skip Tracing (Locating) Services and Public Record Research and Retrieval.
Managed all investigations. Wrote comprehensive, concise, and accurate reports regarding each investigation. Hired and trained investigators. Negotiated with clients.

Key Accomplishments

- Effectively developed information for clients to assist with personal decision making and information for businesses to successfully negotiate with collective bargaining units and assist with contract selection.
- One former employee is now a successful police officer and another is now a successful business owner.

United States Army **Military Police Officer / Investigator**
444 BSB, CMR 999, APO, AE 09031 **October 1986 – December 1991**
HHC LEC, Fort Knox, KY 22222 $35,000 per year
Supervisor: MSG Jackson Matthews (Retired), contact information unknown 40+ hours per week

MILITARY POLICE INVESTIGATOR INVESTIGATING GENERAL CRIMES WHILE WORKING IN CIVILIAN CLOTHING AND UNDER LOOSE SUPERVISION. Provided personal protection for dignitaries. Assignments were generated from Central Military Police Dispatch. Scope of investigations were general military misdemeanor crimes. Conducted interviews and prepared sworn statements from victims, witnesses, complainants, suspects, and subjects. Collected evidence and processed according to established guidelines.

TRAFFIC ACCIDENT INVESTIGATOR / SECTION LEADER: Germany assignments: Instructor for radar operations and German / American traffic law for military police companies, local units, and Community Counseling Center. Reviewed all traffic accidents within the jurisdiction and investigated further, when necessary. Conducted interviews with and prepared sworn statements from witnesses, complainants, suspects, subjects, and victims. Worked with a German counterpart for over 3 years. Fort Knox assignments: Developed system to process traffic tickets and maintain military ticket point system. Conducted traffic accident-related interviews. Prepared related reports.

MILITARY POLICE OFFICER (Fort Knox and Germany): Coordinated joint police operations involving American military and German national personnel. Dispatched to a variety of calls for service. Performed police duties including foot and motorized patrol and physical security of military installations. Provided personal protection for designated VIP's. Maintained traffic control and enforced traffic regulations and safety. Participated in civil disturbance and riot control operations. Managed law enforcement investigations. Applied crime prevention measures. Prepared military police reports, including sworn statements, and processed evidence.

PROFESSIONAL LICENSES / CERTIFICATES

- Illinois Private Detective Agency license and Private Security Guard Agency license holder
- Contract Investigator for U.S. Customs background investigations, Omnisec International Investigations, Inc.
- Currently preparing for the Professional Human Resources (PHR) certification examination
- Notary Public for Cook County, commission expires September 3, 2006

PROFESSIONAL MEMBERSHIPS

- Criminal Investigation Division Agents Association (CIDAA), Current Member
- Cook County and Sheriff's Office Training Council, Current Member
- Society for Human Resource Management (SHRM), Current Member
- Illinois Police Corp Selection Board, Illinois State University, Chicago, IL 2001-2002
- Private Detective Agency, PD-3378, State of IL, 1995-1999
- Illinois Council of Private Investigators, Inc., 1995-1999
- Private Security Guard Agency, SG-1665, State of IL, 1995-1997

PROFESSIONAL DEVELOPMENT

- Crisis/Hostage Negotiations Training, Fort Leonard Wood, MO; 2004
- Information Technology Training; Online Training; 2004
- Anti-Terrorism Awareness Training; Online Training; 2003, 2004
- Prevention of Sexual Harassment; Online Training; 2003
- Workshop for Personnel / Human Resource Assistants, Novi, Illinois; 2003
- Recruiting, Managing, & Retaining Generation "X": The New Police Culture; Garden City, MI; 2003
- Pre-Employment Interviewing; Auburn Hills, MI; 2002
- PPCT Defensive Tactics System (Basic Certification); Chicago, IL; 1998, 2002
- REID Hiring the Best, Madison Heights; MI; 2001
- REID Technique of Interviewing and Interrogation (Basic and Advanced Course); Detroit, MI; 2000
- U.S. Department of Justice: Agency Training Coordinator; Canton, MI; 2000
- Dealing with Difficult People / Conflict Situation Seminar; Chicago, IL; 1999
- Microsoft Courses: Access 2000, Word 8.0, Excel 97, Windows NT, PowerPoint, Microsoft Project
- Attack On Principal Protective Services Training; Jackson, MI; 1999
- Effective Listening Seminar; Chicago, IL; 1998
- Managing Multiple Priorities Seminar; Chicago, IL; 1998
- Enlightened Leadership Seminar; Chicago, IL; 1998
- Conflict Resolution Seminar; Chicago, IL; 1998
- Community Policing Training; Chicago, IL; 1998
- U.S. Army Criminal Investigation Course (CID); Fort McClellan, AL; 1995
- Wayne County Regional Police Academy (Academic Portion); Garden City, MI; 1992
- Military Police Investigations Course; Vilseck, Germany; 1991
- Traffic Accident Investigations Course; Vilseck, Germany; 1990
- Primary Leadership Development Course; Kitzingen, Germany; 1988
- Law Enforcement Seminar, Fort Knox; KY; 1986

- Military Police School, Fort McClellan; AL; 1986
- Basic Combat Training, Fort McClellan; AL; 1985

RECOGNITION

- Nominated for Meritorious Service Medal and Department of the Army Staff Identification Badge for accomplishments during mobilization for Operation Noble Eagle, August 2003. Selection pending
- Army Achievement Medal (3OLC) (equivalent of 4); one received for dangerous mission in Baghdad, with the Secretary of Defense in 2004; also 1991, 1990, 1988
- Global War on Terrorism Expeditionary Medal; 2004
- Global War on Terrorism Service Medal; 2004
- Employee of the Year, Cook County Sheriff's Office Support Services; 2003
- Reserve Overseas Training Ribbon; 1999
- Army Commendation Medal; 1998
- National Defense Service Medal; 1991
- Overseas Service Ribbon; 1991
- Army Good Conduct Medal; 1989
- Army Service Ribbon; 1986
- Army Reserve Component Achievement Medal (2OLC) (equivalent of 3)
- Armed Forces Reserve Medal
- Non-Commissioned Officer Professional Development Ribbon (2)

EDUCATION

Currently enrolled in Six Sigma Master's Certificate Program; On-line program through Villanova University, Villanova, PA; completion expected October 2005

Master's Degree: Organizational Leadership and Administration; Concordia University, Ann Arbor, MI; GPA 3.55; November 2002

Bachelor's Degree: Criminal Justice Administration; Concordia College, Ann Arbor, MI; May 1996

Associate's Degree: Law Enforcement; Central Texas College, Killeen, TX – European Campus; December 1991

Community High School, Chicago, IL; Diploma; June 1985

FERNANDO HERBOSO
SSN xxx-yy-zzzz
288th BSB
Unit 27777, Box 22225
APO AE 09234-7535
Home: (44) 999-98-89-888
Comm Work: (44) 999-33-38-888
DSN: 444-8888

Email Home: Herboso6@aol.com
Email Work: herbosof@cmtymail.98asg.army.mil

Typing words per minute: 60;   Steno: 0

WORK EXPERIENCE
May we contact your current supervisor? Yes

77th Personnel Services Battalion (10/10/2000 - Present) - Operations Officer
APO, Armed Forces Overseas Germany
Supervisor: Lester Smith, (66) 999-97-72-222; contact: yes
Salary: $48,000 per year

CHIEF ADVISOR, PROGRAM MANAGER AND ADMINISTRATIVE OFFICER FOR COMMAND PLANS: Chief Advisor to Battalion Operation Manager and Executive Officer for personnel, budget, training, policies, procedures, resources, schools, inspections, travel, manpower needs, security, and correspondence. Evaluate findings and recommendations on efficiency reviews of operations. Develop plans of action and milestones to incorporate needed improvements to correct deficiencies. Arrange and provide numerous briefings on operation requirements. Prepare briefing slides for command visits. Plan and coordinate command inspections.

SUPERVISE THE LARGEST ARMY PERSONNEL SERVICE IN EUROPE: Directly supervise 4 military personnel supporting largest Army Personnel Services organization consisting of 289 soldiers and 93 civilian employees. Provide leadership and manage diverse military personnel programs including leave, awards, personnel requirements, advancement, performance evaluations, educational programs, transfer programs, and personnel assignments.

SUPPORT COMMAND MISSION AND OPERATIONAL TASKINGS: Manage administrative needs relevant to contingency program planning and force modernization, including command mission and function statements, military manning, distribution, classified information, range operations, battalion suspense and operational taskings, and military personnel programs. Plan and coordinate personnel deployments, redeployments. Plan and manage Command's military and civilian TDY travel program, including budget formulation, reports, orders, and arrangements. Oversee battalion's security program, Nuclear Biological Chemical program, communications section, and a $90,000 TDY budget.

Directly support the Executive Officer, Command Sergeant Major, and Commander in obtaining information, tabulating data, composing numerous command level correspondence and summaries. Research, develop, coordinate, and publish multiple command and community policies and review policy guidance. Maintain and track Command Group assignments to ensure timely receipt of actions by units and staff.

TRAINING TO MEET CONTINGENCY AND MISSION OBJECTIVES. Supervise quarterly training briefings and manage field training exercises. Liaison for German Partnership unit to plan, execute, conduct, train German and American units on weapons and physical fitness. Plan and coordinate transition-to-war, contingency peacetime missions, force modernization, and wartime emergency planning policies for the battalion. Review policy guidance for the battalion operation branch and recommend changes to exercise, force modernization, and mass casualty plans.

RECOMMEND LONG RANGE TRAINING OBJECTIVES. Based on program evaluations, recommend training objectives in terms of organizational structure, programs, and milestones to meet training and operational resource requirements and objectives. Perform program evaluations to sustain deployment posture and ensure continued support of personnel and units moving through the 98th ASG and 100th ASG. Prepare and review policy letters, SOPs, and propose changes to USAREUR guidelines. Interview unit commanders and first sergeants to gain information about organizational missions, functions, and work procedures.

MANAGE AND ANALYZE MANPOWER TO MEET TRAINING AND BATTALION EXERCISES. Coordinate Command's military manpower management system. Assure FYDP data accurately reflects budgeted end-strength, billet requirements and authorizations, and accuracy of Command's Enlisted Distribution and Verification Report. Prepare and process unit status reports.

SUPERVISE INTERNAL SECURITY FOR EMERGENCY PLANS, EDUCATION, AND INVESTIGATIONS. Supervise Personnel Security Program directing subordinate unit level Security Managers, classified information and material control, personnel security, security education, emergency plans, security violations and compromises, classification management, security review of information proposed for public release, security records and foreign travel.

ACCOMPLISHMENTS:
Developed a management system that increased efficiency of processing $90,000 in business travel vouchers and achieved 100 percent accuracy during the annual 2002 audit.

Single-handedly coordinated all Force Protection missions for all subordinate companies in 5 different communities.

Flawlessly planned, executed 5 movements involving a total of 150 personnel to Albania, Macedonia, Kosovo, Turkey, and Iraq. Training and assessing these personnel prior to their movement resulted in all personnel accomplishing their jobs and returning safely home.

Began and developed company security program from scratch, resulting in a thriving section that was rated 'best in the company' during inspection of the security and safety program.

Planned, coordinated, trained 260 military personnel in preparation for deployment to Iraq (2003-2004). During

12 month deployment, was tasked twice to deploy a personnel service, casualty and postal team to Najah, Iraq in support of Operation Iraqi Freedom, set up a post office and a Human Resource Center to provide casualty reporting, postal services, and human resources to 2,000 personnel.

77th Personnel Services Battalion (04/03/1994 - 10/09/2000) - Operations Manager
APO, Armed Forces Overseas Germany
Supervisor: Martin Cleary, (66) 999-66-61-111; contact: yes
Salary: $47,000 per year

PERSONNEL / MANPOWER EVALUATION: Supervised Military Personnel Company staffed by 15 civilians, 80 military personnel servicing 20,000+ military, civilians and family members. Provided technical expertise and guidance to managers, supervisors, and employees on training, safety, welfare, discipline, morale, leave, advancement, evaluations, applications for special schools, entitlements, and commissioning programs. Supported Equal Employment Opportunity and other management programs. Reviewed and ensured proper and timely administration of company programs.

Managed supply program, maintenance and serviceability of all assigned equipment; maintained accounts involving $900,000 worth of property and equipment without loss. Monitored procedures and programs for ensuring adequate and timely manpower requirements, and submitted needs projections to senior management. Provided division level supervision of employees.

Senior advisor to the Commander. Managed Army Individual training requirements and resources, including weapons qualification and physical fitness program. Maintained quality of life program, social functions, protocol, receptions, and ceremonies. Maintained rosters on awards and assignments. Ensured soldiers were slotted properly based on military occupational specialty structure. Managed in and out-processing, issuance of meal cards, and accident reporting.

SUPERVISION / EMPLOYEE DEVELOPMENT: Planned work to be accomplished through employees, assigning work based on priorities. Prepared military evaluations for divisional military personnel. Evaluated training needs, developed lesson plan, delivered training, evaluated training effectiveness.

ACCOMPLISHMENTS:
Superb leadership enabled companies to exceed numerous U.S. Army Europe training standards while completing 100 percent of all directed training. Mentored 50 soldiers to complete Army Non-Commission Officers Educational courses. Expertly planned, executed battalion field training exercise that greatly increased the battalion's overall readiness. Key in planning and preparation of battalion command post exercise, focusing on communications, personnel services support, and maintenance operations training.

Greatly improved the company's maintenance readiness levels; raised company's rate from 73 to 100 percent. Coordinated 5 training exercises; executed all world wide contingency field exercise to include preparation of Operation Joint Endeavor in Bosnia.

Coordinated, implemented, led a company into Bosnia to provide personnel services support to 9,500+ soldiers in Operation Joint Endeavor. 100 percent re-enlistment of all eligible soldiers in 1995 due to high unit morale.

Reorganized company's personnel administrative center in 2 weeks upon returning from a 9 month deployment to Bosnia, achieving 100 percent passing on battalion command inspection. Accomplished more work with less resources during FY 98 when average strength levels were at 78 percent.

Personally established a proactive maintenance program, raising equipment readiness by more than 25 percent.

Selected as "best manager" in 1997 during battalion's command post exercise. Cited by Brigade Commander for winning brigade maintenance award for 3 consecutive quarters.

EDUCATION
College/University
City College of Chicago (10/01/1985 - 07/31/2002)
APO, Armed Forces Overseas, Germany
Degree: Associates in Arts- Major: Liberal Arts
GPA: 3.32   Semester Hours: 85

College/University
University of Maryland (09/01/1984 - 04/30/1994)
APO, Armed Forces Overseas, Germany
Semester Hours: 19

ADDITIONAL INFORMATION:
Secret Security Clearance, (07/09/2002)

AWARDS
Meritorious Service Medal (04/27/1998): Selfless service and dedicated leadership greatly improved the company's readiness and performance

Army Commendation Medal (04/15/1997): Displayed superior talent and industry in completing all required task in preparation for deployment in support of Operation Joint Endeavor/Joint Guard. Directly responsible for leading a company into Bosnia without any safety accidents or injuries. Restructure the available work force, originated an ingenious and comprehensive training program for Soldiers to qualify on casualty reporting, Enlisted Department of the Army Systems, and Human Resource Information Systems. Provided direct leadership and guidance to 52 Soldiers in different technical and tactical fields.

Army Superior Unit Award (04/04/1997): Company received the Army Superior Unit Award while deployed to Bosnia.

Army Achievement Medal (05/31/1996): Outstanding leadership while preparing the company for a organization command inspection, which resulted in the company being rated as the best company. Commended for having the best safety, training, equal opportunity, personnel retention, physical security, leaves, and evaluations program.

Army Achievement Medal (08/23/1990): Transformed the monthly pre-separation briefings into an outstanding program. Personal efforts resulted in the smooth transition of soldiers to civilian life. Quality of work was complimented during the 7th Corps community inspector generals' inspection.

CERTIFICATIONS
Master Facilitator Course 40 h (10/15/1999); Certified to conduct equal opportunity training to military personnel and civilians.

Unit Movement Officer Course 80 h (08/07/1996); Certification to plan, coordinate, and conduct rail load operations.

Master Fitness Course 80 h (11/03/1995); Master Fitness Trainer for the company.

Personnel Management 40 h (09/30/1984)

PROFESSIONAL DEVELOPMENT
First Sergeants Course 240 h (10/07/1998); Provide technical expertise, advice and guidance to managers, supervisors, and individual employees on training, safety, welfare, discipline, morale, leave, advancement, evaluations, entitlements and commissioning programs.

Equal Opportunity Leaders Workshop 40 h (05/15/1990); Equal Opportunity Training for leaders.

PROFESSIONAL SUMMARY
Fluency in reading, writing, and speaking Spanish.

Written / Oral Communications: Proficient in written communications, managing all incoming and outgoing correspondence. Professional oral communicator, providing full range of oral presentations, including training, executive briefings, and one-on-one communications.

Leadership and Managerial Skills: Exceptional record of retention and re-enlistments of soldiers exhibiting high productivity and morale. Respected supervisor, effective at gaining meaningful support of employees.

Information Technology: Demonstrated results in streamlining and using information technology to improve efficiency and effectiveness. Computer proficiencies in Microsoft Word, Excel, Outlook, PowerPoint, Works, Access.

Organized /Analytical: Evaluate work processes and apply creativity in developing options to arrive at smarter ways to carry out unit assignments. Professional knowledge of administrative regulations and operating procedures.

Battalion Aviation Materials Officer / Test Pilot, CW-4
Federal Career Objectives: Pilot, GS-2181-11/12/13
Logistics Management Specialist, GS-0346-11/12/13

Steven J Perkins
6236 Austin Parkway
Apt. 229
Austin Creek, NC 27540

Contact Phone: (999) 999-9999
Work Phone: (999) 999-9999
Email Address: steveperkins@nc.rr.com

EXPERIENCE

11/2001 to Present ; 60 hours per Week; Battalion Aviation Materials Officer/ Test Pilot; $ per Annum; last promoted Not Specified; permanent employee; not on a temporary promotion; U.S. Army, 77th Aviation Regiment, Fort Bragg, NC; Samuel Gray, CPT , 999-999-9999; may contact supervisor.

SENIOR LOGISTICS SPECIALIST MANAGING MAINTENANCE AND LOGISTICS PROGRAMS FOR 21 APACHE HELICOPTERS. Analyze and coordinate logistics and support requirements, both short and long term, for all aviation systems during home station operations, field training exercises, and deployments. Prepare and present oral and written briefings, reports, analyses, and recommendations to senior managers. Data then used by Colonel to present to higher level managers. Information consists of expert technical guidance. Use data to make decisions regarding program planning and execution. Develop comprehensive logistics plans to support overall program plans.

MANAGE CLASS IX AIR BUDGET AND RESOURCES. Determine and submit detailed requirements, resulting in budget and resource allowances. Request number of flight hours. Analyze requirements' effects on budget and formulate alternative logistics plans when operations or requirements change to accomplish unit's mission. Analyze allocated resources for funds, manpower, facilities, equipment, supplies, and services. Monitor and approve procurement, production, storage, distribution, maintenance, transportation, utilization, and disposal of materials and facilities. Monitor budget and reconcile differences. Write monthly report to Division Material Management Center.

INTERPRET SPECIALIZED DOCUMENTATION to include Safety of Flight, Aviation Safety Action Message, Modification Work Orders, and Technical Bulletins. Analyze impact on the unit's missions. Coordinate with all levels of the Army supply system to ensure all logistical requirements are met in a timely manner.

TEST PILOT, TROUBLESHOOTING electronic, mechanical, hydraulic, pneumatic, computerized flight controls, rotor, armament systems, and turbine engines. Inspect fuels and lubricants. Perform detailed test flights to determine airworthiness and obtain readings from instrumentation. Analyze data from test flights to determine performance and make adjustments. Acquire raw data from computerized database to aid in diagnosis; involves data in binary format and interpretation. Identify root causes of failures and formulate solutions.

SPECIAL ASSIGNMENTS:

COORDINATE WITH ARMY MATERIEL FIELDING TEAM to ensure adequate provisions of manpower, supplies, equipment, facilities, and services for the unit's transformation to Longbow Apache. Analyze, plan, and execute logistics for modifying support equipment, receiving new equipment, and redistributing specialized equipment. Through fielding conferences, discuss needs and provide feedback on equipment, develop, evaluate and refine plans.

PLANNED, COORDINATED, AND NEGOTIATED TRANSFER OF 21 APACHE HELICOPTERS to the National Guard according to Army Transformation Standards and Regulations. Personally conducted all prior planning and coordination of transfer while simultaneously planning and executing missions. Managed and tracked all flight hours for each aircraft at a subcomponent level to ensure extremely precise management of subcomponent time to overall, which was necessary to meet standards for transfer. Aircraft transfer cited by FORSCOM Action Officer as the best in the Army to date.

ACCOMPLISHMENTS:

ADVISED APACHE SENSORS PROGRAM MANAGEMENT OFFICE on unit level logistical support requirements for fielding of Modernized Target and Designation Sight (MTADS) to shape the Integrated Logistics Support (ILS) for that system. Identified unit level requirements necessary to field an active unit. Collaborated with Program Management office and vendor to establish guidelines and processes to enable unit to continue operations during modification phase. First Unit Equipped was conducted on schedule, which is critical to maintain funding for new systems. Fielding of MTADS is now in process.

MANAGER FOR MAINTENANCE AND LOGISTICS PROGRAM TO RESOURCE A BATTALION during Operation Enduring Freedom III, redeployment to Ft. Bragg, Aviation Reset Program, Reconstitution Operations, and training rotation to the National Training Center (NTC). Used high level of skills, including initiative, management, technical knowledge, conceptualization and visualization of goals and requirements to achieve them, logical reasoning and analysis, judgment, planning, execution, and follow through. Ensured success of unit during each mission. Examples include the following:

OPERATION ENDURING FREEDOM III: Worked under extreme pressure to provide apache air cover 24 / 7. Used established logistics system to keep operations functioning, since parts in place were inadequate and orders from the U.S. required 2 week lead time. Collaborated with engineers for solutions and permission to conduct special repairs. Coordinated and established an effective repair flow, including budget and payment negotiations with Onsite Logistics Repair Facility in Europe for replacement of main transmission clutches resulting in decreased wait time. Developed detailed plans to combat austere flying conditions, including extreme heat, high altitude, and increased operational tempo. Used technical expertise, judgment, and analytical skills to forecast parts needed and ordering schedules to minimize wait time. Developed aggressive preventative maintenance program to counter harsh environment. Built effective relationships with Item Managers to acquire parts that were needed at other Army sites, including Iraq. No mission was cancelled due to maintenance issues, all convoys, ground and air, had armed apache support ensuring their safety. Personally managed resources that allowed the unit to execute 12-day versus 30-day phases and 1,200 flight hours per month during combat operations. Performed over twice the normal operations with same amount of resources.

REDEPLOYMENT TO FORT BRAGG: With unit deployed to Afghanistan, no remaining Apache units remained at Fort Bragg. Foresaw extreme deficiencies and difficulties developing regarding the Apache fleet maintenance and parts availability due to the deployment of Apache units from Fort Bragg to Afghanistan. Worked to resolve issues during deployment while simultaneously supporting ongoing combat operations. Captured and analyzed demand data from prior deployment. Prepared lists of minimum requirements to support operations and projected parts that were available for return to Fort Bragg. Prepared presentations detailing costs of rebuilding stockage levels and estimated operational abilities; acquired approval from Task Force Commander. Coordinated with support units and Army-level material managers to determine resource availability and obtain resources. Efforts resulted in the unloading and assembling of all 21 Apache units and successfully determining all were fully mission capable. Inventory levels were improved enough to allow the unit to begin training operations immediately upon return, giving the Army an asset in a world situation where all recourses were being maximized.

05/2000 to 11/2001; 60 hours per Week; Theater Aviation Intermediate Maintenance, Product; $ per Annum; last promoted Not Specified; permanent employee; not on a temporary promotion; U.S. Army, G Company 52nd Aviation, APO AP 96271 (Republic of Korea); Terence Reeves, LTC , 999-999-9999; may contact supervisor.

COORDINATED, SUPERVISED, AND PRODUCED ALL AVIATION MAINTENANCE AND LOGISTIC SUPPORT at theater-level for two AH-64 Apache Cavalry Squadrons, one UH-60 Blackhawk air ambulance company, and two AH-64 Operational Readiness Float aircraft. Provided second level component repair. Conducted phase maintenance and performed test pilot support. Primary advisor to Theater Support Group Commander concerning all Apache maintenance and logistics issues.

ACCOMPLISHMENTS:

MANAGED AND SUPERVISED PRODUCTION CONTROL for 12 subordinate sections, and 120 civilian contractors and Army personnel, spanning more than 21 different occupational specialties.

IMPROVED LOGISTICAL READINESS AND SUPPORT EFFECTIVENESS by planning and coordinating changes with technical and program specialists and subordinate sections to reduce average time to complete aircraft phase maintenance from 60 days to 26 days.

CONTACTED AND FACILITATED ACQUISITION OF TECHNICAL EXPERT. Coordinated with technical expert and analyzed two non-functioning Electronic Equipment Test Facilities. Identified problems and deficiencies, determined logistic objectives and goals. Planned, coordinated, and implemented corrective actions restoring both Electronic Equipment Test Facilities to operation. Increased theater-level readiness. Optimized financial resources and saved over $2.5 million in cost avoidance.

ANALYZED WORK ORDER BACKLOG. Analyzed budgetary and resource limitations. Developed alternative solutions by identifying resources available at theater level. Wrote letters of justification, creating five contractor positions that ultimately resulted in reduction in work order backlog. Streamlined work order procedures for critical component repair, allowing same day return to customers.

8/1998 to 05/2000; 60 hours per Week; Production Control Officer; $ per Annum; last promoted Not Specified; permanent employee; not on a temporary promotion; U.S. Army, 273rd Aviation Regiment, Ft. Bragg, NC; Kent Anderson, COL., 999-999-9999; may contact supervisor.

COORDINATED AND PROVIDED CENTRALIZED CONTROL OVER ALL ASPECTS OF AIRCRAFT MAINTENANCE FOR 24 APACHE HELICOPTERS. Received and processed work requests. Coordinated and scheduled jobs into various shops. Monitored status of aircraft parts and shop reports. Coordinated inspections and test flights, as well as the return of repaired aircraft and equipment to supported units. Evaluated and reported status of logistic readiness and identified potential impact. Managed phase maintenance program and aircraft phase flow. Ensured adequate aircraft hours were available for all operations including a detachment deployment to Bosnia. Prioritized and synchronized work efforts to maximize resources that would maintain readiness rates above Army standards. Ensured compliance with all Safety of Flights, Aircraft Safety Action Messages, Modification Work Orders, and Technical Bulletins while limiting the impact on aircraft availability.

SUPERVISED SEVEN SUBORDINATE SECTIONS, 87 PERSONNEL spanning more than 11 different occupational specialties. Established work priorities and work flow guidelines at unit level and to support facilities. Monitored and evaluated performance. Mentored employees. Wrote award nominations. Monitored and approved leave. Resolved technical problems within existing guidelines. Promoted cooperative working relationships among personnel and ensured staff functioned as a cohesive team.

9/1996 to 8/1998; 60 hours per Week; Maintenance Officer / Test Pilot; $ per Annum; last promoted Not Specified; permanent employee; not on a temporary promotion; U.S. Army, 66th Aviation Regiment, Ft. Bragg, NC ; Martin Smith, MAJ , 999-999-9999 ; may contact supervisor.

MANAGED THE MAINTENANCE AND QUALITY CONTROL OF EIGHT APACHE HELICOPTERS. Managed diagnosis and repair of aircraft malfunctions. Conducted maintenance test flights to determine aircraft performance and airworthiness. Used extensive technical knowledge to communicate intricate details of plans to maintenance crewmembers who had various levels of experience.

SUPERVISED 15 MAINTENANCE PERSONNEL. Managed training, welfare, and discipline. Established work priorities and work flow guidelines to support facilities. Monitored and evaluated performance. Mentored employees. Wrote award nominations. Monitored and approved leave. Resolved technical problems within existing guidelines. Promoted cooperative working relationships among personnel and ensured staff functioned as a cohesive team.

ACCOMPLISHMENTS:

SUPERVISED FIRST LOADING OF AN APACHE HELICOPTER ON A C-17. Identified requirements for aircraft modification, resulting in policies and procedures put in place to enable deployment of Apaches worldwide on C-17's.

CONCEPTUALIZED AND IMPLEMENTED PLAN to modify, inspect, and test engines on 24 aircraft in one week to comply with Safety of Flight message. Efforts resulted in the prevention of accidents and casualties due to known safety issues.

12/1989 to 9/1996; 60 hours per Week; Platoon Leader / Attack Pilot; $ per Annum; last promoted Not Specified; permanent employee; not on a temporary promotion; U.S. Army, Various Units, Various Locations;

MANAGED THE MAINTENANCE AND OPERATIONS OF SIX HELICOPTERS AND ALL RELATED SUPPORT EQUIPMENT. Planned, approved, and monitored the turn in and issue of over $100 million worth of equipment during transformation of the unit. SCHEDULED LOGISTICS FLIGHTS.

SUPERVISED UNIT OF 13 PERSONNEL: Managed training, welfare, and discipline of eight warrant officer pilots, one platoon sergeant, and four crew chiefs. Established work priorities and work flow guidelines to support facilities. Monitored and evaluated performance.

SPECIAL ASSIGNMENT:

TRACKED ALL ARMY AIRCRAFT DURING OPERATION UPHOLD DEMOCRACY. Successfully coordinated with other Department of Defense agencies to resolve airspace use conflicts.

ACCOMPLISHMENT:

QUALIFIED TO FLY AS UNIT TRAINER ON THE RESTRICTED ZONE ALONG THE NORTH KOREAN BORDER. Instructed and certified 26 pilots.

EDUCATION
Lake Wales Sr. High School, Lake Wales, FL; 1984 High School Diploma
Embry-Riddle Aeronautical University, Ft. Bragg, NC; Bachelor in Professional Aeronautics , 2005; 3.0 out of 4 Point GPA; 114 Semester Hours

PROFESSIONAL TRAINING
1999; Aviation Warrant Officer Advanced Course, 411 Hours; Distinguished Honor Graduate
1997; Air Movement Operations Course, 100 Hours, Honor Graduate
1997; Ah-64 Maintenance Manager/Maintenance Test Pilot, 219 Hours
1997; Aviation Maintenance Manager, 366 Hours
1995; Aircrew Coordination Training, 40 Hours
1995; Assistant Instructor Training Course Sincgars, 40 Hours
1995; Combat Lifesaver, 40 Hours
1992; Aviation Leader Maintenance / Supply Course, 40 Hours
1992; Ah-64 Aviator Qualification, 430 Hours
1989; Initial Entry Rotary-Wing Aviator Ah-1, 772 Hours
1989; Initial Entry Rotary-Wing Aviator Common Core, 764 Hours
1989; Rotary Wing Qualification, 600 Hours
1988; Warrant Officer Candidate, 410 Hours
1988; Primary Leadership Development Course, 213 Hour
PROFESSIONAL LICENSES/CERTIFICATES
Commercial Pilot Certificate (Rotorcraft Helicopter, Instrument Helicopter); current
FCC Radiotelephone Operator Permit; current

PROFESSIONAL RATINGS, AWARDS, AND RECOGNITIONS
2005; Master Aviator Badge
2005; Legion of Merit
2004, 2004, 2003, 1999, 1996, 1995, 1987; Army Commendation Medal

2003; Bronze Star Medal
2003, 1994, 1991, 1987; Army Achievement Medal
2002, 1990; National Defense Service Medal
2002; Armed Forces Expeditionary Medal
2002; Global War on Terrorism Service Medal
2001, 2000; Meritorious Service Medal
2001, 1996, 1991, 1987; Overseas Service Ribbon
2001; Global War on Terrorism Expeditionary Medal
1999; Distinguished Honor Graduate, Aviation Warrant Officer Advanced Course
1997; Honor Graduate, Air Movement Operations Course
1996; Korean Defense Service Medal
1995; Joint Service Achievement Medal

OTHER INFORMATION
Expert knowledge and abilities in all phases of logistics and maintenance programs with over 15 years of experience as Senior Logistics Specialist and Manager. Results oriented leader with extensive planning and organizational skills. Excellent reputation for treating co-workers and subordinates with professionalism and respect. Mature values coupled with strong work ethic and polished professional image. Self-starter. Strong written and oral communication skills. Security Clearance: Secret

Computer Proficiencies: MS Office Suite (Word, Excel, Outlook, Access), Internet navigation. Army Aviation and DOD Logistics systems: FEDLOG, Electronic Technical Manuals (ETMs), Integrated Electronic Technical Manuals (IETM), Integrated Logistic Analysis Program (ILAP), Total Asset Visibility (TAV), Visual Logistic Information Processing System (VLIPS), and Web-based Customer Account Tracking System (WEBCATS

U.S. MILITARY SERVICE INFORMATION
Active Duty: 07/1985 to Present - U.S. Army
Campaign badges and/or expeditionary medals received: Master Aviator Badge, Legion of Merit, Bronze Star Medal, National Defense Service Medal, Armed Forces Expeditionary Medal, Global War on Terrorism Service Medal, Overseas Service Ribbon, Global War on Terrorism Expeditionary Medal, Korean Defense Service Medal, Joint Service Achievement Medal
Honorable Discharge

ADDITIONAL DATA SHEET
Steven J Perkins
1. Appointment Eligibility:
    Veterans Employment Opportunity Act Eligible
2. Citizenship: Yes
3. Appt Preference:
    Term (positions lasting 1 year or more, but less than 4 years)
4. Willing to Travel: 6 or More Days
5. Vet Preference: 5-Point Preference
6. Low Salary Accept: **None Specified
7. High PP/GR Held: **None Specified
8. Qualified Typist: Yes
9. Birth Date: **None Specified
10. Geo Preference: NC, Fort Bragg

RACE/ETHNIC STATUS: White
SEX: Male

ELECTRONIC MILITARY FEDERAL RESUME
8,400 characters (with spaces), 3 pages

Chief, Aviation Resource Management
Federal Career Objectives: **Administrative Officer, GS-0341-13
Logistics Management, GS-0346-13/14**

THOMAS ROBERTS, CPM

SSN: 000-00-0000
4905 Alamo Blvd.
San Diego, CA 78000
Home: (972) 555-1111
Work: (817) 888-9999
E-Mail: TCRCPM@yahoo.com
U. S. Citizen: YES

WORK HISTORY:

06/2002 to 05/2005, United States Army, Ft. Sam Houston, TX
Supervisor: LTC Steven McCloud. Phone: (210) 555-3333.
Chief, Aviation Resource Management, Major

DESIGNED AVIATION STANDARDIZATION FOR 141 AVIATION UNITS IN 21 STATES. Coordinated and implemented aviation standardization policies and procedures to ensure quality assurance and quality control in the areas of safety, maintenance, operations, training, logistics and security for 141 aviation units throughout 21 states. Managed a staff of 8 inspectors and 1 administrator. Forecasted and executed annual travel and operations budgets in excess of $300,000.

IMPLEMENTED AVIATION RESOURCE MANAGEMENT SURVEYS (ARMS): Conducted over 180 days of inspections annually to ensure standardization and compliance with regulations, directives, and training guidance.

TRAINED PERSONNEL IN OPERATIONAL READINESS: Served as primary trainer for the ARMS Chief in the western area. Advised in technical and tactical expertise for Operational Readiness Evaluations for aviation units. Subject matter expert for Training Management and Aviation Operations for the entire Fifth Army area.

ACCOMPLISHMENTS:
Emergency operations center: established Aviation Center.
Developed Standard Operating Procedures for The Aviation Center.
Information Management Systems: implemented new data management systems.

SPECIAL ASSIGNMENT: Raised $1.2 Million in four months, 08/1999 to 12/1999, United Way, San Diego, CA. Executive Fundraiser: Represented the Armed Forces in community service during the United Way and Combined Federal campaign. Coordinated fundraising and collection procedures at Kelly AFB. Served as Liaison and Public Relations speaker for both campaigns simultaneously. Developed campaign strategies and successfully recruited and trained 200 personnel to perform fund raising, collections and administrative procedures.

04/1998 to 05/2002, United States Army, Seoul, South Korea.
Battalion Executive Director, Major

DIRECTED FORWARD DEPLOYED ARMY AIR TRAFFIC SERVICES. Directed administrative, operations, training, intelligence, and quality assurance and liaison sections of the most forward deployed Army Air Traffic Services (ATS) Battalion in the U. S. Army.

AIR TRAFFIC SERVICE OPERATIONS WITH 400 EMPLOYEES: Coordinated operations encompassing 400 employees including administrative, logistical, training, maintenance and fiscal areas of control geographically located at seven sites across the South Korean peninsula. Managed a $2M operating budget and maintained detailed accountability of over $40M in equipment. Conducted manpower surveys to cut waste and increase efficiency while maintaining personnel positions. Managed the Battalion's Force Modernization and Command Inspection Programs (CIP).

ACCOMPLISHMENTS: DEVELOPED A FORCE MODERNIZATION PROGRAM INCREASING EQUIPMENT INVENTORY BY 17%. Developed the force modernization program increasing the unit's equipment inventory and resulted in a 17 percent increase in air traffic following capabilities. Liaison with the South Korean government resulted in flight following procedures for civilian and military flight corridors. Led flight operations and coordinated all visits by Heads of State and visits by the President and Vice President of the United States.

PERFORMANCE REVIEW NOTED: "…developed a first class staff that is eager to serve and consistently turns out quality work…a teacher, motivator, and leader…providing the continuity so important when changing Battalion Commanders…effective management of the battalion's administrative tasks…performance has been outstanding…articulate, resourceful, and competent..."

05/1996 to 04/1998, United States Army, Seoul, South Korea.
Battalion Operations and Security Manager, Major

DIRECTED AIR TRAFFIC SERVICES. Directed air traffic services and airspace management for the entire South Korean peninsula, including the sensitive demilitarized zone. Managed the tactical and operational training of 400 soldiers at 12 major and remote sites or contingency and wartime operations.

ACCOMPLISHMENTS:
Improved operations/tactics and awarded highest (28 of 28) evaluation rating among air traffic services units. Selected as the Air Liaison Officer/Security during the President's visit to Korea.

10/1992 to 04/1996, United States Army, Ft. Sam Houston, TX.
Aviation Training and Operations Manager, Major

ADMINISTRATIVE AND BUDGET MANAGER FOR 82 AVIATION UNITS. Managed training and operations of 82 ARNG and USAR aviation units and flight facilities covering 8 states in the Fifth Army area. Provided advice, assistance, and support to improve readiness for mobilization and rapid transition to wartime status. Served as Administrative Officer and Budget Manager. Revised Army Readiness Group (ARG) budget, revised proposed Tactical Distribution Allowances (TDA) to Forces Command (FORSCOM), developed travel schedule, and selected ARG assistance team in support of 135 Reserve Component aviation units. RESULTS: Saved

$15,000 in travel funds by using Centralized Army Aviation Scheduling Office, allowing the ARG to provide additional assistance and training to units in need.

EDUCATION

M.A., Acquisition/Procurement Management, Webster University, St. Louis, MO, 12/1995; GPA: 3.5
B.A., Business Administration, Eastern New Mexico University, Portales, NM, 05/1980
A.A., New Mexico Jr. College, Hobbs, NM, 1977

SPECIALIZED TRAINING

Command and General Staff College, 1995. Combined Arms and Service Staff School, 1988. Supply Staff Officer, 1986. Quartermaster Officer (Advanced), 1984. Quartermaster Officer (Basic), 1980.

LICENSES/CERTIFICATES

Hazard Communication, 1995. Fixed Wing Multi-Engine Qualification, 1990. Rotary Wing Aviator, 1985

AWARDS

4 Meritorious Service Awards. 2 Army Achievement Medals. Army Commendation Medal. National Defense Service Medal. Armed Forces Reserve Medal. Army Service Ribbon. Two Overseas Service Ribbons. Army Aviator Badge. Army Fitness Award. Recipient of Athletic (Gymnastics) Scholarship.

OTHER INFORMATION

Summary: Managed operations, personnel, and resources of large scale organizations and projects. Executive management professional, able to identify trends, develop teams, and determine modus operandi to implement strategic plans. Frontline professional with proven background in managing and implementing high dollar projects. Establish and ensure sound operations, quality assurance, and quality control. Leadership ability to optimize team production and maximize group motivation through synergy, empowerment, and open communications. Exemplary public relations and public speaking abilities.

Professional Knowledge, Skills, and Abilities: Knowledge of Federal procurement laws, rules, and regulations in work for Master's degree, supplemented with reading of Federal Acquisition Regulations and Defense Acquisition Regulations, and self-paced studies from DOD websites. Utilize weighted matrices, linear regressions, PERT, and other decision making formats to arrive at the "best" supplier, offering most value added. Utilize Request for Quotes (RFQs) and Requests for Information (RFIs) for bid proposals on standard contracts.

Oral Communications Skills: Negotiated contracts involving subcontracting and third party installments. Frequently incorporated time leveraging and setting concessions for job to be completed on time and at a reduced cost. Liaison for military, federal, and municipal agencies during Combined Federal Campaign and United Way for the City of San Antonio. Led team that raised more than $1M in a two-month period.

JOHN RODRIQUEZ
12500 Wilson Boulevard, #320
San Diego, CA 92126
Phone: (858) 555-0000
Email: JRod2005@aol.com

Vacancy Announcement:

Social Security No: 123-45-6789
Citizenship: U.S.
Veteran's Preference: 10 point/30 percent compensable

PROFESSIONAL EXPERIENCE

May 2003 – present, BUDGET TECHNICIAN, GS-0561-07, step 3
40 hrs per week, Salary: $36,949 per year
U.S. Marine Corps (USMC), Commanding General, (FA Adjutant Division)
MCAS Miramar, P.O. Box 452000, San Diego, CA 92145-2000
Supervisor: Paul Mason; (858) 555-7777; May be contacted.

Compile data and formulate timely, accurate budget reports for the USMC Commanding General.

FORMULATED BUDGET AND DESIGNED SPREADSHEETS FOR HQ ORGANIZATIONS: Analyze and monitor sub-fund administrator's historical data for budget formulation including actual data on executed annual funds. Develop total budget estimate based on prior year's execution. Produce in-depth, well-organized spreadsheets and narratives in approved formats for headquarters organizations.

JUSTIFIED BUDGET FOR FUNDED AND UNFUNDED ITEMS: Develop justification for each itemized budget requirement. Provide unfunded requirements lists developed at local level to request additional funds. Assemble data and deliver PowerPoint presentations to headquarters officials.

PLANNED, FORECASTED AND REPROGRAMMED FUNDS TO ACCOMMODATE BUDGET CHANGES: Forecast requirements, allowing for unanticipated events to avoid over obligation of funds. Develop quarterly reports submitted headquarters. Coordinate response to mid-year review data requirements, including historical data for analysis by headquarters. Establish measures for senior managers measures relative to spending goals in form of percentage of authorized funds spent. Assist comptroller for year-end close-out reporting. Reprogram funds to accommodate budget changes.

EFFICIENTLY EXECUTED BUDGET AND COMMUNICATED PROJECTIONS: Ensure that each step of the budget process is completed within time constraints. Prepare budget for execution, including establishing local budget based on prior year's performance of funds spent. Communicate projections for coming year and add planned projects. Receive funding authorization and process requests, such as obligations of programmed funds.

November 1984 – January 2002, ACCOUNTING CHIEF, E-6, 40+ hrs per week
U.S. Marine Corps, AC/S Comptroller, Bldg 1160, Camp Pendleton, CA 92055-5010
Supervisor: Lt. Col Nathan Kojak (retired); (760) 555-8888; May be contacted.

Promoted from E-1 to E-6 through series of increasingly responsible assignments. Each level included developing and delivering various training modules, establishing fund administrators, planning, budgeting, auditing fund administrator accounts, and communicating comptroller requirements to organizations within the scope of the comptroller.

SUPERVISED MILITARY AND CIVILIANS: Supervised 5-10 military and civilian personnel having a variety accounting functions. Exercised full supervisory authority and discretion for military personnel; advised managers on civilian employees' performance for annual review. Mentored and counseled civilian employees regarding performance and opportunities for promotion.

ADVISED SENIOR MANAGEMENT IN ACCOUNTING AND MILITARY PERSONNEL RECORDS: Advised upper management concerning $10-20 million in accounting data, including military personnel records pertaining to performance reports. Reviewed and analyzed accounting functions including presenting and executing operating budget to ensure valid data.

ADMINISTERED FUNDS AND AUDITED EXECUTED BUDGETS: Applied knowledge of rules, regulations, and government policies to write and edit 30-45 fund administrator requests annually. Analyzed budget data and budget requests. Ensured budgets were processed correctly in accounting system. Advised decision-makers on alternative methods of funding, spending, and accounting of authorized funds. Annually audited, monitored, and analyzed each executed budget for authorized spending.

MONITORED AND CONTROLLED PERFORMANCE OF FUNDS: Reviewed fund administrators' performance and advised on reprogramming of funds to support new or revised requirements during the course of the fiscal year. Continually reviewed comptroller programs to ensure data, reports, and staffing were at acceptable levels. Delivered training and supplied appropriate reference materials to correct misunderstandings of accounting systems and procedures.

ANALYZED ACCOUNTING REPORTS AND BUDGETS FOR CONTROLLER: Read and screened classified information and data to evaluate importance to comptroller's office. Coordinated and supervised fund administrator audit teams that conducted reviews to oversee each authorized budget. Maintained and reconciled official accounting records, including official accounting reports after each accounting cycle.

SPECIAL ASSIGNMENT: Designed and delivered training, including step-by-step instructions, tested for impromptu application, the application now used as the standard for data retrieval in U.S. Marine Corps accounting system.

KEY ACCOMPLISHMENTS: Served as initial point of contact for establishment of Oracle-based SABRS Management Analysis Retrieval Tool System (SMARTS) application. Trained 30-40 personnel prior to launching application on individual computers. Coordinated technical phone assistance and troubleshooting. Modified training module to suit specific needs of three major military commands.

PROFESSIONAL DEVELOPMENT
Financial Management Certificate; USDA Graduate School; pending completion.

Introduction to Financial Management; USDA Graduate School; 2004, 40 classroom hrs.
Appropriations Law; USDA Graduate School; 2004, 40 classroom hrs.
Introduction to Federal Budgeting; USDA Graduate School; 2004, 32 classroom hrs.
Accounting for Non-Accountants, USDA Graduate School; 2003, 32 classroom hrs.
Basic Government Purchasing Class; 2000, 2003, 40 classroom hrs.
Impromptu Application (data retrieval system for SABRS); 2001, 32 classroom hrs.
Microsoft Access, Beginner to Advanced; November 2000, 24 classroom hrs.
Microsoft Office Applications: Excel, Word, PowerPoint; 2000, 40 classroom hrs.
7 Habits of Highly Effective People Franklin Covey; 2000, 24 classroom hrs.
Terminal Area Security Officer Assistant for 3270 Access; 1993, 1999, 24 classroom hrs.
Basic Natural Programming Course; 1998, 40 classroom hrs.

MEMBERSHIPS
American Society of Military Comptrollers; member since 1987.
Veterans of Foreign Wars; continual support; March 1999.

AWARDS, HONORS, RECOGNITIONS
Letter of Appreciation for providing training in government accounting, established reconciliation system; 1999.
Letters of Appreciation for providing outstanding assistance, researching, providing additional funds for project completion; June 1992.

MILITARY SERVICE
USMC; Active Duty Service, August 1967 – January 1970.
USMC Reserves; May 1976 – November 1984.
USMC; Active Duty Service November 1984 – January 2002 (retired).

EDUCATION
B. S., Information Systems / Database Administration; National University; San Diego, CA; October 2003.
A. A., Major: System Analyst; Truckee Community College, Reno, NV; June 1977.

OTHER INFORMATION
PROFESSIONAL SUMMARY: In-depth knowledge of Federal financial management practices, procedures, accounting, budget processes. Experienced supervisor with knowledge of employment policies pertaining to government accounting functions. Skilled in identifying key policy issues, making recommendations to upper management. Proficient at gathering, compiling, analyzing financial, budget auditing information. Technically proficient with Microsoft products. Excellent reputation of working well with people, providing excellent customer service, promoting team work.

ELECTRONIC MILITARY FEDERAL RESUME
8,535 characters (with spaces), 3 pages

Human Resources Planner, Workforce Planner, Recruiter, E-8
Federal Career Objectives: Human Resources, GS-0201-11/12
Administrative Officer, Management Analyst, GS-0340-11/12

MARK L. SIMMONS, JR.

Social Security No: 333-22-4444
307 Victory Lane
Fredericksburg, VA 22444
Home: (540) 222-1234
E-mail: mlsimmonsjr@aol.com

EXPERIENCE

04/2002 to 12/2004, Human Resource Planner, E-8, 40 hrs/wk
U. S. Army Human Resources Command, 200 Stovall Street, Alexandria, VA 22332-0400
William Sullivan; (703) 333-5555; may be contacted.

Team Leader and Director of 20 Human Resource Specialists and Professional Development Managers. Directed recruitment for Army combat readiness personnel for supporting the Global War on Terrorism.

DIRECTED RECRUITMENT ACTIVITIES TO SUPPORT COMBAT READINESS: Oversaw the worldwide assignment of 34,000 enlisted personnel, including recruitment, accessions, staffing, professional development and retention.

DESIGNED INNOVATIVE STAFFING AND WORKFORCE STRUCTURES: Developed recommendations and implemented actions to support enlisted personnel structure changes. Studied work of employee relations specialists located on-site and off-site to determine if it would be appropriate to establish a team structure and recommended a pilot project for six months to test this concept. The pilot was evaluated and the results were successful. With minor adjustments the team structure, with a team leader, was approved and implemented.

DESIGNED AN EFFECTIVE LEADERSHIP DEVELOPMENT PROGRAM TO CREATE A PIPELINE OF FUTURE LEADERS: Determined that a leadership development program would help the facility in its human capital objectives to have people trained to assume tomorrow's leadership positions. Led a workgroup that designed a process that included holding focus group meetings to develop leadership competencies. Once these were validated by an outside, independent source, we developed a training curricula that would help provide the training to help candidates acquire these leadership competencies. The program has been successfully graduating 30 candidates for each of the past three years.

WROTE SURVEY AND CREATED RETENTION PLAN: Surveyed 3,000 employees with over 20 years on the job to determine what they liked about their jobs and work environment; analyzed data, and presented a report to Commander with recommendations on what to continue doing and what to stop doing in the workplace.

ADVISED ON EMPLOYEE RIGHTS AND LABOR RELATIONS: Analyzed and interpreted negotiated labor agreement when acting as intermediary between supervisor and bargaining unit members concerning labor relations issues. Provided advice concerning employer and employee rights, job descriptions, placement, merit promotion, leave administration, performance management and Alternative Dispute Resolution.

HUMAN RESOURCES ADVISOR, ENCOURAGING CULTURALLY DIVERSE RECRUITMENT: Advised branch manager, team members, and customers on recruitment challenges, with particular emphasis on under-representation of Hispanics in the workforce as compared to percentage in the general population. Demonstrated expert knowledge of Federal laws, Executive Orders, manpower regulations, operating policies and procedures in personnel management. Especially instrumental in overhaul of the Command's Performance Evaluation System in redesigning performance standards of each employee to be linked to the mission objectives of the Command. Led redesign effort and massive training initiative.

REPRESENTED AGENCY FOR FORCE STABILIZATION THROUGH ARMY TRANSFORMATION: Represented Branch as Human Resources Analyst on numerous task forces addressing force stabilization, unit staffing, lifecycle management practices, and other concerns in support of Army transformation. Served on the Human Resources Reform working group that designed the process and training for delegation of classification authority to a lower level in the organization.

BRIEFED COMMAND LEADERSHIP: Presented all quarterly briefings to Human Resources Command leadership, staff, installation commanders and family members covering personnel management issues. Conducted periodic reviews in managing strategic approach to unit manning, force stabilization initiatives across Army's manning system, application to government contractors.

ACCOMPLISHMENTS: Recognized discrepancies between system-projected requirements and real personnel requirements and made appropriate adjustments in staffing data. Negotiated solutions and resolved problems in high level interest cases requiring change of assignment. Earned professional performance ranking in top 10% of U.S. Army.

05/2001 to 03/2002, Human Resources Development Manager, E-8, 40 hrs/wk
U.S. Army Human Resources Command, 200 Stovall Street, Alexandria, VA 22332-0400
Mary Jane Quisenberry; (703) 777-8888; may be contacted.

DESIGNED PROFESSIONAL DEVELOPMENT PROGRAM AND MANAGED CAREERS OF 6,313 SERVICE MEMBERS: Point of contact in branch for assignment management and professional development of enlisted service members. Managed careers of 6,313 service members assigned from White House to Iraq. Coordinated with appropriate personnel on high-level interest cases (Congressional, White House, General Officers, other VIPs) requiring change in staffing requests. Authored and presented technical reports, staff action memoranda, and briefings on inquiries, assignments, and related issues upon request of supervisor, managers, and senior staff.

ADVISED AND INTERPRETED CHANGING PERSONNEL GUIDELINES: Served as authoritative source in interpretation of new personnel guidelines, policies, and Federal laws, Executive Orders, Department of Defense (DOD) directives in order to provide liaisons with White House Staff, Congress, major Army commands, supervisors and team members. Reconstructed and verified a variety of facts in connection with staffing personnel.

UTILIZED INFORMATION MANAGEMENT SYSTEMS TO ANALYZE PERSONNEL DATA: Used Enlisted Distribution Assignment System (EDAS), Army Training Requirements and Resources System, Personnel Electronic Record System Management System to request personnel assignments, deletions, and professional development. Analyzed, extracted data from EDAS when screening personnel data. Coordinated with Enlisted Distribution Division, other internal, external agencies for loading, cancellation of requests for staffing, to resolve discrepancies between projected, actual personnel requirements.

ANALYZED MANPOWER FOR WORKFORCE PLANNING: Screened current and projected rosters to monitor strength conditions of commands affected by military occupational specialties to ensure strength equity among units. Screened and selected personnel returning from overseas locations for next assignment locations. Responded to telephone, electronic and written inquires from soldiers, family members, commanders, and divisions within Army Human Resources Command.

EDUCATION

MPA, Public Management, Leadership; In Progress, Troy State University, Fort Belvoir, VA
MS in Administration with Honors, Organizational Behavior, 2004. GPA, 3.64, Central Michigan University, Mt. Pleasant, MI
MBA with Honors, Human Resource Management, 2003. GPA, 3.89, Strayer University, Woodbridge, VA
Anderson High School, Anderson, IN; Graduated 1975

PROFESSIONAL DEVELOPMENT

Effective Briefings/Presentations Workshop, 16 hrs, 2004; Change Management Workshop, 24 hrs, 2004; Working with Difficult People Workshop, 16 hrs, 2004; EEO Seminar for Managers and Supervisors, 16 hrs, 2004; Manager Development Course, 80 hrs, 2000; Supervisor Development Course, 40 hrs, 2000; Senior Enlisted Equal Opportunity Course, 24 hrs, 1999; Instructor Training Course, 40 hrs, 1995

PROFESSIONAL AFFILIATIONS

Member, Noncommissioned Officers Association, 1989-Present

AWARDS and COMMENDATIONS

Meritorious Service Medals, 2004, 2001, and 1996; Army Commendation Medals, 1994, 1992, 1991, and 1988; Army Achievement Medals, 1993, 1988, 1987, and 1986

OTHER INFORMATION

PROFILE: Results-oriented, highly dedicated Human Resources professional with proven career as head of staffing, retention, and development for highly skilled information technology and telecommunications workers. Exceptional leadership and team-building skills. Excel at motivating teams to overachieve. Versatile and proactive problem-solver with high level of integrity. Successful supervisor, managing, monitoring, coordinating work and mentoring up to 156 employees. Mature values, coupled with excellent written, oral communication skills and a polished professional image. Proficient in use of Microsoft products, military personnel management databases, and conducting Internet research.
MILITARY SERVICE: U.S. Army: Active Duty, December 1981 – December 2004

THE RESUME PLACE, INC.
FEDERAL CAREER RESOURCES FOR FEDERAL JOBSEEKERS BY KATHRYN TROUTMAN

Military to Federal Career Guide & CD-ROM
$38.95 + $8.00 postage

ISBN 0-9647025-7-6, 8 x 10, 237 pages, soft cover
Ten steps to transforming your military experience into a Federal resume
The first guide on Military to Federal, including the new Military Federal Resume format, samples and templates. Important Find Your Federal Job ChartTM with 48 announcements interpreted for 40 military MOS. Learn how to STAND OUT above your federal competition!

Federal Resume Guidebook & CD-ROM, 3rd Ed.
$38.95 + $8.00 postage

ISBN 1-56370-925-2, 8 ½ x 11, 400 pages, soft cover
20 more sample Federal Resumes in Word to use as templates! Specialized chapters on Senior Executive Service applications, converting a scientific CV to a Federal resume and insight for writing an IT Specialist, HR Specialist, Program & Management Analyst, Wage Grade (Trades), Contract Specialist, and Administrative Federal Resume.
*The CD-ROM for this book is available only through The Resume Place, www.resume-place.com.

Ten Steps to a Federal Job & CD-ROM
$38.95 + $8.00 postage

ISBN 0-9647025-3-3, 8 x 10, 240 pages, soft cover
Won Careers Best Book of the Year, 2003, Publisher's Marketing Association
Great book for the first-time federal applicant—the original Ten Steps book.
20 more sample Federal Resumes for private industry to Federal jobseekers, plus KSAs.

Ten Steps to a Federal Job – Jobseeker Guide
$18.95 + $7.00 postage

ISBN 0-9647025-4-1, 120 pages, 8 ½ x 11, soft cover
Bulk purchases available for Ten Step Training programs.
This succinct book is used as a handout in Military Career Transition Centers extensively throughout the world.

Ten Steps to a Federal Job – Trainer's Guide
$99.95 + $7.00 postage

ISBN 0-9647025-5-X (For Trainers), 48 pages, 8 ½ x 11, soft cover
Curriculum for the Ten Step Program for Certified Federal Job Search Trainers.

Student's Federal Career Guide & CD-ROM
$21.95 + $7.00 postage

Written with Emily K. Troutman
ISBN 0-9647025-6-8, 185 pages, 5 x 7, soft cover
Won Careers Best Book of the Year, 2004, Publisher's Marketing Association
Just returned to college or finished a certification program to advance or change your career? This book is a MUST. Emphasizes courses, training, projects, internships, team projects. Your Federal resume should feature your education. Samples in this book will help you change careers using your new degree!

Creating Your High School Resume, 2nd Ed.
$12.95 + $7.00 postage

ISBN 1-56370-902-3, 180 pages, 8 ½ x 11, soft cover
High School students need a resume for jobs and college applications! Outstanding samples, case studies, and job search stories for high school juniors and seniors. Teacher's guide, PowerPoints available for instructors.

CUSTOMER ORDER INFORMATION

Individual Name: _____

Agency / Office: _____

Shipping address: _____

_____

Billing address: _____

_____

Telephone: _____
Fax: _____
Email: _____

Credit Card: (Please circle one) Amex | Visa | MC | Discover
Card Number: _____
Expiration: _____

Signature: _____

ORDER INFORMATION
Call: The Resume Place, Inc., (410) 744-4324 or (888) 480-8265
Fax: (410) 744-0112
Order on-line: *www.resume-place.com*
Mail: The Resume Place, Inc., 89 Mellor Avenue, Baltimore, MD 21228

Forms of Payment:
All credit cards, Government Impact Cards, Direct Deposit, Purchase Orders, Training Forms, Checks

About Resume Place for Government Contracting:
Small, woman-owned business, CCR registered, GSA Schedule-69 pending

Questions? Customer Service? Federal Employee Training program inquiries?
(410) 744-4324, M-F, 9-5 p.m. ET

RP MILITARY FEDERAL RESUME WRITING AND EDITING SERVICES

Resume Place, Inc., (410) 744-4324 or (888) 480-8265; Fax: (410) 744-0112; *www.resume-place.com*
89 Mellor Avenue, Baltimore, MD 21228

Which professional writing and consulting service is best suited to help with your federal job search campaign?

FEDERAL CAREER COACHING – Professional Federal Career Coach will coach you in
multiple sessions throughout your Federal Job Campaign from the beginning through selection of
announcements to application and interview preparation.

Description: Is this campaign really important? Do you need help with the federal employment process?
Don't want to waste time guessing about which announcements are the best and endlessly writing/editing
your resumes? The coaching service is usually multiple telephone or in-person meetings to help you
manage your federal job campaign and career change. We provide education and coaching in: Federal job
interest and skills analysis; how to get started; how to find vacancy announcements; how to understand
and interpret the announcements; what is needed for the best resume for you; selection of job titles
and best grade for your experience; how to apply; review of announcements as you search for the best
vacancies plus interpretation for the best "fit" for your experience.

**EDITING – Do it yourself service. You like what you've written, you just need an expert technical
editor.**

Description: Professional editors will proofread and provide heavy and/or light technical editing
and formatting on your draft, fine-tuning your materials. YOU will provide your best draft. WE will
complete the final editing.

**FULL-SERVICE WRITING – Professional Certified Federal Resume Writers will draft the best
resume possible from your documents and Basic Resume.**

Description: You will provide your basic resume outline, dates, descriptions, OERs, training forms,
and any printed materials. We will interview you concerning your accomplishments and interests and
ask questions about needed information to write the best possible electronic or paper federal resume.
This is a true writing collaboration to get the best resume written, focused and targeted toward your
selected positions.

Step 1. Assessment Guide – you will need to submit your draft resume (or outline) and announcement
to our Assessment Guide for a review and development of cost estimate. There is a small,
reasonable fee for assessments and estimates for full-service writing.
Step 2. After reviewing the Proposal, make a decision about the writing project.

INTERVIEW TRAINING – Expert Interview Trainers will prepare you for your Federal Job Interview

Description: Available in increments of 1, 2, 3 or more hours, expert federal career counselors will prepare you for a variety of federal job interview formats, including Behavior-based and Technical. Interview preparation for telephone interviews, one-on-one, panel interviews. It is highly recommended that you research, write, prepare, and practice to WIN THE JOB!

FEDERAL CAREER TRAINING FOR VETERANS

Resume Place, Inc. is a Federal Career Training Organization through Veterans Affairs, Veteran's Rehabilitation & Education Centers (VRE). Ask your Counselor about continuing federal employment and job development services.

Federal Resume Writing and Career Coaching Services
www.resume-place.com

FEDERAL CAREER TRAINING FOR
FEDERAL EMPLOYEES AND AGENCIES

Resume Place, Inc. Federal Career Training for agency-sponsored, in-house programs
President and author Kathryn Troutman and Certified Federal Job Search Trainers are available to come to your agency to train employees in the following popular off-the-shelf programs (customized for your agency):

Resumix (CHART), QuickHire and Electronic Resume Writing
KSA Writing
Interview Preparation
SES Applications
Federal Career Change & Promotion Strategies

Write to *Kathryn@resume-place.com* for career training information.

FEDERAL CAREER TRAINING FOR CAREER COUNSELORS AND TRAINERS
Certified Federal Job Search Trainer Program

Get Certified as a Federal Job Search Trainer. If you are a career counselor, transition counselor or other career or human resources advisor, you would be qualified to be certified in the Ten Steps to a Federal Job training program designed and published by Kathryn Troutman. More than 200 career professionals from military services, universities, Veterans organizations, workforce centers, and federal agencies are certified and teaching this easy-to-learn, simplified federal job search program.

This is a 3-day, in-person program taught in Columbia, Maryland by Kathryn Troutman and Federal Job Search Trainers. Hands-on, computer-room training provides expertise in Federal career advisement and training techniques for federal job search.

Read more at *www.resume-place.com*.

FEDERAL CAREER WEB SEMINARS FOR ALL JOBSEEKERS

Web Seminars sponsored by *www.resume-place.com*
Open to ANYONE—sit at your desk and learn the basics about federal applications!

Free One-Hour Teleclass
3-part Federal Career Course: Federal Resume Writing, KSAs and Interview Preparation ($300)
3-part SES ECQ Writing workshop for writing ECQs ($300)

Read about the web seminars at *www.resume-place.com*.

ABOUT THE AUTHOR

KATHRYN KRAEMER TROUTMAN
President and Founder, The Resume Place, Inc.™, 1973 to present
Federal Career Coach™
Certified Federal Job Search Trainer
Certified Federal Resume Writer & Coach
Certified Career Management Coach (CCMC)

Kathryn Troutman wrote the first book on Federal Resume Writing in 1996 – the *Federal Resume Guidebook*. This book and resume style became the industry standard for Federal HR and everyone who wants to apply for a federal job. Ms. Troutman has since written *Ten Steps to a Federal Job* and, with her daughter Emily, *The Student's Federal Career Guide*. Both books won Best Career Book of the Year by Publisher's Marketing Association.

Ms. Troutman designed the first-ever Federal Job Search Training Certification program based on the Ten Step curriculum. Now, career counselors are teaching the federal job search program in more than 100 military TAP and Spouse Employment Career Transition classes today! The President and founder of *www.resume-place.com*, she and her professional writers provide expert writing and consulting services to more than 1,000 clients per year. Ms. Troutman is also a leading Federal Career Trainer in more than 50 government agencies each year and she is the Government/Public Service Board Federal Career Coach for *www.monster.com*. Kathryn lives in Baltimore, MD and is the proud mother of three children who are successful in their careers!

Update 2006

To: The Resume Place, Inc., 89 Mellor Ave., Baltimore, MD 21228
Fax: (410) 744-0112
Email: *resume@resume-place.com*

We would like to keep this book up-to-date with publications on an annual or bi-annual basis. Please submit any recommendations or ideas to enhance the usability of this book for veterans seeking federal jobs.

I would recommend that you add this information to your next edition of this publication:

_____

I cannot find the following information and I believe it should be added into the next edition:

_____

Helpful websites and tips for federal job search by veterans:

_____

Success story about how you landed a federal job. Let us know if we can quote your name, rank or service.

_____

Name: _____

Email: _____